D1135323

PENGUIN BOOKS

Compose Yourself

Harry Blamires, a graduate of University College, Oxford, was formerly Dean of Arts and Sciences at King Alfred's College, Winchester. He was Visiting Professor of English Literature at Wheaton College, Illinois, in 1987. The University of Southampton has awarded him a D.Litt. in recognition of his achievements as a writer. His total output of some thirty books includes fiction and theology, but he is widely known for his works of literary history and criticism. These include *A Short History of English Literature* (Routledge) and *Twentieth-Century English Literature* (Macmillan). For over three decades students in the USA and the UK have benefited from his classic guide to Joyce's *Ulysses*, *The New Bloomsday Book*. He is also the author of *The Penguin Guide to Plain English*.

HARRY BLAMIRES

DE

Compose Yourself

and Write Good English

PENGUIN BOOKS

PENGUIN BOOKS

Published by the Penguin Group
Penguin Books Ltd, 80 Strand, London WC2R 0RL, England
Penguin Putnam Inc., 375 Hudson Street, New York, New York 10014, USA
Penguin Books Australia Ltd, 250 Camberwell Road, Camberwell, Victoria 3124, Australia
Penguin Books Canada Ltd, 10 Alcorn Avenue, Toronto, Ontario, Canada M4V 3B2
Penguin Books India (P) Ltd, 11 Community Centre, Panchsheel Park, New Delhi – 110 017, India
Penguin Books (NZ) Ltd, Cnr Rosedale and Airborne Roads, Albany, Auckland, New Zealand
Penguin Books (South Africa) (Pty) Ltd, 24 Sturdee Avenue, Rosebank 2196, South Africa

Penguin Books Ltd, Registered Offices: 80 Strand, London WC2R 0RL, England

www.penguin.com

First published 2003
1

Set in 9/12 pt Swift
Typeset by Rowland Phototypesetting Ltd, Bury St Edmunds, Suffolk
Printed in England by Clays Ltd, St Ives plc

Contents

Introduction   1

1 Finding the Right Word   9
2 Topic and Treatment   36
3 The Nuts and Bolts of Writing   57
4 Assembling and Separating   78
5 Blending Word with Word   103
6 'In a Manner of Speaking'   129
7 'What are You Talking About?'   151
8 Compression and Omission   174
9 Sense and Nonsense   199
10 Reasoning and Explaining   222

Index   243

Introduction

Learning to Write

This book is directed at readers who want to be able to express their thoughts on paper clearly and logically. We first learn to write in the same way as we first learn to speak, by practice and imitation. The human race has been peculiarly successful in handing on the ability to speak. Somehow we succeed in educating the young within the first few years of life to manipulate what is really one of humanity's most complex techniques. The development happens all around us – from animal squeaks and dribbles to coherent speech in six years of intellectual immaturity. How is it done? Researchers have counted in thousands the number of words that the average child of three or four utters in a day. Clearly constant practice matters, but that practice is solidly based on imitation, not on formal instruction in 'How to Speak'. We do not introduce our toddlers to grammatical rules or formulations, yet somehow they readily learn that 'John kicked Jane' means something different from 'Jane kicked John'.

The importance of the imitative factor in learning to speak is evident in the different accents, dialects, and indeed degrees of 'correctness' that we hear around us. And since learning to write is equally a matter of practice and imitation, it is obvious that what we read will determine how well or badly we write. Good English usage is picked up by infection from what we hear and read. In the same way, however, bad usage is picked up by infection from what we hear and read. In that respect how healthy is the usage climate that we inhabit? Clearly we cannot expect to progress in expressing ourselves effectively on paper if the printed material we pick up day by day abounds in slovenly and inaccurate usage. Yet of recent years much has been revealed about the increasing faultiness in the English usage of such media as the daily press, magazines and the radio. I have myself made more than one attempt to display in print the kind of errors habitually made and to show how they could be best avoided.

Some of those who have paid attention to this problem have spoken as though it were chiefly due to a general ignorance of grammar. While it cannot be denied that grammatical error plays a part in damaging current usage, it has never seemed to me that the remedy for this situation was to be found simply in stuffing more and more grammatical formulations into the heads of either children or adults. One cannot investigate current usage for its defects without discovering that ignorance of grammar is not the gravest deficiency in it. Some of the faultiest sentences we read and hear nowadays are not in the least ungrammatical.

Getting a correct grammatical structure in a sentence is one thing. Using words meaningfully in a sentence is a different thing. The two matters are of course closely related. It would be difficult to think of a sentence which would be unambiguously sound and precise in the message it conveyed and yet which would be grammatically incorrect. But conversely it is easy to construct grammatically correct sentences which are deficient in meaning and offend common sense. There is nothing grammatically wrong with the following sentences: 'Three and four make five', 'Snails often suffer from schizophrenia', 'If you drink too much tea, you may explode'.

Unless we recognize what an enormous amount of error in writing is due to careless thinking, we shall probably overestimate the damage caused by neglect of grammatical formulations. In my years in higher education I found that crude grammatical slips formed a small proportion of the total errors in written English. Indeed I sometimes found an unerring instinct for faultless grammar existing alongside a tendency to lose one's head over simple logical sequences. I remember once setting a test for mature students in which they were asked to improve or correct a series of faulty sentences derived from their own work. One of the sentences ran:

These intelligent and imaginative children are the result of our
educational reforms.

I was astonished to find that most of the 'improved' or 'corrected'
versions ran: 'These intelligent and imaginative children are the *results*
of our educational reforms.' It seemed to me that instruction in
formal grammar would not meet the crying need of these students.
Grammatically, it seemed, they were keenly on the alert. Their need
was simply to learn to think clearly; to ask themselves not 'Should
the word *result* be singular or plural?' but '*What* is a result?' and 'Can
a child, however intelligent or imaginative, be defined as the *result* of
an educational reform?'

The Need for Sound Thinking

It is sound thinking that produces good English; it is unsound thinking that produces incorrect English. And by 'good English' we mean
wording that clearly and effectively conveys what we want it to convey.
People tend to think that 'good English' is just one of the options on
offer for conveying what they have to convey. Indeed one comes across
the assumption that 'good English' imposes a rather troublesome
demand to do something according to special rules which could be
done just as well and much more easily without them. The reasoning
is false. You might choose between various options if you had to make
a journey to Manchester. You might go by train, by car or even by taxi.
The point about these options is that they all deliver the same result.
They all get you to Manchester. Faulty English is unlikely to convey
exactly the same message as correct English. I have just heard a voice
on the radio declaring that applicants for a certain requirement
'must say where they live and where their postcode is'. Might not an
applicant respond to this demand by saying: 'My postcode is in my
diary along with my PIN number'? The question 'Where is John's
address?' is not the same question as 'What is John's address?' The
same applies to the word 'postcode'. Clearly the speaker should have
said 'where they live and what their postcode is'.

There were centuries in the history of our own civilization when logic was one of the inescapable disciplines in educational courses. Logic is that branch of study in which there is careful analysis of the patterns of reasoning that we follow when arguing a case. It trains us to be exact in our thinking and precise in our utterance, oral or written. The discipline that we must accept if we are to write well is a discipline that first of all directs our thinking. What are the most basic rules for writing correctly and convincingly? You have to make up your mind in advance what (or who) you are talking about. When you actually start to write you must continue to keep in mind exactly what you are talking about. And you must go on talking about it until the sentence ends, or until you specifically change the subject. Saying what you mean is essentially a matter of keeping a straight course and a clear head. Let us look at something I have read in my daily paper. It is concerned with a recent controversy over the use of the MMR vaccine. The journalist is reporting an outbreak of measles in London, where many of the cases are connected with a cluster in Lambeth, Southwark and Lewisham health authority.

> This hotspot of the virus, centred on the White House school in Clapham, has continued to spread since it took hold in February.

This sentence is grammatically correct. Moreover, there is not a single word, considered in isolation, that the writer does not properly understand. Yet it perfectly illustrates what is most often wrong with current journalism in the use of our language. For it tells you that 'this hotspot ... has continued to spread since it took hold'. That is what we are told. Apparently a 'hotspot' is something that can 'take hold' and then 'spread'. The journalist started to talk about a hot spot and then mentally shifted to talking about the virus without allowing her wording to keep up with her. All that was needed to make the sentence above logical was for the writer to keep in mind the difference between a hotspot and a virus and to recognize when she was talking about the one and when she was talking about the other. 'The hotspot of the virus was centred on the White House school in Clapham, and the virus has continued to spread since it took hold there in February.'

We are concerned with the spoken as well as the written word. We are as likely to hear sloppy use of English on the radio as to read it in the newspaper. I have just heard an announcer speak of a calamitous terrorist bomb attack on a night club and speculate about what might happen 'if a similar attack were to recur'. This is a fascinating slip-up. If a second attack occurs that is 'similar' to the first, it represents a 'recurrence' of the first attack. But if that 'similar' attack were to 'recur', that would presumably constitute a third such attack. In other words, it is not the 'similar' attack that 'recurs'. What 'recurs', that is repeats itself, is the first attack, not a 'similar' one.

The radio provides us with notable examples of such loose thinking. I heard a commentator putting the government under pressure on the subject of arms being supplied by UK companies to the Israelis. The government's claim to have an 'ethical' foreign policy was cited. The commentator put on his most outraged, most dialectically power-ful voice: 'Is this a total change in government policy or a recognition of what the real situation is?' Here indeed, seemingly, was the opportu-nity to trap someone. But the supposed alternatives are false ones, for clearly a logical reply might be: 'Both.' The two are not mutually exclusive. You can perhaps create a moment of dialectical tension by asking 'Is this a masterpiece or a load of rubbish?' But you can't create a moment of dialectical tension by asking 'Is this a masterpiece or a work of art?' Yet such false alternatives are regularly put excitedly before us by the BBC news commentators.

We live in a verbally infected environment. It is infected in that simplicity and directness are undervalued. I buy a new electric radio alarm clock. The information about its use is headed 'Functional Overview', which apparently means 'How it Works'. More gravely, our verbal environment is one in which too many of those who address us are not thinking before they speak or write. They have a stock of words and phrases from which material is culled without rational analysis. I recently heard a speaker on a news programme defending a certain plan that had been put into practice. 'In terms of results, it was effective.' That was what he said. And the question arises whether any plan could be 'effective' except 'in terms of its results'. When you say that a plan was effective, you mean that it achieved the results intended. But expressions like 'in terms of' are part of the stock of available vocabulary supposedly appropriate at any point to fill a space.

Compose Yourself

This book is partly about not automatically falling back on that stock of available usage, so often unreliable. It is about thinking before you utter. It is about composing your thoughts for rational discourse. There was a time when schools called lessons in writing 'composition' lessons. It was a useful word for what it conveyed both of inventing material and of imposing order on it. We use the words 'compose' and 'composition' widely of artistic products in music and the arts. They were once used more of agreements and compacts. In Shakespeare's *Antony and Cleopatra* an attempt is made to patch up an agreement between Octavius Caesar and Mark Antony, the two rival masters of the Roman world. As Antony comes along to negotiate with Caesar, he turns to one of his followers and says: 'If we compose well here, to Parthia.' In other words: 'If we get a satisfactory settlement agreed here, then we shall move into Parthia.' To 'compose' is to make satisfactory terms and come to an agreement. In *Macbeth* the defeated king of Norway 'craves composition', in other words, seeks a peace agreement. Especially interesting, in connection with the work in hand here, are the words with which the Duke of Venice opens the council scene in *Othello*. Various conflicting reports have been received about threatening movements of the Turkish fleet. 'There is no composition in these news,' the Duke complains, which would make the information credible. 'Composition' implies consistency and coherence. Anyone concerned for good English usage must be aware that to 'compose' well in speech or on paper is to produce a fabric in which the parts fit together harmoniously. This notion of orderliness, as opposed to inner conflict, is basic to 'composition' of all kinds. 'Compose yourself!' is generally advice to get rid of any disquiet, confusion or turmoil that may be disturbing the system. The word 'composure', implying a settled and unruffled attitude, derives from the same Latin word as 'composition'.

Thus it is that, in the process of correcting faulty English, the expressions which come most frequently to mind are concerned with disorder as opposed to order: 'This word does not properly balance that one', 'This expression does not connect coherently with that one',

'This assertion does not follow properly on that one', 'You cannot put this word here if that word is there'. It is effective 'composition' that produces lucid and meaningful English. And perhaps we shall best understand the character of effective 'composition' if we contrast it with what we know of decomposition. It is the difference between a coherently organized organism working meaningfully in all its separate parts and functions and a defunct, decaying mass of squalid remains. How far our civilization and culture, our institutions and social patterns are more generally affected by decomposition is not a matter for discussion here, but the case could be made that the decay of coherence and precision in our use of words is a symptom that ought to be urgently treated on other grounds than mere interest in making oneself clear.

Be that as it may, the immediate aim here is to guide and encourage readers to come to the task of expressing themselves on paper with two firm purposes in mind. The first is mentally to clear the decks of the accumulated verbal detritus deposited there by daily exposure to today's media. The second is to organize their thoughts for articulation by fixing their eyes on the virtues of directness and clarity. We don't want what we have to say to be marred by modish cliché or laden with fashionable wordiness. It is to cater for these two aims that we scrutinize defective practices in the verbal environment we inhabit and try to show how we may escape their influence. It is often said that we learn from our mistakes and no doubt that is true of certain activities. So far as the art of writing is concerned, however, there is an awful lot that we can learn from the mistakes of others.

1

Finding the Right Word

The right word in any context is the word that fits there and pulls its weight there. There are words which usage has rendered almost incapable of pulling any weight at all. They are words which slip into our use by habit, bypassing the proper process of real thinking. They are overused words which you should think twice about when they come to mind as you are writing, or even as you are speaking if the context is a formal one. Frequency of use is not, of course, in itself necessarily damaging to words. You may use the words 'cup of tea' several times a day, and the words retain their fitness. You don't even damage the words if you regularly use them metaphorically, describing a new television programme that attracts your children as 'not my cup of tea'. The words we are here concerned with are to be handled with especial restraint, not just because they are overused but because they have been overused in a way which has reduced their value. They plant themselves in our minds through force of thoughtless habit. If we actually paused to recall what they are supposed to mean and compare it with what we are making them mean, then we should not utter or write them. We turn first to a distinctive category of words which have already been vandalized, a few of that group of words that is raided day after day, not in order to be used for their proper meaning, but to have that meaning drained away.

Threadbare Words

Consider how the writer chooses to use the word 'terrific' in the following:

> Interesting garden forms of meadow cranesbill, *Geranium pratense*
> are terrific and really thrive on dry alkaline soil.

Here the word 'terrific' is used simply as a term of vague approval. The dictionary meaning of the word – 'very great, intense, frightening' – is ignored. Yet the obvious connection of the word with the words 'terror' and 'terrify' indicates what a powerful connotation it once had. Does the loose use of it matter? Only in the sense that, overused in this way, the word is not available for effective use when it is really wanted. If you want to convey that there is news of a truly 'terrific' disaster, a natural disaster or a calamitous train accident, you cannot convey the magnitude of the event if you have recently been using the word as the gardener used it above. One day you have a 'terrific' headache, the next day a 'terrific' new summer outfit, then a 'terrific' let-down because the price of the item has been halved in the sale. If we can't avoid this unnecessary recourse to the word in daily chatter, we must at least do so when we write or speak formally.

In the same gardening magazine I read of how some enthusiasts renovated a historic garden under the scrutiny of television viewers:

> When we opened the garden to the public, the sun was shining
> and the response was just incredible.

And in another magazine I read:

> I admit that, as a teenager in the late 70s and early 80s, I was
> incredibly impressed with what working-class boys on club doors
> could achieve.

In neither case is it appropriate to introduce notions of incredibility. What is 'incredible' is beyond belief or understanding. Appropriately applied to accounts of seeming preternatural manifestations the word carries its proper weight. Perhaps the careless misuse of the words 'incredible' and 'incredibly' is more damaging than the careless misuse of the word 'terrific', because when we want to define something in terms of magnitude and terror we have lots of words to go at – 'vast', 'immense', 'huge', 'massive', 'horrifying' and 'overwhelming' for instance – but when we want to describe something as utterly beyond belief we have only the words 'unbelievable' and 'incredible'. And 'incredible' has become all but useless because its connotation has been diluted to the point of near meaninglessness.

The fact is that we use lots of words regularly of such a kind and in such a way that if we were asked 'Did you really mean that?' we should have to say no. We didn't really mean that the costume was 'fantastically' cheap but the shoes 'dreadfully' expensive. We didn't really mean that the restaurant was 'beautifully' clean but the chairs 'horribly' uncomfortable. We were just mentally underlining the words 'cheap' and 'expensive', 'clean' and 'uncomfortable'. The over-worked additional words are just devices to intensify the meaning of the words they accompany, virtually putting the words that follow them into italics. It is when we are making statements in the approval mode or the disapproval mode that these intensifiers come fully into their own. It was a 'beastly' cold morning, we say. We happened to get up late and we were 'frantically' trying to make up for it. But the fridge was almost 'literally' empty. Added to which, the postman came 'impossibly' late. So we talk, and the intensifying words 'beastly', 'frantically', 'literally' and 'impossibly' are all but empty of meaning. We really meant that it was a very cold morning, we overslept and were trying hard to make up for it, the fridge was nearly empty and the postman came very late.

It is perhaps worth making the point that, if we try to be resourceful and original in our use of 'intensifiers' we may only add to the damage done to our language. If we say 'It was a deliriously happy occasion', using 'deliriously' as a mere intensifier, then we hasten the coming of the time when 'deliriously' will go the way of 'frantically'. Journalists, of course, have a vested interest in adding to the list of intensifiers, because a newly adopted intensifier carries imaginative clout and an air of refreshing novelty. So the proliferation of intensifiers is presumably bound to increase. We hear or see someone condemned as 'infernally intrusive' or 'unconscionably demanding'. We find someone praised as 'staggeringly clever' or 'captivatingly beautiful'.

Whenever a useful descriptive term is used for purely exaggerative emphasis its connotation is weakened and its progress hastened towards becoming a mere intensifier all but useless for its proper function.

Fashion brings changes in this respect. In one decade the word 'great' stamps things with our approval, in another decade the favourite word is 'fabulous' and then that gives way to 'cool'. Yet each usage is kept alive, and not always happily. It may still be acceptable for us to flatter a friend by telling her that she looks 'great' in the new outfit she has bought. No hint of magnitude hangs about the usage of 'great' there. However, there are contexts in which this appreciative usage of 'great' might be inappropriate.

> Tesco pharmacies sell a wide range of products at great prices for
> you and your family . . .

A really clear thinker could not put that on paper, knowing that the ambiguity inherent in the word 'great' is going to make the claim seem comic. It is safer to advertise as does a restaurant I passed yesterday: 'Fabulous Fish!' No one is going to make the mistake of expecting a steak from the Loch Ness Monster.

One might argue that the world of advertising would be duller without such ventures. Similarly our conversation would be intolerably colourless if we scrapped all the words that save us the trouble of peppering our talk with repetitions of 'very' and 'highly', 'good' and 'bad', 'pleasant' and 'unpleasant'. However, we are here primarily concerned with the importance of habitually using the right words on paper, and that means establishing a habit, word by word, of meaning what we say.

Draining Words of Meaning

We turn now to look more specifically at the process of decay that knocks the real stuffing out of words. There are plenty of words now overused in such a way as to drain them of meaning. We can still employ them in some contexts to carry a valid connotation, but increasingly inexact overuse is debilitating them. Some of them are abstract terms with clear connotations in various fields of scholarship and the arts which have long been taken into more common use. In leaving the more rarified contexts for the domain of day-to-day use, they tend to lose connotative clarity. Then indeed, thrown about by publicists and advertisers, such words are gradually emptied of meaning and become mere counters. It may be argued that the words we have described as 'intensifiers' do at least perform a function, if it is only that of telling you to read the words that follow them in bold type. But some of these 'counters' are being turned into little more than noises in the air or marks on a piece of paper. For our examples let us look at some usages of a group of words now popular with advertisers and journalists. The word 'concept' is one.

> Our special attraction at the show will be special concept cars of the 21st century sponsored by the AA.

Since a 'concept' is an idea in the abstract, the word has recently been exploited where what is required is the notion of some novel product of the inventive mind. Thus we find a firm advertising 'the Atkinson's concept of retaining your kitchen or bedroom carcases and replacing only the facia'.

While the word 'concept' is borrowed from psychology, the word 'theme' has been borrowed from the world of the arts.

> She already had a brass toothbrush holder, so she added to that theme by buying a toilet roll holder and towel ring in the same style.

To suggest that a brass toothbrush holder constitutes a 'theme' to which additions may be made is to wear away the connotative quality of the word 'theme'. Those to whom a 'theme' is something enunciated at the opening of a symphony or an epic poem, and charged with significance, will sense a cheapening of our linguistic currency.

> The interior of the main saloon follows the same design theme to the earlier ships.

The addition of the word 'design' here is interesting because it prepares us for the following advertisement:

> Come to our showroom where our helpful staff will be pleased to
> assist you with queries, designs or theme concepts.

We have had a 'design theme'. Now we have 'theme concepts'. And another firm selling fitments for kitchens and bathrooms claims this for its work:

> It's a total design concept that lets you mix and match to create
> an infinite number of possibilities.

It begins to look as though the terms 'concept', 'design' and 'theme' can also be mixed and matched to create an infinite number of possibilities.

The clear thinker will resist the temptation to join in the campaign of verbal vandalism. It is a campaign that picks words up from any speciality of life or thought and squeezes out of them whatever real significance they bear. One of the firms quoted above claims that it 'redefines the role of the kitchen and dining room'. Serious interpretation of those words would surely convey that there was to be a change from using the kitchen for cooking and the dining room for eating, for such are the roles of those rooms. But what the advertisement really achieves is to redefine the role of utterance, which ought to be to preserve or enrich meaning, not to eradicate it. The word 'role', especially useful in the world of drama, has been divested of its rich connotative quality and used seemingly as the equivalent of 'function'. But only 'seemingly'. For by no stretch of imagination can it be pretended that refurnishing a kitchen or a dining room with the latest in equipment and furniture is generally undertaken in order to alter the function of either.

It would be neglectful to leave this topic without reverting to the way the advertiser used the word 'infinite' above ('infinite number of possibilities'). This is an exaggerative use of a word whose real meaning is totally disproportionate to what is intended by the writer. We have long used expressions such as 'I shall be eternally grateful to you' when we know that we can't really vouch for our 'eternal' destiny. In the same way we have heard people say 'He is a man of infinite patience' when what was meant was that he was a very patient man indeed. Exaggeration in such contexts might be excused as an aspect of human courtesy, but it is a rather different matter when one reads of a garden:

> It is obvious that this is a garden that gives its owners a great deal
> of pleasure. The infinite amount of intimate personal touches
> throughout makes it feel well cared for and loved.

If 'infinite' is now allowed to slip off the tongue or the pen as a ready substitute for 'numerous' or 'many', it will be a pity. That development has happened with 'finite'.

> With only a finite amount of each fabric available, orders will be
> handled on a first come, first served basis.

It is useful to have the word 'finite' as the opposite of 'infinite', the notion of what is bounded by space and time with what is not so bounded. The writer who values logical clarity will not throw away a word so useful in order to convey that the supply of a certain curtain material on sale will run out in due course.

When the word 'finite' is used to mean 'limited' and the word 'infinite' to mean 'numerous' there is an exaggeration that weakens the words. The more such usages are repeated, the more the proper, tight connotations of the words are dissipated. The process of dissipation is happening around us to many, many words. We have taken part in it whenever we have thoughtlessly repeated the word 'unique' to mean remarkable or very effective. It has happened to the word 'myth'. I have just read:

> It is assumed that men who cross-dress must be gay, but this is a
> myth.

'Myth' is a rich word for those stories of gods and goddesses of the ancient world which somehow comprehend through the substance of their narratives sometimes perceptive, sometimes profound interpretations of the universe and our place within it. It is natural that the characteristics of the invented and the fantastic that these stories have should have left us with the notion that 'myth' is one thing and factual history a very different thing. So the mythical gets contrasted with the historical. The word 'myth' is loosely bandied about as a convenient way of casting doubt on the truth of some story or related facts. The clear thinker will always say 'that is false' rather than 'that is a myth', if that is what is really meant.

A similar cheapening of meaning has occurred with the word 'legendary'. Narratives like the story of Theseus are properly described as 'legendary'. They belong to ancient legend and have acquired the mystique of venerableness and remoteness. It is natural that the word should have been used when writers were anxious to create an aura of extreme grandeur around some person or event. 'His generosity was legendary,' the obituarist writes. It is a pity perhaps that he does. But it is surely not quite as damaging as this advertisement for outdoor clothing.

> Durability is legendary and far greater than that of performance
> fabric derived from the petrochemical industry.

Logically examined, the sentence makes nonsense. 'Durability is legendary' is just not true. 'Its durability is legendary' is what is meant, and it is crude misuse of a rich word.

Although perhaps advertisers are most prone to this kind of exaggeration, deeply stirred feelings, either of approval or disapproval, send speakers and writers reaching for hyperbole.

> Fish were still being dragged from the lower river in obscene
> numbers . . .

So an outraged angler writes. 'Obscene' is a strong word and it cannot literally be applied to numbers. The angler reaches for a word which will reveal his disgust with what is happening.

Some Words in Danger

We have looked at words so overused that they have already lost their usefulness. We have observed the process by which words have their proper meanings drained away. We turn now to look more closely at some words currently suffering the kind of careless handling that empties them of exactness in their connotation.

answer

An answer is a reply to a question. The word is used strictly thus on examination papers. If there are pressing problems in the air, we now tend to say 'What's the answer?' But this use of the word presupposes a question or a problem in the background. It is lax to use the word 'answer' where no such query arises.

> There are no right or wrong answers to these issues.

An 'issue', in that context, is a matter or topic of concern. It may call for consideration and discussion, but it does not call for an 'answer'. If the word 'answers' is kept, then the word 'issues' must go: 'There are no right and wrong answers to these questions.' The current fondness for overstretching this word 'answer' is well illustrated in this piece from the world of horse-racing:

> Nevertheless there was a sizeable entry that resulted in 10 combinations finding the answers to a technical track, which was raised considerably for the jump-off.

Whatever physical obstacles and traps impeded the progress of the competitors in this event, it seems unnecessary to describe their successful negotiation as a matter of 'finding answers'.

aspect

The word 'aspect' is surely among the most overused words today. It is properly used of an appearance, a distinct feature, or a particular way of considering some issue, and it comes in useful in numerous contexts. There are contexts, however, in which it seems to function to no clear purpose at all. Here is a piece about reviving airships:

> The memory of Count von Zeppelin was an important aspect in restarting this development from a historical point of view.

In this case the word 'aspect' seems to have been chosen, not for want of any other word, but for want of a clear meaning in the sentence. Nothing would be lost if the sentence were rewritten so as to remove the word. We might suggest 'The memory of Count von Zeppelin influenced us in restarting this development' or even 'encouraged us to restart this development'. Each of those two versions conveys a meaning, whereas the original wording ('was an important aspect in') is evasive of meaning.

background

An interesting kind of verbal misuse can occur as a result of stretching the connotation of a word on the basis of already established idiomatic practice. That is what has happened to the word 'background'. We know what a background is, literally speaking. Yet we tend to extend the meaning of the word conversationally when we are told of some struggle arising between people and we ask 'What is the background to all this?' We are asking to have events accounted for by explanation of how the struggle arose. We are asking for something like the causes and the history of the situation. That usage of the word 'background' is no doubt defensible. But what are we to make of the following? It is concerned with controversy over licensing cruising boats on canals by British Waterways:

> The background to this meeting long predated the continuous cruising license proposals but was to explore problems perceived by BW to be caused by continuously cruising boats and their mooring habits.

It would have been satisfactory to describe how the controversy developed after using the words 'The background to this meeting', but to say that 'the background predated' certain events is to turn the word 'background' into the equivalent of some such word as 'origin' or 'cause'. To make matters worse, the 'background' is then said to have been 'to explore' certain problems. So the background, having first functioned as 'origin' now functions as something roughly equivalent to 'agenda' or 'plan'. 'Background' has been turned into an all-purpose word devoid of any clarity of definition. The sentence should begin: 'This meeting was concerned with issues dating back before the continuous cruising licence proposals . . .'

climate

At the time of crisis after the destruction of the New York skyscrapers by terrorists a BBC announcement told how items such as knives were being taken from passengers boarding planes at UK airports. The action was described as an understandable inconvenience 'during the present climate'. But a climate is not a stretch of time during which things may or may not occur and the use of the word 'during' was out of place. Expressions such as 'climate of opinion' and 'emotional climate' are useful metaphors and the word 'climate' has gradually established itself as a shorthand word for the state of public feeling generally prevalent. However, that usage would scarcely justify the following statement from a local authority reporting on local conditions:

> The bad news in recent months has built on a general climate of
> decline that has been going on for ten years and more.

To say that bad news has 'built on a climate' is to throw words about without respect for connotation. And to speak of a 'decline' as 'going on' is inelegant to say the least. What is conveyed by the sentence can be said without reference to 'news' or 'climate'. The topic under discussion is unemployment and what we learn is that the situation in that respect is continuing to deteriorate.

convenience

A rather surprising popularity seems to have descended upon the word 'convenience' as used in the business world. Of course, it carries useful associations of what is readily available and helpful, and therefore gets applied to provisions made for the benefit of customers, but here we have an example of how the word is being misused in a quite different context. The topic is the controversy about allowing women to become members of Lord's.

> Traditionalists are portrayed as blimps and dinosaurs, but that is
> just a cheap convenience.

To most of us a 'cheap convenience' would be a public lavatory that made no charge. Here a journalist uses the expression when what he appears to mean is that representing the traditionalists as blimps and dinosaurs is an easy way of discrediting them. It appears that 'convenience' is used of something that is ready to hand or easily accessible, and 'cheap' of something that is rather unworthy. So why not say 'but that is a ready-made jibe'?

deliver

The verb to 'deliver' is now scattered over statements from the business world. It was once a word with a much more restricted use than it has now. Time was when postmen delivered the mail and doctors or midwives delivered new-born babies. Yet now I read:

> Of course the LTA should ensure that tennis reaches as wide a base as possible and schools must be the focus for delivering initiatives.

Need 'initiatives' acquire the status of junk mail? What is wrong with just 'taking' initiatives or even 'inspiring' them? The truth is that a remarkable variety of items is now being 'delivered' regularly in the press.

> We believe there is a powerful argument to suggest that a single management focus on delivering safety and quality will produce better results than a diverse matrix of integrated contracts.

This is a statement from the transport industry. To the mind of someone sensitive to words, concern with 'safety' and 'quality' is certainly something to be looked after by a transport system, but the transport industry's business is not a matter of delivering abstractions. It is passengers and freight that have to be efficiently delivered to their destinations. Yet from the same industry we take the following:

> I sense that passengers and London's businesses want us to deliver improvements sooner rather than later.

Why does making bus and train services better have to become a matter of 'delivering improvements'. In simple English 'improvements' are things that you 'make'. It is goods that you 'deliver'. Yet the sentence above was followed shortly after by this:

> Richard Bowker promised to focus on two areas: first, to restore stability and confidence allowing the railway to deliver the basics every day and, second, to design and implement the vision for the railway the country wanted.

We have already heard of the railway 'delivering' safety, quality and improvements. Now it is going to 'deliver' basics and every day of the week. That, along with designing and implementing a 'vision', seems to constitute the system's modus operandi.

focused

In the business world there seems to be a now well-established stylized verbal menu that supplies items for filling up space on paper. The word 'focused' is one of them. This comes from the railway industry:

> He put engineering centre stage. He called for clear, competent, focused leadership. SRA would, he insisted, be pro-active, energetic, an asker of tough questions and a maker of tough decisions.

Does the word 'focused' add anything here? One asks because it is one of the terms now sprinkled over business statements with the seeming desire to make them all sound the same. What would be the use of 'unfocused' leadership? Can any practical task be achieved without focus upon it? And what is the force here of the word 'proactive'? All business leaders should be ready to take initiatives and the word 'proactive' cannot convey anything other than that readiness. The tendency in the business world to pick up a watering-can-type container overflowing with such expressions and to douse printed statements from this fount of overdone clichés is wholly unbusinesslike.

functional

It is happening to the word 'functional'. Something that is 'functional' is something that performs a function, in other words, that works. So to read of the planning of a garden that 'the scheme should be functional' says no more than that the scheme will come off and the garden will be able to be treated as a garden. Surely that ought not to need saying of any scheme or plan. And consider the following from an account of protective clothing for anglers:

> The hood volume can be adjusted by means of a simple, but functional, exterior tape-and-buckle arrangement . . .

The writer is recommending the garment. To remind the reader that the device for adjusting the hood actually works ought surely to be superfluous. A non-functional adjustment system would represent a contradiction in terms.

identify

A now rapidly decaying word is the verb to 'identify'. My dictionary tells me of its use in speaking of proving or recognizing the identity of a person or thing, or of recognizing equivalence between items. But we find a usage far removed from that in sentences such as the following:

> The Chief Constable of Northamptonshire makes a number of points with which many people working in the criminal justice system will identify.

This current tendency to use the word 'identify' as the equivalent of 'sympathize' is surely lax and insensitive. There is no logical justification for this usage. No human being should be asked to 'identify' with a list of points, however valid. The sentence should end 'with which many people working in the criminal justice system will sympathize'.

implement

In any short list of the most overused words in business today 'implement' would have to take its place alongside 'deliver' and 'focus'. We have already heard (under 'deliver') of the railway management's pledge, not only to deliver daily basics, but also to 'design and implement the vision' the country is crying out for. There is more in the same vein:

> Railway Safety is determined that any lessons learned from such incidents are quickly implemented for the benefit of the travelling public.

> We intend to maintain this cooperation with partner organizations to implement the actions identified in the Wye Salmon Action Plan.

The verb to 'implement' means to carry out or put into effect some plan. Its connection with the noun 'implement' indicates its proper range of usage. And here, in the three sentences, we have talk of implementing a 'vision', a 'lesson' and certain 'actions'. In face of the fashion of the moment one would like to plead for a little more variety. Expressions like 'realize', 'fulfil', 'carry out', 'put into practice', 'put into effect' and 'bring about' suggest themselves.

question

Use of the word 'question' clearly exemplifies the way a word's connotation can melt away by excessive and careless usage in the media. It can be argued that 'journalese' is a special kind of utterance and no doubt certain idiomatic freedoms have to be allowed for in that connection, but indisciplined use of the word 'question' can offend common sense. We may smile when we read the heading:

> Asthma and Other Questions Answered

We know that asthma is not a 'question' but a disease, and that diseases require cures, not answers. But the effect of carelessness of this kind is to turn the words 'question' and 'answer' into the equivalents of vague terms such as 'matter' on the one hand and 'opinion' on the other. Here is a sentence from an article on horse-racing that discusses how courses for competitions should test competitors:

> But we can't go back to the more difficult questions like unfilled
> corners, because you can't guarantee that everyone will ride them
> correctly.

Here we are faced with the somewhat bizarre suggestion that 'unfilled corners' represent one of a series of 'questions' and that people can't be guaranteed to 'ride' these questions 'correctly'. Obviously the word 'questions' would have been better avoided.

solution

The word 'solution' is suffering the same fate as the word 'answer'. Just as the word 'answer' floats too far away from its dependence on the word 'question' so the word 'solution' floats too far away from its connection with the word 'problem'.

> Brian Ranwell and his advisers work closely with you to develop
> the ideal solution for your home.

This is from an advertisement for furniture, and one might find many comparable examples of the usage, especially in the advertising world. It seems that a 'solution' must be regarded as representing the thing most sought after in our problematic world. Someone has pointed out that on Victorian gravestones the word 'peace' recurs time and time again as representing the state most to be envied in the lot of the departed. Would it be frivolous perhaps to suggest that the word 'solution' has a comparable hold on the contemporary mind and ought to figure more in inscriptions in the cemetery? Certainly the sentence above uses the word 'solution' for an all-purpose set of desiderata. If you were to observe that you already had all the most necessary conveniences of modern life in your home and did not particularly want to add a solution, you would be accused of missing the point. The fact remains that problems demand solutions but houses do not need them. Here, moreover, someone is wanting to provide a solution for the garden as well as for the house:

> This path doesn't need to be an expensive paved solution, as materials such as gravel and bark are just as effective.

Admittedly there had been talk here of the unpleasantness of having to tread through mud. Nevertheless, to conjure up the notion of a 'paved solution' is to go in for gobbledegook.

vulnerable
This has become a fashionable word. Here is a piece about a possible threat to our vegetables from superbugs resistant to insecticides:

> It is certainly quite possible that a combination of resistant insects and removal of insecticides through regulation could leave us vulnerable to a situation where we would have to bring these vegetables in from abroad.

What is the point of drawing in the notion of 'vulnerability' here? If, instead of saying 'My cold might prevent me from going to work tomorrow', I said 'My cold might leave me vulnerable to a situation in which I could not go to work tomorrow' I should surely leave myself vulnerable to the situation in which I was accused of long-windedness. But that is the way the word 'vulnerable' is being used, in the interests of wordiness. The word should go: 'It is certainly quite possible that through a combination of resistant insects and removal of insecticides we might have to bring in these vegetables from abroad.'

way

The word 'way' is now used with a breadth of application that offends the logical mind. Here is a typical case from an advertisement:

> Viners 18/10 stainless-steel three-piece steamer is one of the healthiest ways to cook.

A means of cooking or a piece of equipment used in cooking is not a 'way' to cook, but a device for cooking. And a more interesting misusage is the following:

> The group is consulting UK broking firms on ways they believe the LSE should be developed . . .

What the writer means is that the group is consulting UK broking firms on 'how they believe the LSE should be developed'. If you are tempted to write the word 'way', check up that there is not some clearer usage to hand, especially some expression beginning with 'how' – 'how' we do this or that, not 'the way' we do it.

Near Misses and Not so Near

Getting the right word is obviously a matter of not using any of the wrong ones. It is interesting that the mistakes in speech or writing which we tend to find most absurd and laughable are often not the result of illogical thinking but of simple ignorance or indeed forgetfulness. I recall a dear old friend, long dead, who would remark on a close summer day, 'Oh, what a paltry hot day it is!' To confuse the word 'paltry' with the word 'sultry' is not the mark of a mind untrained in logical thinking but of a mind lacking the right information on a particular point. When the seemingly educated speaker on the radio spoke of 'Mr William Hague's precipitous retirement from the leadership of the Conservative party', he was displaying similar ignorance of the proper meaning of the word 'precipitous' and confusing it with the word 'precipitate'. A 'precipitate' decision or action is one which is too quickly reached or undertaken, but 'precipitous' means 'steep' and is often applied to hillsides. There are no questions of grammar or of logic at issue here. Educated people will rightly squirm when the familiar confusions are made between the words 'flaunt' and 'flout', but the slips do not indicate an ill-functioning mind so much as an inadequately informed mind. We should not think ill of a foreigner whose first language was not English for picking the wrong words in cases of this kind.

For every instance of such misuse, which results from confusing different words that are similar in sound, there must surely be hundreds of cases of misuse which result from mistakenly trying to make a word do a job that it is not fitted for. Very often the effect of so doing is to link one word with another in an illogical connection. We are here looking at some words that have been used where their true meaning makes them inapplicable, and at some words mishandled in the constructions used.

condone

The writer often has to choose a word from a group of words that share close similarities, yet each has its own sphere in usage. Mistakes in selection can make a bad impression on the intelligent reader. Here, a journalist is writing about the judging of competitive events:

> You can't condone those who abuse the judges, though, any more than you can condone biased judging.

The verb to 'condone' means to overlook an offence, to let it pass without condemnation. It is not used of people. One 'condones' an offence, but one 'forgives' a person. 'Forgive' is not the word required here, however, and there is no exactly parallel verb to the verb 'condone' that can be applied to people. The best reading here would omit 'those who': 'You cannot condone abuse of judges, though, any more than you can condone biased judging.'

cure

The innovative mind naturally tries to avoid the obvious and the commonplace. In the use of language, avoiding the obvious may produce the stuff of poetry; or it may produce illogicality. To use a word outside its normal referential context is legitimate provided that the word fits appropriately into the novel context. But if it comes dragging a significance which is inappropriate to the new context, then the experiment does not enrich language but damages the word. That is what happens here:

> However, the remorseless downward trend in the numbers taking engineering at university will not be cured by teaching the subject in schools and certainly not at GCSE level.

The verb to 'cure' is a powerful verb and the contexts appropriate for using it effectively are numerous. But stopping a downward trend in students taking engineering at university is not one of them. We do not 'cure' downward trends. If need be, we 'reverse' them or 'halt' them, or at least 'slow' them. There are plenty of words available for checking trends and ameliorating situations without recourse to a word so richly useful in its proper contexts as 'cure'.

curtail

This word has a certain overlap with the word 'reduce', but the following usage is extravagantly out of place:

> We must be eagle-eyed to ensure that the government and its agencies do not seek to curtail all our lives and pleasures while we are focused elsewhere.

This was written by a sportsman worried about opposition to hunting and shooting. The word 'curtail' means to abridge, to cut short. The only way to curtail someone's life is to kill them. And it is difficult to picture how even one's pleasure could be 'curtailed' if one was 'focused elsewhere'. The wrong word was chosen. The writer was really complaining about a possible limitation imposed on his activities and on his pleasures. He was fearful of being deprived of them. Curtailment, limitation and deprivation should not be confused. A better word here than 'curtail' would have been 'restrict'.

deprive

> The vastness of the day's first 2,000 ft top deprives intimate views of the upper Ullswater scene, although it retains a sizeable portion of the lake's lower reaches.

The climber here is going up Helvellyn and seemingly lamenting that he loses sight of upper Ullswater. He is there 'deprived' of a certain view, but his wording seems to tell us that, in losing sight of certain stretches of Ullswater, vastness functions as the depriver while it is intimate views that are deprived of a 'scene'. If only he had spoken simply of gaining views or losing views and left the irrelevant notion of 'deprivation' aside, he might have written a satisfactory sentence. 'As one reaches the first 2,000 ft peak, one loses sight of the upper Ullswater scene, although a sizeable portion of the lake's lower reaches is still visible.'

dismantle

A glaring transition from concrete to abstract is provided by a letter-writer to *The Times* on the subject of the parliamentary debate after the destruction of the New York skyscrapers.

> All civilized people share the outrage at the barbarism of September 11. But we should heed those backbenchers in all parties who in Parliament on Friday warned against inflicting terrorism in response (Tam Dalyell); who spoke of dismantling the hatred on which terrorism breeds (Alex Salmond) . . .

It is illogical to speak of 'dismantling' hatred. The act of dismantling is a concrete one. Statesmen have rightly spoken of 'dismantling the network' of terrorism. But to try to take over the notion of dismantling without mentioning something that could indeed be 'dismantled', such as a network, will not do. Moreover, it is equally illogical to speak of 'inflicting terrorism'. Great miseries are 'inflicted', that is, imposed on people without their consent, but terrorism is not what is 'inflicted', it is itself the act of inflicting it.

fob off

A slight slip does damage to the following sentence:

> The wines I tasted were miles away in spirit from the dire local style fobbed off on innocent tourists at inflated prices.

The verb 'to fob off' with this or that means to trick someone by passing something off on them that is inadequate to the need or demand. 'She sought a full explanation for the power failure, but was fobbed off with a feeble excuse.' Notice that there, where 'fobbed off' is used in the passive voice, it is the person who is 'fobbed off'. It would be incorrect to say instead 'but a feeble excuse was fobbed off on her'. Yet that is what has happened in the sentence above. It is wrong to say that the cheap wines were 'fobbed off' on tourists when what is meant is that 'innocent tourists were fobbed off with them'.

happen

Let us take a light-hearted example of a strictly inapt use of the verb to 'happen':

> I long for small, pretty feet, but that's never going to happen.

The pedant may well ask 'What is it that is never going to occur?' The verb 'to happen' is one of the most used verbs in our daily conversation. So common is it that we recognize that this journalist is misusing it intentionally, with raised eyebrow, to make her point chattily and intimately. However, taking that kind of liberty can assume a different aspect:

> A spokeswoman for Comet said of the hostage-taking: 'We regret
> the fact that happened but in the interests of customer service
> we have offered her a new machine.'

This is not journalistic licence but crude ill-usage. 'Facts' do not 'happen'. Events happen. The hostage-taking happened, but the fact that it happened did not happen. The fact was an abstraction from the events, something known only in the mind, so the word 'fact' intrudes illogically here. The spokeswoman should have said 'We regret what happened.'

Again, when computer trouble brought dealings on the London Stock Exchange to a halt, we heard this announcement on the radio:

> A spokesman for the Stock Exchange said they didn't know why
> the problem had happened.

Do problems 'happen'? We should not have considered the statement odd if the wording had been 'they didn't know why the problem had arisen'. It is worth while to examine traditional usage here. The technological breakdown is not a 'problem'; it is an event. It produced a 'problem' for the people at the Stock Exchange, but it was the breakdown that 'happened'.

install

We turn to a less direct specimen of verbal confusion. We have here a sentence taken from a write-up in praise of an airport's car-parking facilities:

> In order to meet increased demand, we have recently expanded the size of our long-term car park by adding 2,300 spaces. At the same time, we have taken the opportunity to install closed circuit television and other security measures which have enabled us to apply for recognition by the Association of Chief Police Officers as having a secure car park.

To begin with, the word 'size' is redundant. We expand car parks, we don't expand their 'size'. Secondly, the word 'measures' covers any kind of actions taken to secure a particular end. One such 'measure' is the installation of closed circuit television. The closed circuit television is 'installed', but the 'other measures' are not 'installed'. The verb 'install' is being required to do a job it cannot do. What is meant is: 'At the same time we have installed closed circuit television and taken other security measures.' Care must be taken when using the word 'and' to make sure that proper parallelisms are maintained. You would not say 'We have fitted up a new kitchen and other improvements' because the 'improvements' were not 'fitted up', but 'made'.

oblivious

Here is a sentence about a paedophile charged with taking snaps of children.

> The photographs were taken on unidentified beaches while the children played – their parents oblivious to O'Carroll's lens.

Srictly speaking, to be 'oblivious' of something is to be forgetful of it. The element of forgetfulness is crucial in sensitive use of the word. Here the parents were not forgetful of something, but just 'unaware' of what was happening.

obtain

Sometimes it is difficult to understand how a misuse can have occurred at all, so odd it seems at first sight.

> Some of the mills in Hebden Bridge have been recycled into small workshops and craft centres, but there is still just enough real work done here to obtain a healthy sense of reality.

The 'sense of reality' is surely something perceived by the visitor. It is not something that he or she 'obtains'. Nor is it something that the town 'obtains' so much as something that the town 'conveys'. And since real work has been done at Hebden Bridge for more than a century, the notion that the town is now 'obtaining' this sense is historically misleading. Why not 'there is still just enough real work done here to preserve a healthy sense of reality'?

overstep

Another obvious verbal misfire occurs in this piece about the treatment of children:

> Maybe children could do more by themselves. Sometimes we overstep the help they need rather than letting them come to us.

To overstep is to go beyond the proper limit and it would be proper to say 'Sometimes we overstep the mark in helping them' or 'Sometimes we go too far in helping them' but this is not to 'overstep' the help they need. Rather it is to 'over-supply the help they need', which wording makes sense, though it is not very elegant.

raise

> Funding is still being raised for the project.

'Funding' is the provision of funds. Therefore this should be 'Funding is still being sought.' We 'raise' funds, but 'funding' is the supply of those funds, and we 'seek' it.

relinquish

Here is an unusual failure to get the right word:

> All the assessors I spoke to enjoyed the challenge and the opportu-
> nity of their increased work, often relinquishing their own time
> to ensure adequate time was made available to the student.

We may 'use' time well or badly. We may 'spend' it in this way or that, 'waste' it or 'make the most of' it. But we do not 'relinquish' it. To 'relinquish' something is to abandon, renounce, or release our grip on it. These admirable assessors can be praised for 'giving up their own time', but time is our natural earthly dimension and only at death do we relinquish it.

side

This is a useful word in such statements as 'There's another side to that matter'. It makes sense because two sides of the same thing, a coin for instance, represent very different aspects of the item.

> Stoke City, a club which once counted among its playing staff such
> legends of the game as Stanley Matthews and George Estham, is
> trying to overcome a shameful side. A sizeable section of the
> club's fans are among the most troublesome in the country.

One scarcely knows which is worst, to speak of the problem of the club's misbehaving fans as a 'side' or to speak of 'overcoming' that side. Why not speak clearly of 'tackling the club's troublesome fans'?

speculate

Words descriptive of the thinking process are numerous. Any thesaurus would give you a long list under the word 'think'. One of these is the verb 'to speculate', for which the dictionary meaning is to conjecture without knowing all the facts. Although it has a specialized use in the world of finance, it is not a word that opens up a range of possible uses. And one thing is unquestionable: it is an intransitive verb, and cannot govern an object. It follows that it cannot be used in the passive voice.

> Taxes will rise over the next few years, but not by as much, or in
> such draconian ways, as is now being speculated.

What is 'being speculated'? You can 'throw' a stone and the stone is thereby 'thrown'. But since you cannot 'speculate' anything, nothing can ever 'be speculated'. The journalist should have used a transitive verb: 'as is now being suggested', 'being mooted' or 'being considered'.

subsidize

> If we must continue to subsidize huge amounts to keep the trains
> running, let's use the money to improve the passengers' lot, not
> the shareholders'.

This letter to the press seems to assume that the verb 'to subsidize' can be used like the verb to 'pay'. You can pay ten pounds for a tie. Or you can pay the shop assistant for the tie. Usage allows us to pay money or to pay the vendor. But this does not mean that we can either 'subsidize' the railways or 'subsidize' huge amounts of money. The dictionary tells us that to 'subsidize' is to 'aid or support with money'. To subsidize, in other words, is to supply monetary assistance. In this case a simple correction is called for. Change the word 'subsidize' to the word 'supply'.

substitute

This word and the word 'substitution' are now used improperly as often as they are used properly. The idea seems to have established itself among the general public that to 'substitute' means the same thing as to 'replace', and that 'substitution' is the same thing as 'replacement'. The following is from a letter to the press:

> The resignation of Gerald Corbett and his substitution as chief
> executive by the former Railtrack finance director merely replaces
> like with like.

Gerald Corbett has been 'replaced' as chief executive. The sentence should speak of 'the resignation of Gerald Corbett and his replacement as chief executive by the former Railtrack finance director'. This former Railtrack finance director has been 'substituted' for him. If there is to be use of the word 'substitution' here it must be applied to the man thus substituted, not to the man he replaces. This misuse is especially grave because it frequently produces a reversal of the intended meaning.

> What's more, by substituting healthy food for drink, heavy
> drinkers often lose out on many of the nutrients which can
> actively help prevent cancer.

To 'substitute healthy food for drink' is to replace drink by healthy food. So this writer is telling us that taking in healthy food instead of drink damages people. We must assume that something very different was intended. To make the sentence accurate, while keeping the word 'substitute', a total reversal is required: 'What's more, by substituting drink for healthy food, heavy drinkers often lose out on many of the nutrients which can actively help prevent cancer.' It is a serious matter to say the opposite of what you intend to say. When in doubt, do not use the word 'substitute' but the word 'replace'. The writer here could have thus avoided risk, speaking of 'replacing healthy food by drink'.

undo

An even stranger illogicality is here committed with this use of the verb to 'undo'. The writer is lamenting that standards of safety in residential neighbourhoods are no longer what they once were:

> We are brought up to believe that some things are inviolate, but
> a taboo has been broken which we cannot undo.

What is it that 'we cannot undo'? It appears from the sentence construction to be the 'taboo'. But we know that is not what is meant. The writer means that a taboo has been broken and cannot be restored. It is the 'breaking' of the taboo which cannot be 'undone' but, as the sentence stands, the word 'which' cannot refer back to anything other than the word 'taboo'. It should read 'but a taboo has been broken which we cannot restore'.

voluminous

The vocabulary we have to express largeness is extensive, but there are many kinds of largeness and therefore the various words for it are not interchangeable. The following sentence illustrates the point.

> All the time, Taylor's drug habit was growing ever more volu-
> minous.

The word 'voluminous' implies largeness of volume, that is to say, large in the amount of space something occupies. The drug habit does not grow in the amount of space it occupies. If the word 'habit' is kept, say: 'The habit was growing more demanding/irresistible.' Otherwise say: 'The drug consumption was increasing.'

2

Topic and Treatment

Many of the topics which we touch on in speech or writing in daily life come to our minds in the company of a ready-made vocabulary. And often that vocabulary bears the marks of repeated mishandling. Indeed there are many usages widely current in the world of communication around us that are defective, some of them to the extent of being glaringly illogical. Among them are words which should act as danger signals to the writer when they come to mind. This is not to say that they always lead one into crude error, but very often they are picked up in order to convey some meaning which could be much better conveyed in quite different terminology. Useful and correct as they can be in the right context, when misplaced they mark the user as less than precise and thoughtful. We have to be prepared to face the fact that the usages everyone around us seems to accept may yet turn out to be unsound when the logical mind closely examines them. The unsoundness may reside in sheer inappropriateness of connotation or perhaps in vagueness of connotation, for there is a tendency to evade the precise word in favour of a woollier one. We are to look in this chapter at some areas of discourse where care must be taken to avoid familiar errors.

Quantities, Subdivisions and Proportions

What we say is often concerned with quantities, 'a little of this' or 'a lot of that'. Often proportions are involved, and we report: 'Most of the members were sympathetic but a number of them opposed us.' We have a substantial vocabulary to go at in this sphere, yet there is a tendency to choose terms which are imprecise or in other ways inappropriate. Indeed there is remarkable variety in the way writers fail in precision when verbally sectionalizing, partitioning or dealing divisively with objects, entities or living beings.

cross-section

Talking about samples or specimens can sometimes produce a degree of incongruity which the logical mind is uncomfortable with. Here is the comment of a writer who has just sampled a firm's new range of cars:

> Having driven a cross-section of the range, I can say they offer
> high levels of comfort and ambience.

One might reasonably speak of 'sampling a cross-section of the range' because the words 'sample' and 'cross-section' belong to the same field of discourse. The word 'cross-section' has long ago shed its basic limitation as meaning a plane surface formed by cutting across a solid, but the word 'drive' has concrete association with motor vehicles and as used here jerks the reader into mental discomfiture. In short, we drive cars but we don't drive cross-sections.

element

It is not unusual to find the word 'element' applied to a number of people in a given body who are being grouped in the mind of the writer for their common attitude. 'There is an element who are dissatisfied' we may say, and used thus the word makes good sense. That is not the case in the following however:

> But the frail Muhajidin coalition was destined not to last long.
> Its elements were soon at each other's throats, with constant
> heavy fighting in Kabul and the surrounding provinces.

Groups of people thus differentiated cannot happily be described as 'elements', especially when actions are being ascribed to them. The ancient poets were fond of telling us how the elements were at war in storm and tempest, but sectionalization of warring human communities into 'elements' is inappropriate. A fitter usage here would be: 'Factions were soon at each other's throats.'

Oddly enough, the word 'element' in loose usage acquires what we might call a 'pseudo-causal' flavour. 'The help his mother gave him was a big element in his success.' We hear that kind of thing and it makes sense conversationally. But in print a similar usage can look shabby. Here is a leading article about education:

> If Labour is to secure a second term and make the sort of progress here to which it rightly aspires then Ofsted and the Chief Inspector of Schools will be a vital element.

A point we have made earlier is relevant here. The expression 'a vital element' rolls off the tongue, or here the pen, too readily. If one means that 'Ofsted and the Chief Inspector of Schools will play a crucial part', then why not say so?

in excess of

It is a good idea, before penning any sentence which involves a reference to quantity, to seek the simplest terms. More often than not expressions involving words like 'majority' and 'percentage', as well as terms like 'large numbers' can be happily replaced by 'most', 'many' or 'few'. The same applies to the words 'in excess of'.

> In excess of 350,000 people have visited the botanic garden since it opened in May last year.

Clearly nothing but a hint of unnecessary artifice is gained by not writing: 'More than 350,000 people have visited the botanic garden since it opened in May last year.'

less

On this matter of talking about quantities, the old advice about misusing the word 'less' seems to be for ever relevant.

> When I spoke to Michael O'Leary he also explained that less and less ex-factory items are now being stocked.

This really tells us that the items in stock are getting smaller and smaller. The words needed here are 'fewer and fewer ex-factory items'. And a now equally common misuse of 'less' is to treat it as though it had no comparative meaning.

> Working lone fathers also reported that they felt they had less
> support from their male colleagues.

'Less' than who or what? From the context it is clear that the writer has no intention of making the kind of comparison that the word 'less' should introduce. The meaning is 'Working lone fathers also reported that they felt they lacked support from their male colleagues' or 'they had insufficient support from their male colleagues'.

majority

A fashion has developed of misusing the word 'majority'. Clearly it is most properly used when there is a collection of units to refer to – 'a majority of rail-passengers' or 'a majority of school children', but when one hears in a weather forecast that a given area 'will miss the majority of the showers' the notion of referring to showers as though they were voting MPs seems most inappropriate. And what of the following?

> Remember, work is the place where you spend the majority of
> your time.

What is wrong with the simple and obvious words 'the place where you spend most of your time'? And far worse than that infelicity is the following from a railway magazine article on the restoration of an old engine:

> The majority of the boiler now fitted is therefore new.

If there is a 'majority', there must also be a 'minority', whatever we are talking about; and to divide up a piece of engineering equipment such as a boiler into a 'majority' and a 'minority' is surely inapt.

part

Like 'section' and 'element', the word 'part' can slide too easily into a writer's mind.

> Research commissioned by the European Commission revealed
> that 60% of consumers across the European Union feel they 'don't
> know enough' about an event that will alter one of the most
> important parts of their lives – their money – forever. A statistic

which belies the fact that the euro could eventually rival the
dollar, or the yen, as a global reserve currency.

Satisfactory usage of 'part' when applied to 'life' might make it refer
to a period of time or a special personal activity, but surely not to a
possession such as money. Even the loose word 'things' would be
better here: 'one of the most important things in life'. But there is a
more subtle linguistic failure in the use of the words 'belies the fact'.
The prophecy in question, 'that the euro could eventually rival the
dollar or the yen', is not a 'fact' but a possibility, and a possibility
cannot be 'belied' (that is, shown to be false). A more logical version
of the case would be: 'A statistic which casts doubt on the possibility
that the euro could eventually rival the dollar, or the yen, as a global
reserve currency.'

A case might be made that the precise writer could generally be
distinguished from the sloppy writer by their use of the word 'part'.

Everyone knows Tony and it occurs to us that many who do not
habitually attend the Awards will want to make a special effort
this time, to be part of, and identified with, this once-only
occasion.

What does it mean to 'be part of' an Awards, part of an 'occasion'?
We all know what it means to 'take part in' an Awards ceremony.
Why not use that meaningful expression? As for wanting to be 'identi-
fied with' an occasion, that is the terminology of media non-thought.
Nobody really wants to be labelled as a section of an 'occasion' or
mistaken for an 'occasion'. We have dealt already with that misuse.
As so often 'identified with' here could better be replaced by 'associ-
ated with'.

When one keeps a lookout for the word, it is really surprising to
discover, not only how widely, but also how variously the word 'part'
is now misused. On the Queen Mother's death a Radio 4 commentator
proclaimed: 'This is a moment in history and people want to be part
of that moment.' It is difficult to conceive exactly what 'being' a
part of a moment involves, but the word 'part' gets used even more
irrationally than that. Here is an opposition politician criticizing the
Chancellor's taxation changes for pension funds:

> David Willette, Shadow Social Security Secretary, said the tax-raid
> was 'part of the Government killing the goose that laid the golden
> egg'.

It is not even clear here whether 'part of the Government' refers to the Treasury and its policies or whether the text means that the tax-raid was one element in the Government's policy of killing the goose.

We see misuse of 'part' at its worst when it is applied to a human being directly, as it is in this reference to a champion horse-trainer:

> Martin Pipe is part of the progress made in modern-day training.

It is a poor way of paying tribute to define the champion as a section of 'progress' instead of as one who contributed largely to that progress.

Sometimes the misuse of the word 'part' is due to a writer's strange reluctance to use the word 'partly'. That is the case in the following:

> Part of the improvement comes through operational gearing,
> part comes because the group keeps constant and determined
> pressure on costs.

To sectionalize an 'improvement' in that way is clumsy. The natural way of making the point would be to say: 'The improvement comes partly through operational gearing and partly through a constant and determined pressure on costs.'

There is a comparable carelessness in the following sentence by a reviewer who was praising a performance of Benjamin Britten's opera *Albert Herring* given by Opera North:

> Part of the interpretation's success is having the chamber orches-
> tra on stage taking part in the action when they are not busy
> playing (and sometimes when they are).

The success of a production may be 'due' to certain features of it, thus 'partly' due to this and 'partly' to that, but that 'success' cannot logically be divided into sections. In any case the use of the words 'interpretation's success' instead of the 'success of the interpretation' is clumsy. 'The success of the interpretation is partly due to having the chamber orchestra on stage taking part in the action.'

percentage
There is a current tendency to use the word 'percentage' infelicitously. It is after all a word with a clear numerical connotation.

> Following the amount of publicity by the media, it would appear
> that a small percentage of the motoring public has failed to heed
> the warnings and continue to consume alcohol and drive.

To begin with, the word 'amount' conveys nothing here. There can be a small amount or a large amount. It would appear from the context to be the latter that is intended. But the main complaint we have is that 'a small percentage of the motoring public' is a clumsy way of saying 'some few motorists'. And, by the way, 'a small percentage' is first given a single verb 'has failed' and then a plural verb 'continue'. The verbs should be brought into line, either 'has failed and continues' or 'have failed and continue'. Incidentally the plural verb is most unhappily used in the following statement about the Ridgeway National Trail:

> The recently completed survey shows that 51 per cent of the Trail
> do not meet the surface standard.

What are the things that 'do not' meet the standard? Are they yards or miles? It would be better to say '51 per cent of the Trail does not meet the surface standard'.

What is crucial in using the word 'percentage' is to keep in mind exactly what the total is of which the 'percentage' is a part. Failure to do so can lead to absurdities.

> As she recovered from her illness, she began thinking about why
> so few women – just 12.5 per cent, according to statistics – occupy
> America's executive suites, and why so many leave corporations
> to start their own businesses.

The woman in question is an American. I do not know what the population of the United States is or whether the female part of it is really half the total. But there would actually be millions of them who have made it into executive suites, were there really an eighth of the total number of women, as this implies. Clearly the writer meant to convey that only 12.5 per cent of the people occupying executive suites were women. She should have said so: 'As she recovered from her illness, she began thinking about why so few of those who occupy America's executive suites are women – just 12.5 per cent of them, according to statistics.'

section
The problem that arises in choosing the right word when dealing with numbers of people is closely related to the problem of confusing the personal and impersonal categories in choice of vocabulary, a matter we turn to in a later chapter. I have just heard the sentence: 'A larger section of the population began to use the co-ops.' There is a kind of inappropriateness here that results from mental laziness. The word 'section' is properly used of a part or subdivision that can be separated from the main body of, say, a country, a book or a plan laid out on paper. For the most part its significance is impersonal, often mechanical, though there are certain contexts in which the word can be fitly used of groups of people. When men and women are gathered together in an orchestra or a choir, it is logical and useful to speak of the 'string section', the 'woodwind section', the 'contralto section', and so on; but it should be noted that this usage is appropriate only in fairly technical consideration of musical matters. One might say 'the brass section is ill placed' and there might even be an occasion for saying 'the brass section is unhappy with the choice of conductor' but one would be less likely to say 'the brass section is too fat'. The fact is that the people who use the co-ops do not represent a differentiated body of that kind, and if one wants to say 'More people began to use the co-ops' there is no point in dragging in the word 'section' at all. Why is it there? I would argue that it is there because what comes to the speaker's mind here is not the word 'section' and then the words 'of the population' but the combined expression 'section of the population'. Our ordinary conversation is chockful of such established expressions that roll through the mind unchecked by conscious attention to each individual word.

sector
If 'section' is a word that can be used unhappily of groups of people, the word 'sector' can be even more unhappily so used. The geometrical

basis of the word cannot be easily forgotten. When it is applied to groups of people as contributing to the economy, 'the private sector' or 'the public sector', it is convenient and useful, but when people are under consideration as human beings with souls and bodies use of the word can jar, as in the following:

> The scheme represents a new era in reproductive medicine and
> helps certain sectors who before couldn't get treatment.

When you are considering men or women wanting treatment for infertility or suffering from physical limitations in their sex life, then to speak of them as 'sectors' is crudely inappropriate. All that is needed here is 'and helps people who before couldn't get treatment'.

There is perhaps slightly more justification for the word 'sector' in the following:

> One of the most unedifying sights of the last few years has been
> the continual bickering and backstabbing process carried out by
> many sectors of the industry on a regular and very public basis.

Nevertheless, the words 'bickering' and 'backstabbing' carry highly charged personal associations. It is not 'sectors' that go in for bickering and backstabbing, but men and women. It would be better merely to use the word 'people' or 'workers' or 'employees'. Moreover, what is the word 'process' doing there? And the words 'carried out'? Both expressions are redundant and should be removed: 'continual bickering and backstabbing among workers in the industry'.

some

Here is a sentence from a leading article written just after the air disasters in New York and Washington:

> Haphazardly, and amid considerable confusion, air traffic in
> America is recovering some of its position in the nation's life.

Does the expression 'some of its position' make any sense at all? We know what it means to speak of someone gradually recovering their position after some setback or accident. Even so, in reply to the question 'Has he recovered his position yet?' one would not reply 'Some of it'. 'Positions' cannot be sectionalized, divided into portions or segments. Having lost a former 'position', one cannot scoop it up shovelful by shovelful until it is fully regained. It would be better to write 'air traffic is beginning to recover its position in the nation's life'.

Comparisons of Magnitude and Quantity

It has to be said that making comparisons of size or extent seems to put a heavy strain on the sense of logicality which we ought to be able to expect from those who write professionally. There is a peculiar waywardness in using the expression 'just as' or 'as . . . as'.

> We may even convince ourselves that we could be just as happy
> with five channels than 140.

What is the word 'than' doing there? 'She is just as tall as me' we say, not 'She is just as tall than me'. The above should read 'just as happy with five channels as with 140'. Yet the habit seems to be catching. Here we are told about the health threat of rheumatoid arthritis:

> It is more than three times as likely to affect men than women.

There again the word 'than' should be 'as'. The error seems to derive from mixing up the construction intended here with the construction 'It affects three times more men than women' where 'more . . . than' is the proper usage. The error seems common enough.

> Remote-controlled photography showed that I had twice as many
> foxes visiting my garden than I had realized.

This too should be either 'twice as many foxes visiting my garden as I had realized', or 'twice more foxes visiting my garden than I had realized'. It is the construction 'as many as' that must always be followed by 'as'.

We can find this error now in a publication of the maximum respectability:

> A study in Seattle, which analysed 26,000 car crashes, showed
> that, for instance, people who weigh between 15st 10lb and 18st
> 10lb were two-and-a-half times as likely to be killed in crashes
> than those who weighed less than 9st 6lb.

If an error is repeated frequently enough in respectable publications, then it becomes officially 'correct'. Despairingly, therefore, one makes the point that this should read 'two and a half times as likely to be killed in crashes as those who weighed less than 9st 6oz'. Despairingly, because it is sound logic as well as grammar that is at risk. 'He is bigger than I am' is sound enough. 'He is twice as big as I am' is likewise sound. But the bogus mixture 'He is twice as big than I am' will not do.

Even when a sentence is sound enough in construction for the 'as much as' construction to be handled without any recourse to the irrelevant word 'than', there can still be serious blunders.

> He is, in short, a fairly normal member of the metropolitan middle class, an electorally pivotal slice of humanity with whom Tories currently have as much in common as they do Albanian peasants.

It would be (logically) correct to say 'You have as much in common with me as you do with a Neanderthal' but incorrect to say 'You have as much in common with me as you do a Neanderthal'. So the above must be amended to 'an electorally pivotal slice of humanity with whom Tories currently have as much in common as they do with Albanian peasants'.

Matters of Opinion

We turn from matters of quantity and magnitude to look at some broader areas of reasoning, where judgements are passed and opinions aired. In the first place we examine some usages that are now widely accepted but which raise questions for the logically minded. They show how the connotation of much-used words decays as precise meanings are neglected.

mean
When we ask 'What does it mean?' we are generally seeking to know what something signifies or 'stands for' ('A "vegetarian" meal means a "meat-free" meal'). We also use the verb to explain hidden purposes ('The thieves meant to take all the jewels') and to say what certain

phenomena portend ('The cloudy sky means rain ahead'). It would be foolish to be over-pedantic in dealing with a word which has given us such vivid expressions as 'The new head means business', 'She means well' and 'She doesn't mean any harm'. However the frequency with which the verb is used today and the multiplicity of purposes it serves suggests that some attention should be paid to it here. In a book of this kind it is the first of the above usages that must come frequently into play. Yet our usage of the word on these pages has little in common with the following usage in a passage giving advice to a young woman preoccupied with losing weight:

> Although she has set herself a thinness goal she feels will mean happiness when she achieves it, the reality is the process can only result in misery.

Why do we insist on saying that something or other will 'mean' happiness when we want to convey that it will 'bring' happiness? And consider the following:

> The choice of flowers means that in spring this garden is a riot of colour.

What is conveyed here is that the choice of flowers 'makes' this garden a riot of colour. At the back of this sentence is the matter of showing a causal connection. It is the particular choice of flowers that has 'caused' the garden to be a riot of colour in spring. We have got into the habit of expressing causal connections like that by using the verb 'to mean' and evading clear reference to cause and effect. Here is a vivid specimen of the evasive usage. It is a description of a coat.

> It has a Permatex breathable membrane that gives maximum protection from wind and rain and a unique double placket that comes up to the neck to ensure the coat is extra snug and means there is no need for a scarf.

In actual fact this is a case where the word 'mean' is not only evasive but redundant. There is again no question of 'meaning' but of cause and effect, and that matter has been covered by the verb 'to ensure'. Correct it to 'comes up to the neck to ensure that the coat is snug and that there is no need for a scarf'.

> Never go to party on a night before an interview or you may not
> look your best next morning, meaning the job goes to someone
> else.

What is conveyed here is: 'You may not look your best next morning,
with the result that the job goes to someone else.' But, the colloquial
tone being what it is, the word 'meaning' is again really redundant.
For the word 'meaning' one could just substitute 'and': 'you may not
look your best next morning, and the job goes to someone else.'

The effect of our overuse of the verb 'to mean' is to turn it into an
all-purpose device for avoiding other verbs. Here is the obituary of a
distinguished writer clearly from the pen of a literary scholar:

> The length of her career meant not only adventurous development
> in her style, but great changes in the world to be written about.

The writer should have asked himself or herself what the real connection was between the length of the woman's career and developments
in her style and in the world she wrote about. The connection was
again one of cause and effect. 'Her career lasted long enough to allow
not only adventurous development in her style, but also [note the *also*]
great changes in the world to be written about.'

need

The word 'need', both as verb and as noun, has become as carelessly
used as the verb 'to mean'. Even when it is correctly used, one can
often feel that it is not the best word in the context.

> . . . The Director of the Daycare Trust argues that the Government
> needs to put more investment into delivering universal childcare.
> 'It needs to become part of the local infrastructure . . .'

Why the word 'needs', twice used? Why not 'the Government has to'
or 'ought to' or 'must' or 'should'? And why not give 'It needs' the
same treatment? So often the verb 'need' nowadays merely stands in
like that for the common verbs of obligation. If this seems to the
reader like nit-picking, one has to reply that the word 'need' is forever
hitting one in the eye these days, as it does three times in this sentence
from a letter to the press:

> Our road system is in chaos – it needs modernization across the
> country, rural areas need consideration and congestion in our
> cities needs action.

Three requirements are postulated here: 'modernization' for our road
system, 'consideration' for rural areas, and 'action' for urban congestion. The vagueness of these specifications indicates the laxity which
use of the verb 'need' seems to encourage.

However, the more serious problem arising with the word 'need'
comes with its use as a noun.

> New Finish 3-in-1 is the first tab in the UK to provide all your
> dishwashing needs. There's no need to check your salt, detergent
> or rinse agent.

Here the writer has used the word 'need' twice, only two words
intervening between them. The second use raises no questions, but in
the first case 'provide all your dishwashing needs' really means
'answer all your dishwashing requirements'. Strictly speaking, to talk
of 'providing' people with 'needs' is logically like offering to supply
them with deprivations such as poverty or hunger. My latest dictionary treats the meaning of the word 'need' in terms of lack, requirement, necessity, distress and poverty. The notion that whatever does
away with any of these deficiencies might be called a 'need' is not
allowed for. Yet both as a verb and as a noun meaning either 'requirement' or 'provision' the word 'need' is suffering from an epidemic of
overuse.

> We need a radical new approach to wildlife conservation in urban
> areas . . . Local authorities need long-term plans to accommodate
> the needs of wildlife across an urban area.

Here the writer has used the word 'need' twice as a verb and once as
a noun within a comparatively short passage. Why not 'We must have
a radical new approach to wildlife conservation in urban areas'? And
why not 'Local authorities must make long-term plans to cater for
wildlife across an urban area'?

From this extraordinary overuse of the word something like verbal
chaos can result:

> Professor David Begg and his helpers would surely be better employed formulating proposals showing how best to integrate the various transport needs of the country instead of simply hoping he can find a way to make the real needs of the road haulier and motorist disappear.

'Needs' as requirements and 'needs' as provisions answering those requirements seem to be confusingly related here.

Evaluations

When we want to express a high degree of approval or disapproval we tend to use words that carry a disproportionate degree of weight. Instead of saying 'I like the sound of that' we say 'That's a magnificent idea'. And instead of saying 'His suggestions don't impress me' we say 'He hasn't an idea in his head'. In the ordinary exchanges of life our desire to put a special stress on something leads us to exclaim 'That's absolutely astonishing' when we really mean 'You surprise me'. There is a proper place for exaggeration in the use of words. Poetry is full of it. But when we are trying to convey our thoughts with the maximum clarity it is likely that touches of exaggeration will militate against precision and also probably do damage to the words we use. For in reaching for words that carry a special weight of meaning we sometimes misuse words that cannot properly allow modification of their full connotation. A most obvious case is presented by the word 'unique'. Nothing can be properly called 'unique' unless it is the only one of its kind. When the advertiser offers us another 'unique opportunity' we know better than to be overly impressed. More to the point here, however, is to recall the limitations that the word's exact meaning imposes on its use. Strict awareness of the word's meaning would preclude such expressions as 'more unique' or 'very unique'.

There are some idiomatic expressions in regular use which encourage sloppy thinking in that respect. Although one would not hear anyone saying 'This set of chessmen is very complete', one can hear careless generalizations such as 'His conversion to vegetarianism is very complete'. That is a way of underlining the completeness of the conversion, but it is bad in that it implies that there can be degrees of completeness, that one thing might be 'completer' than another. The word 'complete' is like the word 'full', the word 'whole' or the word 'intact'. No vessel can be 'very full' or 'fuller' than another full vessel. No one's reputation can be 'very intact' or 'more intact' than someone else's intact reputation. Yet there is a tendency to make such statements as 'I cannot imagine a more complete breakdown in communications' or 'I could not imagine a site more full of buildings', usages in which the negatives somehow hide the illogicalities. And one hears statements like 'I thought the attendance at the meeting was exceptionally full', which again implies different levels of 'fullness'.

We are concerned with descriptive terms which have a kind of absoluteness. That is to say, further qualifying terms (such as 'more' or 'less') cannot be applied to them. The same logic applies, even more strictly, to certain descriptive terms that are extemporized and achieve usefulness.

all-time

This expression is a case in point. It matches such words as 'best' and 'worst' in characterizing an ultimate superlative. If the temperature reaches an 'all-time' high, then there can be no high 'more all-time' than that. Yet we hear a speaker on the radio declare:

> Confidence in the Euro is at a very all-time low.

The desire to qualify 'all-time low' is illogical. The error is parallel to that which would be made if one said 'He comes to see me very always'.

currently

A recent use of this word raises a comparable question about the word 'current'. In an article on the attractions of the moorland country-side around Halifax a journalist writes enthusiastically about:

> the fascination to be found in these previously (and in some cases
> very currently) grimy valleys.

We understand what the writer is trying to say, but the notion of degrees of 'currency' (conveyed by the words 'very currently') is not a happy one. My dictionary defines the word 'current' as meaning 'of the immediate present' or 'in progress'. It would have been better to write 'and in some cases very recently'. That is what is meant.

cutting-edge

New fashions in words of late tend to make the most of compounds. This is an expressive combination with a metaphorical basis. The sharp edge of a blade is what cuts into things and the words 'cutting-edge' usefully define the sharp impact of an argument, a theory or a plan. Excessive use of such terms leads to a kind of verbal anarchy in which they are dragged from their basic function.

> I never saw anything more cutting-edge than her water-colours.

Unfortunately, this is not an isolated specimen of the new fashion. Another such sentence opens an article thus:

> Knitting is the new sex . . . Yes, right now there isn't a thing more cutting-edge.

To turn 'cutting-edge' into an adjective and to use it in the comparative form ('more cutting-edge') as though there were degrees of 'cutting-edginess' is inexcusable. We do not inhabit a linguistic environment in which one thing may be claimed to be 'cutting-edgier' than another, and there remains something else that is the 'cutting-edgiest' of all.

key

The popularization of the word 'key' as a descriptive term has also produced some bad usages. To say that John Smith was a 'key figure' in a firm's reorganization is acceptable. But surely that would not give John Smith the right to go home and tell his wife 'I'm key now' or 'I'm as key as John Jones'. I make that point after reading the following tribute in a magazine:

> Amongst a small number of people who have been key in the Society over the years stands, prominently, Mr John Smith, who stood down as our chairman at the AGM this summer.

Plainly the word is taking on a life of its own in journalism. This is what is said of a champion yachtswoman:

> The key to her, however, is that she is also possessed of a technical
> mind . . .

We understand that usage, 'key' being more or less equivalent to 'the
secret of her success', but of the same woman we read:

> Ellen's success is instrumental and key in taking women's yacht-
> ing one step further.

Here we are, back again with 'key' as an adjective, and it plainly adds
nothing, since what it might mean is already covered by the word
'instrumental'. And a speaker on the radio began:

> The Saudis, who play a very key role in this . . .'

Nothing can be said to be 'very' key any more than an issue could be
said to be 'more key' ('keyer') than another issue.

major

Just as 'all-time' is superlative in its connotation, so the word 'major'
is originally comparative in its connotation. That is to say the adjective
'major' was basically the equivalent of 'greater'. This puts a question
mark over a usage heard on the radio referring to 'some of the most
major conflagrations of history'. For the pedant that usage is really
equivalent to speaking of 'some of the greatest greater conflagrations
of history'. The word 'most' adds nothing. It is verbally lax to think of
events as 'more major' or 'less major' than others.

niche

We turn to another innovation. When a question arose about a proposal to introduce lap-dancing to activities at Henley, the press
reported:

> Julie Davies, who works for a local theatre company, said 'It's a
> bit shocking and I think it's a very niche market.'

The use of 'very' implies that there are degrees of 'nicheness' or
'nichehood'. In which case one market might be 'nicher' or 'more
niche' than another and indeed that there might be a market that
was the 'most niche' or the 'nichest' of all. It is a pity when idioms

which have a certain novel usefulness (like the use of 'niche' and 'key' above) should be rendered ridiculous in this way.

one-off

The expression 'one-off' appears to be the colloquial equivalent of 'unique'. Yet on a *You and Yours* programme on Radio 4 a speaker argued:

> Is that not a very one-off case?

Once more it has to be pointed out that if something can be said to be 'very' one-off, then presumably it would be 'more one-off' (or 'one-offer') than something which is merely 'one-off'. Moreover, such reasoning would seem to allow for something to be declared 'the one-offest of all'.

true

The word 'true' is certainly unqualifiable. We say 'Yes, that's very true', but strictly the use of 'very' is illogical. No truth can be 'truer' than any other truth.

> This time of year is always exciting and for me, as your new Food
> & Wine Ed, that's especially true.

Nothing can be 'especially' true. What the writer really means to convey is that the excitingness of the season is something felt notably in her professional work.

truth

What applies to the word 'true' applies to the word 'truth'. The word 'true' should not be turned into 'truer' or 'more true'. In the same way the word 'truth' must not be qualified so as to suggest that there are degrees of 'truth'. The press recently reported discoveries that provided new evidence of the fate of Richard II.

> In *Richard II*, one of Shakespeare's most poignant plays, the weak
> Boy King is murdered at Pontefract castle. But the truth was less
> certain, leading one of the most reliable contemporary writers,
> Froissart, to state 'On the manner of Richard's death I know
> nothing.'

Truth is truth. What is true is true. Truths cannot be graded in degrees of 'certainty'. There is not a truth that can be 'less certain' than another truth. What is meant here is that the facts as known would not directly confirm Shakespeare's view of Richard's end. The writers (there were two of them) should have said: 'But it is not certain that this version of things is true.' Indeed they might better have said: 'But it is not certain that Shakespeare's view represents the truth.' That is the proper status of the concept 'truth' in this context.

Shifting Connotations

We turn to a different kind of laxity in usage. It arises especially when we refer by name to people, places, books and many other items. Extreme care has to be exercised to prevent any sliding between one connotation and another. I have just heard a news announcement which exemplifies a quite appropriate liberty that may be taken with proper names:

> Scotland travelled to Rome to meet Italy.

Although I am not an interested follower of soccer or rugby, this announcement made on the radio did not confuse me. The context was that part of the news devoted to sport. But clearly there could be situations where a statement of that kind might cause difficulty to a foreigner with a limited command of our language. What is important is that no one should use words with a specialized and limited connotation – such as 'Scotland' there, which means the soccer team – alongside other usages with a more general connotation. Yet you will hear this kind of statement from football enthusiasts.

> I always support Southampton because it's my home town.

Strictly speaking, this is incorrect. The word 'Southampton' here means the football team, and the football team cannot be the speaker's 'home town'. That habit of changing the connotation of a word in mid-use makes for nonsense. You would not say 'They were beaten by Southampton, from where you can get a ferry to the Isle of Wight'. Yet comparable abuses of double connotations are to be found.

> On the west coast is Papa Stour, a Viking name meaning the
> island of priests.

The place and its name must be distinguished. This is like saying 'I come from London, which has two vowels and four consonants'.

It is important to recognize this error in its crudest form. For to say 'This is my wife, Rosamund, a noun of three syllables' is not really more absurd than many versions of the error that can be found in print. If the first part of the sentence is about a person and the second part about a word, then logic demands that the differentiation be made clear. One hears such statements as: 'You ought to read *Nicholas Nickleby*. I found him a fascinating character.' There the speaker shifts from speaking about a book to speaking of a character in it, and the two are not one and the same thing. This collapse in logical consistency is not rare. People reviewing books in magazines readily fall into it.

> This is not one of the best-known walking areas though it is
> surrounded by the Lake District, Howgills, the Yorkshire Dales
> and Bowland. It is a booklet of 15 fairly short walks with almost
> two thirds being five miles or less.

'This' refers to an area of countryside, but in the succeeding sentence 'It' refers to a booklet. So quickly and directly to define a stretch of country as a booklet after building up the geographical sense of the region shows total failure of concentration.

The reader may be surprised to learn that this particular error can be found, half-concealed in its context, in learned books. Here is something from a book about Wordsworth:

> Many of the ballads have Lake District settings, like 'The Nut-
> Brown Maid', a favourite, who is sorely tested by her lover . . .

The author is writing about a poem called 'The Nut-Brown Maid' and he tells us that she was 'sorely tested by her lover'. The distinction between ballad and person must be made clear: 'Many of the ballads have Lake District settings, like "The Nut-Brown Maid", a favourite poem about a girl sorely tested by her lover.'

3

The Nuts and Bolts of Writing

So far we have been largely concerned with the choice and use of those words that seem to carry the main weight of our meaning: nouns and verbs, adjectives and adverbs. Such words are the most basic components in the fabric of meaning. The English language has developed in such a way that there are lots of seemingly less significant words which are also crucially important in determining meaning: prepositions, conjunctions and pronouns. Words like 'of' and 'in', 'who' and 'where' are sprinkled over what we say or write, binding utterance in logical sequence as nuts and bolts and rivets hold the sections of a piece of machinery together. We turn first to the short words which form the simplest of linkages, such as 'for', 'of', 'from' and 'in', most often used as prepositions.

Simple Linkages

Now a curious recent development in our habits of utterance, if the media represent us fairly in this respect, is in our use of these, the seemingly simplest of our short words. There are journalists and broadcasters who write and speak as though those words were all kept in a bran tub and, whenever one was required, the hand could be plunged into the tub and the word chancily clasped between the fingers could be inserted in the text. Let us exemplify the kind of misuse which results in the case of some of the commonest words.

for

Here is a sentence about how the Russian people responded to the news of the disastrous loss of the submarine *Kursk*.

> Most people believed what they were hearing from the Western
> world, which shows how much trust the Russian people have for
> their leaders.

We have always used 'in' after the word trust. 'Trust in the Lord' we say, and 'Put not your trust in princes'. What is the point of trying to establish a new usage in this respect? The standard usage may in some cases be more a matter of convention than of logic but the onus of defending innovation must lie with the innovators. Yet I read in a magazine that a certain river has 'consistently been significantly more productive for salmon'. We know what it means to claim that our business has been 'more productive for us' and, surely therefore, it is 'for' the fish salesmen and the general public, the consumers, that the river has been 'more productive'. The salmon have gained nothing from the development. The river has become more productive 'of' salmon. One wonders whether 'for' has become an 'in' word these days. The point is made because a speaker on Radio 4 said 'Ever since Ken Livingstone was elected Mayor for London . . .' Yet ever since the days of Dick Whittington we have had sayings ringing in our minds about the Lord Mayor 'of' London. The distinction between the City's Lord Mayor and London's elected Mayor may carry subtle social overtones, but such grammatical differentiation between the two would surely be invidious. And now a voice on the radio describes the editor of the *Observer* as the editor 'for' the *Observer*.

One version of the misplacement of 'for' results from applying it mistakenly to a verb when it properly goes with a verb similar but not identical in meaning. For instance, we rightly say 'There was no one there who could be mistaken for an American'. But that does not justify a journalist in writing:

> There was nobody in the Sheraton Hotel who could be suspected
> for an American.

The verb 'to suspect' requires a different usage: 'There was nobody in the Sheraton Hotel who could be suspected to be an American' (or: 'who could be suspected of being an American').

There are times when the word 'for' makes an intrusive appearance where no such word is required. The following example comes from a correspondence about whether parents should manipulate victories for their children when they play board games with them. A woman is looking back on her own experience as a child:

> When I finally won, it felt marvellous. I never begrudged him for
> not letting me win.

'To begrudge' is to take with a bad grace someone else's achievement or possession. The achievement or possession must be mentioned, so the usage here is incomplete grammatically. 'I never begrudged him his victories' would make the point.

of

It is sadly true that, to balance false uses of 'for' where 'of' might have been fitly used, one can find the converse error.

> Two Shropshire smallholders have found a way of enthusiasts of
> bell-ringing to make as much noise as they like without fear of
> upsetting the neighbours.

Both the first two uses of 'of' are wrong. The discovered 'way' is the way 'for' bell-ringers to operate, and the bell-ringers are enthusiasts 'for' bell-ringing. A similar misuse occurs in a recommendation for a new therapy system, claiming that it 'can make a very real difference to sufferers of stress and anxiety, poor circulation, rheumatism' and so on. Have you ever heard any one say 'I am suffering of rheumatism' instead of 'from' rheumatism?

And here is a sentence from the record of a speech, which runs:

> A historic mission of eradicating poverty is within our grasp.

But the mission is surely 'to' eradicate poverty. The proper place for 'of' after 'mission' would be in such usages as 'the mission of Dr Barnardo's to serve the poor'. Another comparable and extraordinary predilection for the word 'of' occurs in the following letter about shortfalls in the country's pension funds:

> Not to act decisively now may see the Government charged at
> the next election of standing idly by as the one great welfare
> success of the past century crumbled around them in just a few
> months.

We do not 'charge' people 'of' offences, but 'with' offences. So the
sentence above would better read: 'If the Government does not act
decisively, it may be charged at the next election with standing idly
by . . .' Yet perhaps none of these misuses of the word 'of' matches up
in sheer awkwardness to the misuse in the announcement that came
over the air in connection with the murder of a little girl:

> The pessimism of finding Sarah alive is increasing.

The word 'of' should be replaced by 'about'. The word 'pessimism'
could be followed by 'of' only in such a sentence as 'The pessimism
of the police about finding Sarah alive is increasing'.

One can find the word 'of' intruding even where no such link word
is required. One journal speaks of the present age as one:

> where people are increasingly merely accepting of opulence
> rather than staggered by it.

We may properly be said to 'accept opulence', and to insert the word
'of' into the construction is out of place. And here it appears after the
verb 'befit', a useful word in such sentences as 'Such conduct ill befits
an aristocrat', which means that the behaviour is inappropriate or
unsuitable for an aristocrat. The word carries a faintly archaic air, but
here we see it combined with the latest journalese:

> The grown-up chicness of the flat is wholly befitting of Ruby.

There the word 'of' must go: 'The grown-up chicness of the flat wholly
befits Ruby.'

from

The word 'from' is perhaps less frequently misplaced than either 'for'
or 'of', but the following misuse occurs in the daily press. The piece
records the retirement of a leader in the world of fashion.

> The only doubt in this whole exercise is whether, on past form,

> M. Saint Laurent really intends to bid farewell from the scene
> entirely.

We bid farewell 'to' people and places. Wherever has the journalist heard of people bidding farewell 'from' either? The usage seems to suggest a wilful special visit to the bran tub. And in the same paper I read:

> Nunn pulled off another triumph this year with his production
> of *The Merchant of Venice* from the National Theatre.

If the words 'National Theatre' refer to the company, 'from' should be 'by'. If they refer to the building, 'from' should be 'at'.

There are cases where a preposition can serve seemingly incongruous purposes:

> After many years of suffering from this affliction, some of you
> seem to have found relief from the following remedies.

The two uses of 'from' here are worth examining. We suffer 'from' an affliction ('I suffered *from* a headache') and we get relief 'from' certain remedies ('When I had a headache, I got relief *from* aspirins'). It would be better not to use the two constructions together in the same sentence, as happens in the above. 'After many years of suffering from this affliction, some of you seem to have found relief in the following remedies.'

Occasionally one can find the word 'from' used superfluously.

> The real cause of vandalism is as much from boredom as from
> rebelliousness.

'Boredom' and 'rebelliousness' are possible 'causes' of vandalism and the word 'from' is out of place above.

towards, by, about, against, to, through

One could go on listing innovations of this kind which astonish by their sheer novelty. I read that 'there was considerable dissatisfaction towards the university', and marvel that the word 'towards' has been hit upon, since we usually speak of our dissatisfaction 'with' this or that, and sometimes of our dissatisfaction 'at' this or that. Then a mother complains because her young daughter 'became increasingly interested by media images of thinness'. The proper usage would be 'interested *in*' media images, but what the mother probably wanted to convey needed a stronger word than 'interested', perhaps 'increasingly obsessed with media images'. If the word 'by' is to be kept, the wording would have to be 'increasingly influenced/fascinated by media images'. 'By' is not one of the link words that is often forgotten, yet a reviewer writes thus of a new book:

> Memoirs about childhoods filled with abuse have become so commonplace in recent years that you may be bored as well as repelled at the idea of reading Carolyn Slaughter's *Before the Knife*.

The usage 'bored as well as repelled at the idea' misuses the word 'at'. We may be bored 'with' certain tasks in certain circumstances but we are bored 'by' the thought of having to do them. And that applies to 'repelled' too. One is astonished or flabbergasted 'at' a spectacle, but one is repelled 'by' it.

We turn to a report about crime figures:

> Home Office recorded crime statistics for England and Wales in 1980 were 1225 rapes against females.

The verb to 'rape' is a transitive verb. We speak of 'raping a woman' and of the woman as being the 'victim of rape'. It is no more logical to insert the word 'against' here than it would be to speak of '15 murders against children'. Therefore the wording here should be '1225 rapes of females'. 'Against' is quite the wrong word to use in reference to criminal matters of this kind because we speak of bringing a charge of rape 'against' an offender.

The word 'to' is also misused:

> Driving regulations ban people to drive.

That should be: 'Driving regulations ban people from driving.'

> The price to transport oil from the Middle East . . .

That should be 'The price of transporting oil from the Middle East . . .'
The impression created by the use of the wrong link word is of

lax thinking as well as of lax penmanship. That applies too to the impression created by inserting one of those crucial words where none is needed.

> Paul Morris, an anti-selection campaigner, says that antagonism
> between schools in Ripon permeates through the community.

The verb to 'permeate' means to penetrate, to pervade. The antagonism 'permeates the community'. The word 'through' is out of place.

with

This is probably the most frequently misused word in current journ-alism. Stop yourself immediately if you find yourself writing 'with' at the beginning of a sentence, and indeed anywhere where you are not using the word in its simplest, obvious meaning: 'He came with a brand new car' or 'She went down with flu'. Take the following as a specimen of how *not* to use 'with'.

> With a chambered stomach similar to ruminants, the monkeys
> can digest large quantities of leaves . . .

What the writer meant was: 'Having a chambered stomach, the monkeys can digest large quantities of leaves.'

> With a woman boss, there's a belief she'll be better, more caring
> and sharing.

The word 'with' is an unnecessary intrusion here where the writer simply means: 'There's a belief that a woman boss will be more caring.'

> With the path of the war on terrorism impossible and foolish to
> predict, buyers, sellers and agents are now wary, without running
> scared.

Perhaps there we ought first to look at the most glaring illogicality. If it is 'impossible' to do something, it is unnecessary to say that it would be 'foolish'. But why the word 'with'? What the journalist means is: 'The path of the war on terrorism being impossible to predict . . .' And here again the reader should take note of a most useful construction, much neglected in contemporary English – that particular use of the word 'being' or some parallel word. You will hear people saying 'With plaice being so expensive, I bought some cod', a sentence in which the word 'with' could simply be omitted. The expression 'plaice being so expensive' is a complete and grammatical phrase, but it is turned into a piece of verbal clumsiness by the addition of 'with'.

> Croup is very common, with about ten to twenty per cent of children getting croup in the first two or three years of life.

There again is a sentence from which the word 'with' should be removed. Removing it ought to knock up the marks in the English exam by a sizeable quantity.

> The landing-place was unsatisfactory, with passengers disembarking at low tide being obliged to step out of the boat on to a plank.

The same applies to this sentence: cross out 'with' and it makes good sense. More and more the word 'with' assumes the character of a dangerous trap in the writer's path. I cite the following from a piece giving advice about winter gardening:

> Geraniums, streptocarpus, fuchsias and basket plants should be checked regularly with any diseased leaves being found removed.

'With any diseased leaves being found removed' – what a mouthful! Not only is 'with' an intrusive redundance, so are the words 'being found'. The three words should be replaced by a properly positioned 'and': 'Geraniums, streptocarpus, fuchsias and basket plants should be checked regularly, and any diseased leaves removed.'

The temptation to go on citing instances of 'with' misused is perhaps turning into the writer's obsession, but the point has to be driven home.

> With 230 stores from Inverness to the Isle of Wight, there's a Powerhouse near you.

But if there is a Powerhouse near us, I'm sure there aren't another 200-odd branches there too. The advertiser wanted to convey that the branches being so numerous you are likely to have one nearby. Why didn't he say that? Because he is working in a literary environment in which wherever possible you insert the word 'with'. The sad thing is that one could easily quote a list of bad uses of 'with' that would fill a book of this length. However, perhaps we can all take some comfort from this:

> Whatever the weather with Jacksons Fine Fencing you don't need
> to worry.

Verbal Hinges

We turn now to some of the words that perform a different function in making connections crucial to rational utterance. Where words such as 'of' and 'from' knit terms together, filling out the content of the meaning ('the time *of* year', 'a letter *from* grandma'), the words we are now to examine are used for the purpose of hinging one assertion upon another in some sort of meaningful relationship ('This is the place *where* we keep our souvenirs'). A breakdown in logical linkage can occur by failure to keep in mind the exact character of the relationship. Often it is a case of choosing the wrong word to link two assertions together.

when
The word 'when' establishes temporal connections ('I stay in when it rains'). If the question of time is not involved in a connection made by the word 'when', then it is probably not the best word to use.

> The Prime Minister of Pakistan has accused Indian Intelligence
> Agents of carrying out two recent bomb attacks, one on a bus and
> the second in a hospital when six people died.

The word 'when' establishes the wrong kind of link here. 'Hospital' is not a word with which the word 'when' can properly be connected, nor indeed is the word 'second'. The specimen is an interesting one because there are two possible alternative corrections. Either 'when' must become 'where', thus locating the deaths ('hospital where six people died'), or 'when' must become 'in which', thus linking the deaths to the attack ('the second, in which six people died').

We find a good deal of carelessness in this respect, that is, in ignoring the proper function of the word 'when', that of linking things temporally.

> There are few better ways to enjoy a country walk than when you
> are in the company of a real expert.

The word 'when' directly attached to the word 'ways' establishes a quite illogical connection. If the word 'when' is to be preserved then there must be an appropriate word for it to connect with ('There are few better times to enjoy a country walk than when . . .'). However, there is a strange irony here in that the word 'when', indeed the whole group of words 'when you are' can be happily omitted. Sound logic is restored by their omission: 'There are few better ways to enjoy a country walk than in the company of a real expert.'

A slightly more complex misconnection is represented in the following:

> The amount of paperwork a police officer has to complete follow-
> ing an arrest is enormous, inversely proportionate to the job
> satisfaction when he sees many miscreants escape justice either
> as a result of some technical error or because the court has been
> told the prisons are full.

To speak of 'job satisfaction when . . .' is lax. A simple addition would improve this, an addition that would give the hinge word 'when' a fit term to connect with. Add the word 'felt': 'the job satisfaction felt when he sees many miscreants escape justice'.

Any placing of the word 'when' that leaves the reader guessing about the items it links together is to be avoided. This applies even to sentences which at first just cause a momentary uneasy doubt in the reader's mind before it is quickly washed away by what follows.

> Peeling chestnuts is easier when hot, though you'll need to hold
> them in a cloth.

The last part of the sentence reassures the reader that it is not the person peeling the chestnuts who will find the work facilitated if he or she is hot. The reassurance is needed because there are sentences such as 'Catching a cold is more likely when wet through' where the words leave room for no doubt at all that it is the catcher of the cold and not the cold to which the words 'when wet through' apply.

where

False linkages are established by the word 'where' as well as by the word 'when'. In conversation we happily treat these hinge words with freedom ('This is where I ask to be excused'). Transferring that kind of freedom to the printed word can often be acceptable, but it sometimes involves a degree of inexactitude which verges on the illiterate. Here is a piece from a popular magazine:

> Reading the letter reminded me of an account I read some years ago where a policeman on night duty in a Hampshire village was told there had been a complaint: 'Late at night and sometimes in the early hours a convoy of cars would rush noisily through the village.'

The story here was an amusing one because the dutiful policeman ended up stopping the car carrying the Queen. Our objection is to the use of the word 'where'. The policeman was not on night duty in the account but in the village. After 'account' some word such as 'of' is required ('an account I read some years ago of how a policeman on night duty was told there had been a complaint').

A more direct incompatibility occurs in this sentence from a piece about writers of guidebooks:

> Writers, like editors and publishers, obviously have a responsibility to do their homework and consider what and where they are actually describing and promoting.

It is clear that review writers too have a responsibility to attend to their homework. The word 'where' is totally out of place. If you gave a description of a locality, someone might logically ask 'What are you describing?' but not 'Where are you describing?' The words 'and where' should be omitted from the above.

More subtle slips than that occur in lax use of 'where'. Here is a very questionable sentence heard on the radio on the subject of a meeting between John Major and President Clinton:

> They will also discuss Northern Ireland, where American patience
> with the republicans is beginning to wear thin.

'Where' is quite the wrong word here. It is not in Northern Ireland
that patience is beginning to wear thin. To locate the American
attitude thus is an error. It is on the subject of Northern Ireland that
American patience may be beginning to wear thin. Northern Ireland
is not here a location visited but a topic discussed. That must be made
clear: 'They will also discuss Northern Ireland, a subject on which
American impatience with the republicans is beginning to wear thin.'

who

Misuse of the word 'who' in linking assertions produces similar illogicalities. Here, a writer is commenting on the Greenwich Dome:

> Why did they proceed with the extremely expensive plans for the
> Jubilee Line and the Dome without having established that the
> site could in fact be cleared? Why did the Government proceed
> without having secured a major developer, who had been sought
> unsuccessfully for a decade.

If you advertise a post and have difficulty for a long time in finding a
suitable applicant, you may reasonably speak of seeking such a person
'unsuccessfully'. But if you finally find the right man or woman, you
cannot turn to them and say 'You are the manager who has been
"sought unsuccessfully" for a long time'. The appointee was sought
successfully. This may seem to be a subtle point, but the requisites of
strict logic are sometimes subtle. In the original statement above, the
word 'who' was the wrong word, for if the Government had 'secured
a major developer' that developer would not have been sought 'unsuccessfully'. The sentence should have read: 'Why did the Government
proceed without having secured a major developer after one had been
sought unsuccessfully for a decade?'

as

The most common misuse today involving the word 'as' is illustrated
here in a leading article:

> The late King Hussein married an Ipswich girl, and Princess Muna,

as Toni Gardiner is now known, is held in high esteem as the
mother of King Abdullah.

Toni Gardiner is not now 'known' Princess Muna; she is 'called' Princess Muna. To satisfy the logical mind the sentence should run 'Princess Muna, as Toni Gardiner is now called', because the only logical
alternative would be 'Princess Muna, as Toni Gardiner is now known
as'. We 'call' people this or that but we don't 'know' them this or that.
We 'know' them 'as' this or that. The same criticism applies to the
reference in an academic book to 'Euclid's *Elements*, as the first six books
were collectively known'. The books were not 'known' *Elements*, they
were 'called' *Elements*. The entire media world now seems ignorant of
this elementary distinction.

There is another use of 'as' that raises a similar problem.

> She saw her inheritance as a duty as much as a privilege.

Logically speaking, this should read: 'She saw her inheritance as a
duty as much as as a privilege.' Clearly that will not do. For that
reason one should avoid combining the 'as much as' construction
with another construction involving the word 'as'.

Other Devices for Making Connections

We turn to a handful of expressions that are currently ill used.
The specimens quoted are such that, under examination, they will
certainly offend the logically minded. Yet in fact the usages represented are now becoming so well established that in the eyes of
many they are no doubt regarded as 'correct'.

as regards
This is a peculiarly unattractive expression and always avoidable.

> As regards his actual performance on the field, he is as good as
> any member of the team.

There is no need at all to use the awkward word 'regards'. Replace it
by 'for': 'As for his actual performance on the field, he is as good as
any member of the team.' 'As regards' can generally be replaced thus.

followed by

The expression 'followed by' has to be handled with great care. Before using it the speaker or writer must ask: What is being followed and what is following? Then the following confusion could be avoided:

> Then in the 1980s he became a groundsman at the Roman Villa
> at Vindolanda, followed by several years of work at the Roman
> Army Museum in Greenhead.

There is only one item here which could be 'followed by several years' and that is 'the 1980s'. Certainly, as a groundsman he could not be 'followed by several years'. If 'followed by' is to be kept, then the sentence should read: 'A period in the 1980s spent as a groundsman at the Roman Villa at Vindolanda was followed by several years of work at the Roman Army Museum in Greenhead.' But why preserve the expression 'followed by' at such cost in verbal jugglery when its omission would simplify everything? 'He became groundsman at the Roman Villa at Vindolanda in the 1980s and then worked for several years at the Roman Army Museum in Greenhead.' As so often in making corrections, what improves things is the use of the appropriate verb in 'worked for several years' instead of the noun in 'several years of work'.

We see a comparable lapse in the following sentence about climbing Mont Blanc:

> Its first ascent in 1786 by Michael Picard was followed in 1787 by
> the more scientific Dr Horace Benédict de Saussure . . .

This comes from a scholarly book, yet the blunder is elementary. One ascent can be 'followed' by another, but not by a climber. If the expression 'followed by' is to be used, then what follows it must balance what precedes it. Here the construction would be better avoided. 'It was first climbed in 1786 by Michael Picard, and then in 1787 by the more scientific Dr Horace Benédict de Saussure.'

The trouble is that we have got used to using the verb 'follow' with only the dimmest sense of what it really means. It has become almost a substitute for 'and'. Take this sentence:

> She was initially schooled at St Alfred's School, Hampstead. Then

> a succession of governesses and schools followed as she and her
> family moved about at the Navy's behest.

What are these governesses and schools 'following'? Why introduce
the word? Why picture the incongruous procession of governesses
and schools? Why not say directly 'Then she was taught by various
governesses and at various schools'? Using the words 'she was taught',
instead of building meaning on the noun 'succession', produces simplicity, clarity and directness.

in terms of

This is now a grossly overused expression. As a device for moving from
some generalization to some specific indication of the area to which
it applies 'in terms of' can no doubt be sensibly used.

> In our Cardiac Department you'll find that hands-on means just
> that. In terms of professional backing. In terms of the practical
> experience.

It is perhaps the combination of the idiomatic 'hands-on' with the
repeated 'in terms of' that makes the reader wish the writer had spelt
out the case without recourse to the currently fashionable idioms,
but at least the idioms make sense there, which surely cannot be said
of the following about a cricket captain:

> He has influenced a lot of matches in terms of winning them.

All one can do is to congratulate the cricketer that he was not guilty
of influencing a lot of matches in terms of losing them. But the object
here is to illustrate a far too common usage in terms of mocking it.
Here is a piece about outdoor jackets that are on the market:

> . . . In essence all the materials used by major manufacturers are
> so similar in performance terms within the range of application
> of a jacket type, that though differences can be measured, they
> are so slight in practice as to be almost negligible.

The only thing to say is that all these usages of 'in terms of' by various
writers are so similar in performance terms within the range of
application of such a phrase that the whole lot should be written off
as wasteful and redundant.

similar to

In any comprehensive list of the dangerous words with which to begin a sentence surely the word 'similar' would stand high up.

> Similar to food pricing, all hotels should prominently display the cost of single and double room rates in a position which can be clearly seen by prospective clients, usually in the hotel reception (or an external display sign).

What is 'similar' to food pricing? It cannot be 'all hotels'. Nor, logically, can it be 'the cost of single and double room rates'. The comparison intended is not between prices or pricing but between the methods of publicizing them. So, if the word 'similar' is kept, then the matters between which the similarity is desired should be clearly stated. But our complaints do not end there. The demand that prices should be displayed 'in a position which can be clearly seen' is imprecise, because what is meant is 'in a position from which the display of rates can be clearly seen'. It is no use being able to see the position if the printing thereby displayed is out of sight-range. Moreover it is incorrect to define the required positioning as 'usually in the hotel reception (or an external display sign)' because the information would not be 'in' an external sign. What is meant is 'generally speaking, in the hotel reception or on an external display sign'. Last of all, the expression 'cost of single and double room rates' is incorrect. It is the cost of the rooms that is at issue. The word 'rates' is superfluous. A general rewriting is required. 'Like the price of meals, the cost of single and double rooms should be prominently displayed by all hotels, either in the hotel reception area or on an external notice board.'

like, akin to and *compared to*

The word 'similar' and the word 'like' must both make appropriate matches. It is logical to say: 'Like Britain, Newfoundland has a limited number of native mammal species.' There the comparison between Britain and Newfoundland is direct and clear. But what I read in a magazine article on Newfoundland is 'Like Britain, the number of native mammal species was limited by quirks of glaciation . . .' and no mention is made of Newfoundland in the sentence. The only thing directly compared to Britain is a 'number'. It should be clear from what has been said already that trying to express comparisons in print often provides a graveyard for logic.

> The Gould memos which laid bare a Government astray on 'touch-stone issues' signalled a detachment akin to the Thatcher of the late Eighties.

The straying of the Government on touchstone issues is said to indi-cate a detachment akin to Mrs Thatcher. It is plain that the writer did not accidentally omit the apostrophe that would have made sense of his statement ('a detachment akin to Mrs Thatcher's') or he would not have inserted the word 'the' before the lady's name.

It may be argued, I suppose, that the reader is not really discomfited by having to sort out the real illogicality of the following:

> Compared to the two established stallions, Mendicean still retained a figure more akin to his racing days.

It sounds rather clumsy to have to correct this to 'Mendicean still retained a figure more akin to that of his racing days' but logic requires it, not because the point may be missed but because the logical mind is not content to compare a stallion's figure to his racing days.

The Use of Possessives

One of the closest connections we make in our thinking is that between people and their attributes or possessions. In many contexts the English language supplies us with two alternative devices for making this connection. We naturally prefer to refer to 'John Smith's house' rather than to 'the house of John Smith'. The possessive case formed by the apostrophe is the more convenient and less artificial usage. Are there contexts where this usage is not acceptable? The question arises because of the contrast between two current practices. This is the more usual one:

> The professor's discovery opened a new stage in cancer research.

Compare it with the following piece about a problem with a hot axle-box on a mainline train:

> After the fault's discovery, the train went to Leicester at low speed where it terminated.

We needn't quibble about the seeming preference for a train to 'terminate' rather than to 'stop'. But the workman who spotted the trouble might reasonably claim that it was 'his' discovery, the 'engineer's' discovery. Indeed here is a clear case where the construction with the apostrophe is less than felicitous. The sentence should have read: 'After the discovery of the fault, the train went to Leicester at low speed, where it stopped.'

The preference in that case for the use of 'of' rather than of the apostrophe is surely a matter of clear thinking. The possessive relationship truly exists between the professor and his discovery, as indeed between the engineer and his discovery. It is surely that relationship which is turned on its head if we start to talk about 'the fault's discovery'. We should not think of speaking of 'America's discovery by Columbus' instead of 'Columbus's discovery of America'. Yet I find the following in a nurses' magazine:

> Both staff and managers have benefited in all sorts of ways as a result of the scheme's success.

Again one must protest that the construction with the apostrophe is out of place. Perhaps the staff and managers are being unduly modest about what has happened in attributing to the scheme credit that is really due to the deviser of the scheme (not 'the scheme's deviser'). In any case words could be saved here: 'Both staff and managers have benefited from the success of the scheme.'

It would seem that usage of the clumsier construction is being extended. A letter to the press provides this example:

> Lord Woolf's decision neatly absolves the youth prison service from the difficult task of supervising the murderer's further detention.

The 'detention' is not a possession in the same category as the murderer's home or his wristwatch. It is externally inflicted on him, and once more the apostrophe would be better avoided: 'supervising the further detention of the murderer'. That, however, is not as glaringly inappropiate as the usage found in another letter to the press. A news item had reported that the Tory leader, Iain Duncan Smith, had indicated his readiness to support Steve Norris in a bid to become Mayor of London in 2004.

> I would hope, however, that no one will prejudge any decision of the Central Office Candidates Committee. From my experience as a member of the selection panel during the last process, I do not think that Mr Norris's approval as a candidate should be taken for granted.

Here the writer translates 'approval of Mr Norris's candidature' into 'Mr Norris's approval as a candidate'. Nothing surely could be more inappropriate than to turn 'approval of Mr Norris' into 'Mr Norris's approval'.

To some extent the same issue arises with the use of possessive personal pronouns. When a couple came in for rough handling in the tabloid press we heard the fact announced thus on the radio:

> The couple have attacked their treatment by the media.

It was of course the media's treatment of them that was under fire, and it would have been better to avoid referring to it as the couple's treatment. The expected construction would be: 'The couple criticized the way they were treated by the media.' As so often, we have to deal with usages that the really sensitive writer would have naturally avoided, such as the following advice to gardeners:

> Do give this sort of planting a go. It's really like a herbaceous border with more grasses, but their addition means that the effect is much lighter and airier than a border packed solidly with perennials.

Nothing is gained, except a certain awkwardness of expression, by writing 'their addition' instead of 'adding them'.

Although that use of 'their' in the sentences above does not cause any misunderstanding, there are cases where an element of ambiguity may be produced by the usage.

> Which is where nurses come in. Labour is absolutely dependent
> on NHS staff to deliver its reforms and, with doctors brooding
> over their treatment, nurses hold the key.

May not this be read in two ways? Presumably the doctors are brooding over 'their treatment' by the Government, but 'nurses' are the dominating subject of the sentence and 'their' might be read as referring back to them. In any case, when doctors are involved the words 'their treatment' must almost always refer to their handling of patients. The sentence errs in another matter by its ugly use of the word 'with'. The word should be replaced: '. . . while doctors are brooding over the way they themselves are treated, nurses hold the key'.

We cannot fling around the word 'incorrect' in judgement on all the constructions we are now criticizing, but there is an awkwardness about the usage they represent. Consider this announcement after a murder, 'The houseboy has already confessed to her killing', where 'confessed to killing her' would be preferable. Then again we hear on the air of a suspected murderer about whom more has become known as 'his investigation has progressed'. The investigation by the police cannot possibly be identified as 'his' (the suspect's) investigation. And there is surely something misleading about the following comment made to a pregnant actress by someone else in the public eye: 'A huge media fuss surrounded my birth.' In the context it was clear that she meant her baby's birth.

The Apostrophe

The use of the apostrophe in the sentences at the beginning of the previous section ('the fault's discovery' and the 'scheme's success') must be distinguished from its use in the sentence cited above ('It's really like a herbaceous border'). The crucial distinction is that the apostrophe in 'it's' indicates an omission. In our schooldays we were taught that 'its' does not need an apostrophe unless it is an abbreviation of 'it is' or 'it has'. Yet misplaced apostrophes disfigure the public scene, as an hour's shopping in a suburb or a small town will prove. Nevertheless, I can record with some satisfaction that a restaurant I have passed on my walks for years has suddenly changed its notice board, removing the unwanted apostrophes from the offer of 'Haddock's, Chip's and Pea's' at an attractive price. It is a curious fact that errors with apostrophes almost always consist in putting them in where they should not be, not in omitting them where they should be. I read in a gardening magazine:

> It's compact nature makes it an ideal tree for a small garden.

And the apostrophe there is wrong, because 'its' is not short for either 'it is' or 'it has'. Then consider this specimen sentence from a respectable broadsheet:

> But it's not as if I can pluck another Skincare: Do's and Donts' out of thin air.

There should be no apostrophe in 'Dos' for 'dos' is the plural of 'do' and there is no question of a genitive or possessive case, and no question of an omission. But there should be an apostrophe in 'Don'ts', not after the 't', notice, but before it, because 'Don't' is the abbreviation of 'Do not' and the omitted 'o' has to be allowed for. In another publication, a not particularly vulgar magazine, I find a reference to 'the behaviour of the team at Christmas do's', and once more the apostrophe is a mistake, for 'dos' is simply the plural of 'do'. Writers must always check that they do not give way to the temptation to put an apostrophe before the 's' of a plural. This applies even when abbreviations are used. In a notice that begins 'GP's, surveyors, solicitors . . .' the apostrophe should be removed from 'GPs'.

In our conversation we readily make use of such abbreviations as 'I don't think the newspaper's come yet', where the apostrophe in 'don't' replaces the letter 'o' of 'not', and the apostrophe in 'newspaper's' replaces the 'ha' of 'has'. That kind of usage belongs to dialogue only. It is with distress that one sees a certain caravanning magazine sprinkling its pages with such forms as 'Safety's enforced by a high-level brake light', 'Neither van's at the cutting edge of fashion', 'The site's predominantly given over to statics', 'Salcombe's a small town on the Kingsbridge estuary' and 'Simon Coe's the show director'. This practice of indiscriminately replacing 'is' by an apostrophe has nothing to be said for it.

4

Assembling and Separating

When we look into current usage it is not surprising to find that a good deal of space on paper is filled by writers adding one item to another in making a point or distinguishing one item from others in making a point. In this chapter we shall look at disciplines that will safeguard us from making the errors all too common in the various verbal processes used for these purposes. We turn first to what on the surface might seem to be an area of assertion free of minefields, examining various ways of stringing items or facts together.

Straightforward Successiveness

From our earliest days of putting pen to paper the word 'and' is likely to figure prominently there. It is of course the most common device for linking one item with another. And because the word is so much used and in so many utterly different contexts, bad habits gather round its use. We are sparing of the word when we have a long list of items to add together; we reserve it for the last one: 'some tea, some sugar, some butter and a loaf of bread'.

We do not have to look far in literature for examples of how to list items in sequence logically. Recall those traditional light verses that we still hand on from generation to generation at Christmas and note how the sequence is sustained:

> On the twelfth day of Christmas
> My true love gave to me
> Twelve lords a-leaping,

Eleven ladies dancing,
Ten pipers piping,
Nine drummers drumming . . .

and so on down to the turtle doves and the partridge in the pear tree. The verbal pattern is sustained throughout. Every line from the third onwards depends directly on the second line for its meaning. There is no point at which the singer is required to break the pattern by inserting some such line as 'He threw in a set of coffee-spoons' or 'He was also kind enough to include a bowl of goldfish'. Lines that did not follow directly on 'My true love gave to me' would break the pattern. The whole structure of the sequence is that of a tree whose branches all span out from the same trunk and are utterly dependent on it.

It does not require an acute sense of logic to appreciate that any deviation from the verbal pattern established in this sequence would spoil everything. Yet it is not in the least difficult, scouring today's journalism, to find items accumulated in supposed succession that fail to match. Here is a specimen of the error at its most obvious:

> Elefanten Gore-Tex boots offer all the advantages of providing children with security, comfort and most importantly ensuring natural foot growth.

The reader takes in 'security, comfort and most importantly', then waits for the third item in the list. But it doesn't come. The pattern is broken by the insertion of the word 'ensuring'. The only way to rescue the sentence would be to stick to the pattern: 'all the advantages of providing children with security and comfort, and most importantly of ensuring natural foot growth'.

It is possible for the correct pattern to be broken by the intrusion of a single unwanted word.

> William Henderson (1813–1891) was born into one of the great industrial and commercial families of 19th century Durham whose wealth allowed him to fish the rivers of the north of England, Scotland, Europe but especially in his beloved Tweed.

The word 'in' destroys the pattern. The writer forgets within a few words that he has written 'fished the rivers of the north of England,

Scotland, Europe' and not 'fished *in* the rivers of the north of England', so the intrusive 'in' applied to the Tweed destroys the proper sequence.

The breakdown in consistency can occur in what should be a straighforward series of items.

> Objectivity is neither possible, nor wholly desirable in horsey exams, literary prizes, figure skating, in football referees and cricket umpires.

One may question whether there are any examinations or competitions in which objectivity is not 'wholly desirable', but our main concern here is with the laxity in the listing. The succession of items that begins with 'horsey exams' and is followed later by 'figure skating' is interrupted by 'literary prizes'. The exams and the skating are events, but 'literary prizes' are awards. Having thus mixed up competitions and prizes, the writer then goes on to add people to his list – 'football referees and cricket umpires'. The whole list should be tidied up: 'horsey exams, literary competitions, figure skating contests, football refereeing and cricket umpiring'.

There is often carelessness in this respect when an introductory list of contents is supplied for an account of a series of items to follow.

> A series of free data sheets gives comprehensive information and tips on a variety of camping-related subjects. Choosing the right tent or caravan, how to travel safely, where to camp, security precautions, using gas cylinders and electric hook-ups safely – these are a sample of the sheets available.

Three different verbal patterns are used here in a sequence which could better have preserved one pattern throughout. 'Choosing the right tent or caravan' and the last item 'using gas cylinders and electric hook-ups safely' keep the same verbal pattern. Between them we have 'how to travel safely', which matches 'where to camp', and 'security precautions', which matches nothing. The writer might have brought these into line with the first and last items: 'travelling in safety', 'finding a camp site' and 'taking security precautions', and the whole sequence would have matched. There were two other logical options. One was to bring the whole into line with the second and third items: 'How to choose the right tent or caravan, how to travel safely, where to camp, how to take security precautions, how to use gas cylinders and electric hook-ups safely.' The other option was to take the whole into line with the fourth item: 'The right choice of tent or caravan, safety in travel, choice of camp site, security precautions, and safe use of gas cylinders and electric hook-ups.' The basic mistake made here was to present the chosen items thus as 'camping-related subjects' and then as 'sheets'. Had the writer chosen to make a formal list of titles, 'Choosing the right tent or caravan', 'How to travel safely' and so on, then the same demand for grammatical consistency would not have applied.

The same error has to be recognized when there is no mechanical listing but a sequence of points made in straightforward prose. I read this in a nursing periodical:

> Two important concerns of the students were ensuring that health and safety issues were addressed and where to obtain further guidance in completing their action plans.

This is like saying: 'I want to ensure that my baby is protected and where to buy baby food.' The sentence requires another verb because ensuring something is one process and wanting to know something is another process: 'I want to ensure that my baby is protected and I want to know where to buy baby food.' The offending sentence could read: 'Two important concerns of the students were ensuring that health and safety issues were addressed and learning where to get further guidance in completing their action plans.' That does not make very good English of course. It would be much better to write: 'The students had two important concerns: ensuring that issues of health and safety were dealt with and learning where to get further guidance in completing their action plans.'

A shift in construction no less incongruous mars the following:

> Initially I saw my role as advising and supporting clinical assessors, particularly those new to the role and supporting students for the first time, in resolving problems experienced by students on placement, and to develop a learning environment within the nursing homes.

Having begun the sentence 'I saw my role as advising', the writer should have stuck to wording which followed properly from that beginning. Instead of which she branched out on a pattern of wording which does not fit: 'I saw my role as advising . . . and to develop a learning environment.' Correct this to: 'I saw my role as advising and supporting clinical assessors . . ., as supporting students . . ., resolving problems . . ., and developing a learning environment . . .'

Subtler Failures in Successiveness

It would be wrong to leave the impression that really skilled writers could never be faulted in this respect. The degree of accuracy which the logical mind demands sometimes proves difficult for the professionals to sustain. I cite a leading article about employment in the public services:

> It should extend especially to health and education. The attraction of careers in either field has been undermined by the rigidity with which they are managed, the militancy of public sector unions, the lack of proper career structure, and above all, no sense that merit will find a suitable reward.

The general statement 'The attraction of careers in either field has been undermined by' is followed by three expressions which properly attach themselves to it: 'the rigidity . . .', 'the militancy . . .' and 'the lack . . .'. But no sensitive writer would try to attach the fourth expression used here directly on to what properly should govern it ('The attraction of careers in either field has been undermined . . . by no sense that merit will find a suitable reward'). It requires only a slight alteration to correct this ending, because the word 'lack' has already been used: 'the lack of proper career structure, and above all, of any sense that merit will find a suitable reward'. The error is exactly the same as is committed in the sentence 'The success of the party was undermined by the coldness of the room, the lack of alcohol and above all no music'.

There are occasions when it can be taxing to sustain logical equivalence exactly from specimen to specimen in sequences such as these.

I cite the words of another experienced writer, asking the question 'How did the monarchy survive the 20th century?' He notes the removal of European emperors in the inter-war years, and then adds:

> Britain experienced two World Wars, a Cold War, a world slump,
> the independence of the Empire, and a social revolution.

Four of the items in that list of five are events or developments which Britain can be said to have 'experienced': the two world wars, the cold war, the slump and the social revolution. But Britain did not 'experience' the other item in the list, 'the independence of the Empire'. Britain did not 'experience' independence, but 'granted' it. That should be allowed for: 'Britain experienced two World Wars, a Cold War, a world slump, the granting of independence to the Empire, and a social revolution.'

How easily such failures in consecutiveness can occur is evident in these words from a rather poetic description of Moscow:

> Lenin smiles down, bald and malign, the cleaners, drab in head-
> scarves and downtrodden mien, scrub and mop . . .

The cleaners must not be said to be 'drab in headscarves and downtrodden mien' because it does not make sense to say they were 'drab in downtrodden mien'. Presumably what was meant was 'drab in headscarves and downtrodden in mien'.

More often than not errors in this kind of construction take the form of a single lapse. But occasionally one comes across a string of linked examples in which all share in an unfortunate choice of words.

> LBJ beat Goldwater by a landslide, as did Reagan with Mondale
> and Nixon with McGovern, or indeed Thatcher with Foot and
> Attlee with Churchill . . .

'With' is the wrong word. No doubt the writer was trying to avoid the correct but awkward sequence: 'LBJ beat Goldwater by a landslide, as did Reagan Mondale, Nixon McGovern . . .'. Surely the most satisfactory wording would repeat 'beat': 'LBJ beat Goldwater by a landslide, as Reagan beat Mondale and Nixon beat McGovern, or indeed as Thatcher beat Foot and Attlee beat Churchill.'

We end this section with a sentence from a letter to the press that reveals one of the subtlest ways in which the logic of successiveness can be upset:

> Some ten years ago, as a criminologist at Manchester University, I was author of a major study on police-held criminal records systems in England and Wales and the US. In the book, we highlighted the concerns of many about the slowness of the system, accuracy of information held (at that time by the police), its completeness and confidentiality, and so on.

There are two ways in which we use the word 'concern' in this kind of context. We speak of our concern 'about road accidents', 'road accidents' being something that we wish to be rid of. Let us call that a 'negative' concern. We also speak of our concern 'about road safety', 'road safety' being something we wish to preserve. Let us call that a 'positive' concern. Both usages are reasonable. But, if we are making a list of our concerns, we ought not to mix the two. That is what happens in the above sentence. The writer's concern 'about the slowness of the system' is what we have called a 'negative' concern, for he wants to get rid of the slowness. The other concerns – for 'accuracy', 'completeness' and 'confidentiality' are 'positive' concerns for what the writer approves of. It would be best to alter 'slowness' to 'speed'.

Other Devices for Grouping

It is perhaps not surprising that the kind of laxity which attends grouping items by the use of 'and' should appear when other methods of annexation are used. Preserving the pattern remains just as important.

as well as

The simplest use of this expression presents no problems. 'I'll have the perfume as well as the powder.' In such a sentence no one would fail to preserve the parallelism between 'the perfume' and 'the powder'. But what about the following?

> There'll be plenty of time to sample the café lifestyle of Venice as
> well as taking in a rich and rewarding view of some of its great
> historical, artistic and architectural treasures.

You would not say 'There's plenty of time to talk as well as reading'.
You would say 'There's plenty of time to talk as well as to read'. The
pattern has to be preserved as in all constructions that accumulate
items in succession. 'There'll be plenty of time to sample the café
lifestyle of Venice as well as to take in a rich and rewarding view of
some of its great historical and architectural treasures.' Yet journals
abound in examples of this misuse.

> When a group of post-menopausal women used resistance
> machines twice weekly for a year, they managed to increase their
> density, as well as strengthening their muscles and increasing
> their muscle mass.

That is the now standard laxity. The writer breaks the pattern, shifting
from 'to increase their density' to 'strengthening their muscles'. The
sentence should read: 'they managed to increase their density, as well
as to strengthen their muscles and increase their muscle mass'.

All writers should be warned against ever beginning a sentence
with the words 'as well as'. It is a sure recipe for error.

> As well as the lubrication problems, it was never possible to
> support the overhanging ends of the rails fully, causing them to
> flex, which raised stresses around the boltholes.

There is nothing here at all properly to balance 'the lubrication
problems'. It would have made sense to say 'As well as lubrication
problems there were stress problems'. That kind of balance is required
around the words 'as well as'. As it is, another expression should have
been used ('There were lubrication problems and it was never possible
to support the overhanging ends of the rails fully . . .'). It would be
logical to say 'As well as five children of their own, it was never
possible for them to support two adopted ones', because the 'five
children', like the 'two adopted ones' are the objects of the verb
'support'.

together with, etc.

What applies to the use of 'as well as', in respect of the need for parallelism and balance, applies equally to 'together with', 'along with' and 'in common with'.

> John Hotchkis was elected chairman of the Wye Fisheries Association in 1900 and was instrumental, together with the cooperation of the 8th and 9th Dukes of Beaufort, in resolving the problems.

'John Hotchkis' must not be linked by 'together with' to anything other than another living being. John Hotchkis might have taken a walk together with one of the dukes or even entertained him for supper, but he could not have consorted in that intimate way with 'the cooperation' of the dukes. 'Togetherness' has sometimes been a vaunted ideal for cooperation between living beings, and you might take a stroll 'together with' your dog but you would not take a stroll 'together with' your walking stick or 'together with' your wife's cooperation. 'John Hotchkis was elected chairman of the Wye Fisheries Association in 1900 and, with the support of the 8th and 9th Dukes of Beaufort, was instrumental in resolving the problems.'

We can find the same carelessness in the use of 'along with'. Here is a review of a book on angling:

> The historical development of Shrimp and Spey flies is covered along with a regional guide . . .

The 'regional guide' must not be said to be 'covered'. Once again it is better not to try to cater for the two items with the one verb: 'The historical development of Shrimp and Spey flies is covered, and there is a regional guide . . .'

There can be even more damage to the meaning by misplacing 'in common with'. Here is an account of a caravan site near Edinburgh:

> In common with the other sites, bus and train can be utilized – the former stopping near the site entrance.

A sentence beginning as this begins must continue in the following way: 'In common with the other sites, this site has such and such advantages.' 'Bus and train' must not be said to have anything 'in common with the other sites'. They do not share anything with the other sites. 'In common with' was the wrong expression to choose. 'As is the case at other sites, bus and train can be utilized . . .'

also

We are dealing repeatedly in this section with constructions which link items and which, in doing so, demand perfect balance between the items they link. And with none of those constructions is the demand stricter than with the use of the words 'both . . . and'. Here is a sentence about the equipment needed for towing caravans:

> This is both within the framework of type approvals legislation
> and also for overall towing safety and peace of mind.

To begin with, we do not need to strengthen the force of the words 'both . . . and' by inserting 'also', but in any case all balance is lost. To say something is both 'within' some legislation and 'for' some purpose is to misuse the words 'both . . . and'. And why introduce the word 'framework'? 'This both fits in with type approvals legislation and contributes to towing safety and peace of mind.'

Linking items by using the words 'not only . . . but also' might seem to be a straightforward matter. 'It was not only cold but also wet.' That illustrates the balance again required – between 'cold' and 'wet'. Yet see how the mind can slide away from keeping that balance.

> She had not only major abdominal surgery but also will have
> suffered some degree of surgical shock . . .

The sequence 'She had not only . . . but also will have' is totally unbalanced. Since the statement begins 'She had not only abdominal surgery but also' it must continue by supplying the balancing item to 'abdominal surgery'. Instead the mind of the writer leaps to a different sequence of thought. To complete the sequence logically one needs something like 'She had not only abdominal surgery but also an experience of shock', which would convey what two things she 'had' ('She had not only this but that'). It would be better put: 'She suffered not only major abdominal surgery but also some degree of surgical shock.'

This kind of illogicality can occur with the use of the word 'also' even when the complication of the sequence beginning with 'not only . . .' is lacking.

> Although the job is primarily a pre-publication role, you will also be expected to provide post-publication advice including handling complaints and, if appropriate, litigation.

You cannot be 'also' expected to 'do' anything at all unless something else has already been expected of you. And to say the job is a pre-publication role does not directly present any such expectation. To make sense the sentence should have run: 'Although the job is primarily a pre-publication role, it will also require you to provide post-publication advice . . .' The ironical thing is that there is an easier way still to correct the publisher's advertisement, and that is simply to cut out the word 'also': 'Although the job is primarily a pre-publication role, you will be expected to provide post-publication advice.' Indeed it would seem that there is always room for caution before inserting the word 'also' in a statement. Here is something else to exemplify the point:

> Some are extremely acidic in colour and can appear too harsh and strident under our usually grey sky. I also prefer dramatic dahlias to have plenty of space around them . . .

No preference as such has been stated that would justify the use of the word 'also' before the word 'prefer' in that sentence.

besides, as well as, in addition to
In accumulating points alongside each other we make use of other expressions, such as 'besides', 'as well as' and 'in addition to', which all make the same demand for preservation of balance. It is logical to say 'Besides their London flat, they have a country cottage in the Cotswolds' because the balance is preserved between 'London flat' and 'country cottage'. It is illogical to say 'Besides their London flat, they go off to the Cotswolds at the weekends' because no balance exists between 'their London flat' and 'they go off'. In the same way it is logical to say 'We are both fond of country walks as well as of symphony concerts' because the balance is again preserved. It would be illogical to say 'As well as looking after the cat, they asked us to

collect their post while they were away' because there is no parallelism between 'looking after' and 'to collect'. Usage would not allow the construction 'They asked us looking after the cat'.

The same demand for parallelism is made when one uses the expression 'in addition to'. 'I bought wine and spirits in addition to the usual meat and vegetables' is the correct usage. A slight lapse in the logical sequence can produce absurdity.

> On pensioners, Mr Prescott announced that he had set a new goal
> to wipe out fuel poverty by 2010, in addition to the existing
> £1 billion warm homes programme.

The placing of the expression 'in addition to' suggests that Mr Prescott had the double aim to wipe out both fuel poverty and the existing £1 billion warm homes programme by 2010. It would probably be best to reshape the sentence: 'On pensioners, Mr Prescott announced that, in addition to the existing £1 billion warm homes programme, his new goal was to wipe out fuel poverty by 2010.'

on the one hand . . . on the other hand
Here is another construction that requires a balance to be kept between the two parts, what follows 'on the one hand' and what follows 'on the other hand'. Let us look at a case where such balance is lost. Here is a piece recording French concerns over English beef during the period of the BSE crisis:

> Farmers unions are protesting, on the one hand, against French
> rules that require the slaughter of a whole herd when a single
> case is detected, and on the other are demanding that the Govern-
> ment remove a million animals, born before 1996 when tough
> controls on BSE infection were introduced, from the human food
> chain.

The use of the expression 'on the one hand . . . and on the other' here gets quite out of hand. We may say: 'He is protesting on the one hand against the lack of porridge for breakfast and on the other hand against the charge made for coffee after supper.' That usage is satisfactory because of the balance maintained between 'lack of porridge' and 'charge made for coffee'. Such a balance must always be maintained with the two halves of the construction. But in the sentence cited above the writer forgets how the construction works in the very act of using it. It is not logical to write: 'He is protesting on the one hand against the lack of porridge for breakfast and on the other is demanding free coffee after supper.' That is the equivalent of what this journalist is doing. If the construction is to be kept, the relationship between the two balancing protests must be made clear: 'On the one hand farmers' unions are protesting against French rules ... and on the other hand are demanding that the Government remove a million animals ...' In fact the original would be best corrected by deleting 'on the one hand' and 'on the other'. It would then be perfectly logical. The moral seems to be that one should hesitate before using the construction.

Inclusiveness

include/including

If strict logic is to be preserved, all the rules governing the use of English when listing items in succession apply equally when writers are recording accumulations of supposedly parallel items after words such as 'include' and 'including'.

> Your membership also includes, in selected issues of National Geographic, five bonus full-colour, double-sided supplements, including Mars, ancient Egypt, Treasure Discoveries, Africa and Antarctica.

Here we have two uses of the verb 'include' ('includes' and 'including') which produce the kind of laxity at issue. It is an elementary defect to write 'Your membership includes' this or that when what you mean is 'Your membership entitles you to' this or that. Nevertheless the habit is widespread. And the second misuse here, involving the word 'including', illustrates an equally common illogicality. The supplements are said to include 'Mars, ancient Egypt' and so on, when what is meant is that they include articles and photographs about these localities. Moreover the sentence is made worse by the fact that the homogeneous list of localities ('Mars', 'ancient Egypt', 'Africa' and 'Antarctica') is interrupted by inclusion of the item 'Treasure

Discoveries', which belongs to a totally different category of items. I should offend similarly if I were to recommend a book as 'containing York, Durham, Winchester and Lincoln' instead of as 'containing chapters on York, Durham, Winchester and Lincoln'. And I should be guilty of a worse infelicity if I recommended the book as 'containing York, Durham, recent discoveries, Winchester and Lincoln'.

The world of advertising can provide examples of extreme disorderliness in this respect. Here is an advertisement for digital hearing aids, recommending a publication:

> This authoritative publication both informs the prospective customer of his or her rights and describes certain matters that should be understood before making a decision. It answers many important questions including such points as: Prices of hearing aids/ Benefits of digital hearing/ NHS or private?/ Who is legally entitled to dispense hearing aids?/ Replying to advertisements/ What are my safeguards?

The logical chaos here is inexcusable. To say something 'answers many questions including such points as' presupposes that a question can take the form of a 'point', which plainly it cannot. Then the listing includes six items, three of which are questions and three of which are not. Perhaps those latter three can be regarded as 'points', but in any case the mixture will not do. The writer should have opted either for a series of questions or for a series of points. If the first alternative were adopted then the introductory part of the sentence should read: 'It answers many important questions including the following: . . .' And the subsequent list should read: 'What do hearing aids cost? What are the benefits of digital hearing? Should one use the NHS or the private sector? Who is legally entitled to dispense hearing aids? How does one reply to advertisements? What are the applicant's safeguards?' If the writer chose to list 'points' instead of questions, then the introductory part of the sentence should read: 'It deals with many important points, including the following: . . .' And the subsequent text should read: 'Pricing of hearing aids/ Benefits of digital hearing/ Choosing between NHS and private treatment/ The legal entitlement to dispense hearing aids/ Replying to advertisements/ The patient's safeguards.'

In this matter we allow ourselves certain freedoms in conversation which certainly ought not to be indulged in print. For instance, the following advertisement offends in that way:

> Loctite Super Plastix, is the first system to bond all types of household plastics – including notoriously difficult surfaces such as toys, electrical appliances, and perspex.

In the first place, 'difficult surfaces' should not be classified among 'types of plastics'. And in the second place, toys and electrical appliances are not 'surfaces' and should not be listed as such. Rewrite: 'Loctite Super Plastix is the first system to bond all types of household plastics. It is effective on notoriously difficult surfaces such as those of toys and electrical appliances, and on perspex.'

We are here concerned with what are really breakdowns in logic. The lapse into error after the word 'including' can reveal a direct and crude collision of meanings.

> The Land Reform Policy Group paper suggests various changes, including the need in specific circumstances for public acquisition.

Whatever items follow the words 'various changes including' must themselves be changes. A 'need' cannot possibly be a 'change'. If the word 'changes' is kept, then what follows must be on these lines: 'suggests various changes, including the possible public acquisition of land in specific circumstances'. If the word 'need' were to be kept, then the sentence must begin differently: 'The Land Reform Policy Group drew attention to various requirements, including the need in specific circumstances for the public acquisition of land.'

An awkwardness of a different kind after the word 'including' is represented in the following:

> Pitt was certainly not a republican, but neither was any other politician of any standing at the time, including Fox, the florid, flawed leader of the Whigs.

One would not say 'No one at all turned up for the celebration, including women and children' because the words 'no one' are all-exclusive and it is unnecessary to start exemplifying instances of the excluded. Similarly, once one has said that no politician of any standing at the time was a republican, the use of the word 'including' is infelicitous. It would be slightly better to write 'neither was any other politician of any standing at the time, and that applies to Fox', or perhaps 'neither was any other politician of any standing at the time – not even Fox'.

from . . . to

Experience suggests that the sequence involving the words 'from . . . to' is a dangerous construction to use. Consistency has to be preserved between what follows the word 'from' and what follows the word 'to'. The usage is properly represented by such sentences as: 'The shop stocked everything from tin tacks to electric drills.' There we have a perfect balance between its two halves. 'Tin tacks' are balanced by 'electric drills'. Yet there is a temptation to drift away from that kind of balance.

> His work ranged from studying outbursts of solar particle radi-
> ation to the origin and lifetime of cosmic ray particles from
> nearby regions of the Milky Way.

Parallelism breaks down here. What is needed is: 'His work ranged from studying outbursts of solar particle radiation to studying the origin and lifetime of cosmic ray particles.' If 'studying' is kept after 'from' it must be balanced by a matching word after 'to'. It would be correct to say: 'His work ranged from studying this to working on that' because the balance is preserved between 'studying' and 'working'. Whereas balance is preserved in the sentence 'His offences ranged from stealing money to accumulating huge debts', balance is lost in the sentence 'His offences ranged from stealing money to huge debts'.

A more striking illogicality can occur when what is included between the words 'from' and 'to' does not exemplify what it is supposed to exemplify.

> From Wordsworth through to Wainwright, the English Lake Dis-
> trict has been described and dissected for more than 250 years.

One might say 'From Haweswater in the east to Wastwater in the west, the Lake District has been described and dissected', because

Haweswater and Wastwater are indeed part of the Lake District, but neither Wordsworth nor Wainwright was ever a feature of the terrain. You would not say 'From baby Mary to Granny, our house is beautifully equipped'. The sentence should read: 'From Wordsworth through to Wainwright, writers have described and dissected the Lake District.'

For a more subtle breakdown in logic we turn to a review of an art exhibition on 'The Poetry of Nature'. It first describes the 'centrepiece' of the show, a picture of Greta Bridge, 'the most important example of John Sell Cotman's work'.

> But the other pieces in this show – from the draughtsmanship of the architectural studies to the bright colours of the later works – explore a man's meditations upon the place that he occupies within the natural world.

When the writer turned to talk about the 'other pieces', she should have stuck to that subject. The error she makes is of the same kind as is made in the following: 'The other students in the group – from the cleverness of Jane to the doggednes of Emma – are an interesting bunch.' The point is that 'cleverness' is not a student and 'doggedness' is not a student. What the sentence should say is 'The other students in the group – from clever Jane to dogged Emma – are an interesting bunch.' In the same way 'draughtsmanship' is not a piece in the show and 'bright colours' are not either. The writer should have made up her mind whether she was going to continue by talking about the artist's qualities or about his other pieces. 'But the other pieces in the show – from the finely draughted architectural studies to the brightly coloured later works – explore a man's meditations on the place that he occupies in the natural world.'

If one is looking for the greatest depth of illogicality to be attained by misuse of the 'from ... to' construction, perhaps it is here, in an advertisement from a bank:

> And our expertise spans an enormous range of industries, from manufacturing and information technology to everything in between.

Alternation

We are as likely to use words to separate this item from that as we are to use words to add this to that. Alternation is one of the strictest devices for separating or differentiating one thing from another.

or

Arguing a case often involves invoking alternatives. 'You must grant that (either) this or that is the case' we may say. A proper balance must exist in the wording between what constitutes 'this' and what constitutes 'that' on either side of the word 'or'. There has to be a parallelism in construction as well as in logic. To fail in this respect can be crude indeed. This is how a man retiring from a post after some controversy expressed himself:

> I would have like to have carried on – there was no reason why not to. The problems were in the past, those involved had, or were moving on.

The statement 'those involved had' must be completed by 'moved on'. Here the construction adopted is 'those involved had ... moving on', which will not do. Clumsy as it may seem, there is no logical escape from completing the two verbs: 'those involved had moved on or were moving on'.

Where the notion of strict alternation is present in the form of the sentence, there must be logical validity in that alternation. There is now a habit in the media of positing alternatives which abuse the word 'or'.

> Does parenthood appeal or appal?

Thus Radio 4 trails a coming programme. But it is plain that appealing and appalling are not exclusive alternatives. It would be quite rational to reply to that question by saying 'Neither'. There are plenty of things in life which do not appeal to one and yet certainly do not appal. Here is another choice offered by the BBC:

> Are exams good for children? Or should they be having more fun?

Again the propositions separated by the word 'or' are not genuine alternatives. A proper alternative to 'Are exams good for children?' might be 'Are exams bad for children?' And, whether exams are good or bad for them, it still might apply that children ought to be having more fun. We must not treat light-hearted journalistic usage of this kind too seriously, but there are usages of 'or' in more solemn writing that seem equally ill considered.

> Most of the people who have disliked the Queen Mother, and
> there have been some, have not lived as long as her or feel that
> the occasion of her 100th birthday is not a time for criticism.

Of those who have disliked the Queen Mother there is a majority ('most') which the sentence is about. (The minority are left out of the reasoning.) These dislikers are divided into two categories. There are those who have not lived as long as she has, and since she is nearly 100 at the time of writing, the boundaries of this category do not leave much room for many people outside it. However, nothing more is said of their attitude. But it is explained that the second category of dislikers, seemingly all centenarians, feel that the occasion of a lady's hundredth birthday is not the best time to criticize her, and we may add that surely they of all people ought to know. It is perhaps not worth our while to spend much time on this limited group of commentators. One cannot feel that the reasoning has taken us very far.

whether . . . or
Somehow the use of the word 'whether' before 'or' increases the reader's sense that perfect parallelism must be preserved in the alternatives proposed. You would not say to someone 'It's all the same to me whether you stay or moving away'. Yet in fact that kind of inconsequential alternative can be found offered in print.

> With Christmas and the New Year out of the way, people like to
> get on and do other things, whether hiding in a corner until the
> credit card shows signs of recovery, get out and about more to
> walk off some excess pounds . . . or go to a motor show and buy a
> brand new model.

The sequence here is 'whether hiding in a corner . . ., get out and about . . . or go to a show'. How can the mind forget so quickly what course it is taking through the thickets of the English language? The sentence should read: 'People like to get on and do other things, whether hiding in a corner until the credit card shows signs of recovery, getting out and about more to walk off some excess pounds . . . or going to a motor show and buying a brand new model.'

That kind of thoughtless logical collapse often disfigures magazine journalism. I take another specimen:

> Women often dream about sex with anonymous strangers . . .
> whether it's a man they met at a fancy dress party, or an elaborate
> sexy scenario with the balaclava-clad Milk Tray man . . .

The 'anonymous strangers' are supposed to be exemplified. The first such stranger is a man met at a party, the second is an elaborate scenario. The mind's failure to keep its grip on the train of thought is grotesque. If we must have all that stuff about the 'sexy scenario', then it must come as an attachment to the Milk Tray man and not vice versa. 'Women often dream of sex with anonymous strangers . . . whether it's a man met at a fancy dress party or the balaclava-clad Milk Tray man, taking one into a sexy scenario . . .'

The same breakdown can occur at a much more sophisticated level:

> Every culture, every religion has its foundational charitable narra-
> tives, whether it is the she-wolf who nurtured Romulus and
> Remus or the Good Samaritan's unselfish display of agape.

The writer is supposed to be specifying 'narratives' after 'whether' and 'or', but neither the 'she-wolf' nor the 'unselfish display' of the Good Samaritan is a narrative. There is a double shift from narrative to a character in a narrative and then to the behaviour of a character in a narrative. Moreover, a narrative might be short or long, simple or complex, but it cannot exercise charity. A story about murder does not become a 'murderous story'. Correct the sentence thus: 'Every culture has its foundational narratives of charity, whether it is the story of the she-wolf who nurtured Romulus and Remus or that of the Good Samaritan and his unselfish display of agape.'

It is not difficult to accumulate evidence of the need to think through the construction to the end before beginning a sentence with 'whether'. Here is a passage from an obituary of a brave charity worker:

> On one occasion during the Blitz she led 29 customers to safety when the store suffered a direct hit. Whether inspired by that event, her RAF boyfriend, or more likely to insure against having to work in a war factory, she volunteered for the Women's Auxiliary Air Force in 1941, and worked on radar.

The writer loses his or her way. The sequence beginning with 'Whether inspired by that event' must be completed. It cannot be followed by the words 'or . . . to insure'. If the 'whether . . . or' construction is kept, the sentence must run: 'Whether inspired by that event, by her RAF boyfriend, or by her wish to avoid having to work in a war factory, she volunteered for the Women's Auxiliary Air Force.' The words 'whether inspired by' there are followed by the three logically matching options – 'that', 'the boyfriend', 'the wish to avoid work in a war factory'.

Contrasts

We turn to another mode of differentiation, that of drawing direct contrasts. In drawing such contrasts a balance has to be preserved between the opposed items. The mind has to concentrate on the question 'What am I contrasting with what?' For the truth is that in current usage, time after time, we find that this point has been neglected. Here is a comment on the announcement of an engagement involving an English girl:

> Life in the presidential palace in Damascus will seem very different from a semi in Acton.

The contrast here should be between life in one place and life in another. Yet the wording turns it into a contrast between life in Damascus and a building in Acton. The writer has to watch personal habit like a lynx in this matter. The basic elements of the contrast must be spelt out: 'Life in the presidential palace in Damascus will seem very different from life in a semi in Acton.' There is no escape from this strictness of parallelism except into illogicality. Yet the press abounds in such illogicality.

> If you can prove your income to an adequate level for the mortgage you want, and if you've got two years' accounts, you don't need a mortgage any different from an employed person.

Ponder the meaning of 'a mortgage any different from an employed person'. One must not draw either a comparison or a contrast between a mortgage and a person. It may sounds very awkward to say 'You don't need a mortgage any different from the mortgage of an employed person' but that or something like it has to be said. The wording may be 'a mortgage any different from that of an employed person' or, more naturally, 'a mortgage any different from an employed person's' but the parallelism must be made between two mortgages, not between a mortgage and a mortgagee.

Making such contrasts can easily lead to quite subtle failures of parallelism.

> The Tea-Cosy man is quite the professional these days – a far cry from the stumbling ramshackle nature of his early gigs, though one suspects that much of that was deliberate.

You might say: 'My father is a great reader these days – a far cry from the active young athlete he once was.' For there the parallelism between 'a great reader' and 'the young athlete' is preserved. You would not say: 'My father is a great reader these days – a far cry from the athletic exploits of his youth.' For there is no proper balance between 'my father' and 'the athletic exploits'. In the same way, in the sentence above, there is no proper balance between 'the Tea-Cosy man' and the 'stumbling ramshackle nature of his early gigs'. If the present self cannot be neatly contrasted with the earlier self, then the parallelism must be shifted to the performances: 'The Tea-Cosy man has real professionalism these days – a far cry from the stumbling ramshackle nature of his early gigs . . .'

We have to keep a proper balance too when making statements that fork out into a contrast. 'I don't mean that she was really hostile, but she showed a lack of consideration.' In that statement 'she was really hostile' is balanced by 'she showed a lack of consideration'. Yet here is a sentence from the work of an academic writer in which that balance is lost:

> The point is not that he was influenced by Le Grice, but his total familiarity with this rhetorical manner from college exercises.

The lack of proper balance between 'he was influenced' and 'total familiarity' is notable. The sentence should read: 'The point is not that he was influenced by Le Grice, but that he was totally familiar with this rhetorical manner from college exercises.'

Perhaps the most used word in making contrasts is the word 'unlike'. This raises a problem for the writer on usage, for the word is now so widely misused by the media that claims for the acceptability of their current practice might be made on those grounds. Nevertheless common sense will not allow one to acquiesce in the abuse of the word.

> And, unlike most of the past 40 years, the Government has not had to struggle with a financial crisis and market pressures to take unpopular spending and tax decisions.

If I said 'Unlike Jean, Betty lives in the country', you would recognize the basic contrast between Jean and Betty. But if I said 'Unlike last year, Betty now has a baby', you would rightly remind me that last year would not be capable of having a baby, so the contrast would not make sense. Yet in the sentence above we have precisely that breakdown of logic. The Government must not be said to be 'unlike most of the past 40 years'. The contrast is false. We know quite well that the past 40 years did not struggle with a financial crisis. The governments in power no doubt did. Then why not say so? 'Unlike the governments of the past 40 years, the Government has not had to struggle with a financial crisis.'

It is often quite easy to correct this truly gross illogicality.

> Unlike many modern marriages, Pat and Anne have joint accounts for all their financial affairs.

What on earth makes the writer compare Pat and Anne with other couples' marriages instead of with the couples themselves? Pat and

Anne are not a ceremony or an institution; they do not constitute a 'marriage'. What we need is: 'Unlike many modern married couples, Pat and Anne have joint accounts for all their financial affairs.'

There are occasions, however, when one comes across a confusion which cannot be so easily sorted out.

> Unlike the river downstream of Putney, it is possible to scramble out of the water and reach a towpath at all stages of the tide.

Having begun the sentence with the words 'Unlike the river downstream of Putney', the writer must follow it somewhere with some word to which the expression applies. The nearest thing we get to that is the word 'water'. Rescuing the opening of this sentence would put such a strain on one's syntax that the effort is scarcely worth while. It is better to change the construction: 'At all stages of the tide it is possible here to scramble out of the water and reach a towpath, which could not be said of the river downstream of Putney.' The best advice one can give on this matter is: if you are just going to begin a sentence with 'unlike', don't.

Making Exceptions

The truth is that we are extremely careless in the use of the expression 'apart from', which ought to point to an exception. 'Apart from the starter, I found all the courses very tasteful.' That is the proper use of the expression. The starter is excepted from the judgement passed on the rest of the meal. Yet increasingly we find such usages as the following:

> Apart from giving the children a wonderful treat, the organizers made it a really educative experience.

Here, in her use of the expression 'apart from', the writer is not intending to imply any exception to her generalization. She wants to convey how one benefit was added to another, not to differentiate between the one and the other. In short, 'apart from' was not the best expression to use. The word 'besides' would have served her purposes better. 'Besides giving the children a wonderful treat, the organizers made it a really educative experience.' The following sentence about a new petunia ('Frillytunia Rose') shows how far this misuse can go:

> But apart from the frilly petals it is also notable for its rich rose
> flowers, complemented by light green foliage.

'Apart from' succeeded by 'also' is surely a contradiction in terms. 'Apart from' should separate, while 'also' unites. It would be far better to begin with 'besides' or 'as well as' or even 'in addition to': 'In addition to the frilly petals it is also notable for its rich rose flowers . . .'

The ironical thing is that we find corresponding misuses of the word 'besides'. The form of the word 'be-sides' indicates its function of linking items side by side ('She has many other good qualities besides her friendliness'). This is the very opposite function from that of the word 'apart', which performs a separating function. Yet a habit is developing of treating these two expressions as though they were interchangeable.

> And besides visits to her hairdresser, most of her beauty routines
> go on behind closed doors.

Surely there is a distinction drawn here between going to the hairdresser and otherwise having her beauty treatments at home. Making that distinction calls for the words 'apart from', not 'besides'.

5
Blending Word with Word

Keeping to the Point

The clear-minded writer or speaker gives attention to individual words and is sensitive to their exact meanings, but it is not the choice of this word or that word in isolation that determines whether what is said or written makes logical sense. It is the way words hang together, the way one word connects with others, whether comporting happily or colliding uncomfortably. Coherence in thought and utterance depends on a clear understanding of relationships between concepts and ideas. Our concern here is to show how to avoid one of the most common forms of illogicality, a breakdown in the relationship, between the different words that make up a statement. It is no good choosing the right word if one renders its effect null or absurd by bringing the wrong word to bear on it. Sometimes a degree of sharpness of penetration is required to pinpoint what has gone wrong when a statement proves to be illogical in that respect. But more often than not the clear-headed reader will recoil uncomfortably from inner illogicalities, perhaps even before they are fully recognized, and the clear-headed writer will be forearmed by a native watchfulness against committing them.

Inappropriate relationships between words can have a serious bearing on the meaning of what is conveyed. At its crudest, this kind of error can even produce a brand of inner contradiction, as in this news item:

> Describing her husband as 'one in a million', she appealed for help in catching his killers who she said had left a void in her life which could never be replaced.

A 'void' or emptiness left in one's life by a bereavement is not something which a grieving widow would want to see 'replaced'. 'Replacing' a 'void' achieves nothing. The void has to be 'filled'. The speaker was mentally concerned with the late husband who, she felt, could never be 'replaced'. But applying the verb 'replace' to the void instead of to the lost husband produces a kind of inner contradiction. Oddly enough, it is a confusion that frequently attends use of words such as 'void' and 'gap'. I have heard a new book praised on the grounds that 'it fills a necessary gap'. Seemingly the speaker ignored the fact that if a gap is 'necessary' then the last thing you must do is to try to fill it.

The crucial rule for the writer in this respect can be simply expressed. If you have a good idea for the right word in the first part of the sentence, don't forget that you have used it when you are writing the second part of the sentence. If you begin by talking about a 'void', then keep the word and its meaning in mind when producing the rest of the sentence. The speed with which a writer may lose track of what he is saying is well illustrated in the following:

> His Methodist upbringing soon turned into a thoroughgoing
> humanistic atheism.

Here is a case in point. An 'upbringing' is an upbringing and it cannot be turned into a system of belief or unbelief. The man's upbringing would have remained Methodist even if he had changed his beliefs year by year for the rest of his life. When you begin a sentence by talking about someone's 'upbringing', you must not forget what you are talking about and continue as though you had begun by talking about that person's 'Methodism' or 'Christianity': 'Although brought up as a Methodist, he soon became a thoroughgoing humanistic atheist.'

Let us look at another instance of this seemingly immediate forgetfulness. The article is about hunting, a sport just recovering, at the time the piece was written, from the impact of foot-and-mouth disease.

> The wise old advice to get as much hunting in before Christmas,
> before the weather turns, has not been possible this year and so,

after everything else, it would be nice if Jack Frost could give the
hunting world a bit of a break.

Within the first two lines of her sentence the writer had forgotten
how she began. She surely did not mean to tell us that the wise old
advice had not proved 'possible'. Advice is one thing and carrying out
that advice or acting upon it is another thing. The advice is 'wise' and
'old'. It applies year after year, but 'it has not been possible to follow
it this year'.

We turn from advice on hunting to the business world. Here the
writer hits on a useful word for his purposes, and then continues as
though he had used some other word:

> Continuing advances in production, efficiency and waste re-
> duction enable us to keep a firm brake on costs, which we can
> pass on to you in the form of unbeatable retail prices.

The advertiser no doubt thought it was a good idea to speak of keeping
a 'firm brake' on costs. But the word 'brake', once uttered or written,
was forgotten. For you cannot pass a brake on to your customers, not
even in the form proposed. The word 'which' must go unless the word
'brake' is changed. What is 'passed on' is the gain made from operation
of that brake. Introduction of the 'brake' begins to seem not quite
such a good idea after all. If we keep it, the preservation will probably
be at the cost of a certain awkwardness: 'enables us to keep a firm
brake on costs, and so to benefit you by our unbeatable retail prices'.
Better sacrifice the 'brake': 'enables us to make savings in production,
which we can pass on to you'.

We criticized the ending of the above statement because 'which'
could not properly connect with 'brake'. Here we have a similar,
if less obvious, failure to connect, where no such word as 'which'
is used:

> The name Daphne invariably conjures up thoughts of delightfully
> fragrant flowers, a quality most daphnes have in abundance.

You might say 'He is a man of great honesty, a quality I admire'
because 'a quality I admire' is a fit match for the word 'honesty'. But
you ought not to say 'He is an honest man, a quality I admire', because

the 'quality' has not been mentioned. In the same way 'a quality most daphnes have in abundance' relates back to something that has not been mentioned, 'fragrance'. If the word 'quality' is kept, the word 'fragrance' must somewhere precede it: 'The name Daphne conjures up thoughts of delightful fragrance, a quality most daphnes have in abundance.'

We have been dealing with illogical talk of 'replacing' voids and handing 'brakes' on to customers. Such sentences exemplify a kind of mental crossover from one area of discourse to another. The mind accidentally slides away from one line of logical utterance to another. It is easier to slide thus in speech than in writing. A speaker on the radio spoke thus:

> The chances of winning the Nobel prize for science are going to take a long time.

The speaker began to talk about 'chances' and promptly forgot the fact. He pushed uncomfortably together the notion that chances for winning the Nobel prize do not often occur and the notion that it will therefore be a long time before a Britisher can possibly achieve one. The word 'long' applies to time, but it is not the 'chances' that take up the time. What is meant is: 'The chance of winning the Nobel prize for science arises rarely, and it may well be a long time before a Britisher achieves it.'

Sometimes a switch in thinking of that kind, which leaves the original subject ('chances') high and dry, occurs with a seeming ease that astonishes when the reader actually examines what is being said.

> Not the least of Bob Weighill's achievements was his willingness as an elder statesman of rugby union to modify the somewhat austere views he brought to the game from his service background.

Here again the writer begins by speaking of Bob Weighill's 'achievements', but immediately forgets that he is so doing. If you are listing a man's qualities of character, you may justly speak of his 'willingness to modify austere views brought from a service background'. But the writer here is speaking of his 'achievements' and, welcome and laudable as this 'willingness' of his was, it was certainly not one of his 'achievements'. If 'achievements' are to be mentioned, it must be in some such statement as: 'Bob Weighill's achievements were to some extent due to his willingness as an elder statesman of rugby union to modify the somewhat austere views . . .' But why not just pay direct tribute to the man's character?

Being too Clever

Sometimes failure of this kind to keep to the point seems to be purposeful. The professional writer may seem to have an excessive desire to appear slick and informal:

> I have always admired Japanese designers but have never found them particularly wearable.

We must assume that the writer did not seriously believe that it is possible to 'wear' a designer. She even knew that it is the designer's clothes that may or may not be 'wearable'. Then why did she go out of her way to talk nonsense? The desire to be clever can lead one astray. So can the attempt to be slightly 'different'. An element of pretentiousness often enters into a sentence when the wrong word is chosen from a group of related ones. Here is material from the motoring world:

> The rear panel, so often overlooked, is equally handsome, thanks to the more pronounced sculpting than many of its rivals can muster.

Where several words have an overlap of meaning, it is important not to abuse that overlap. To 'muster' is to gather together, especially used of summoning men for military purposes. The overlap in meaning with words such as 'gather' and 'collect' would not give one the right to speak of 'mustering daffodils' from the fields or 'mustering alms' from worshippers in church. Language does not work like that. The slightly comic, idiomatic usage by which we speak of 'mustering all our resources' when we are summoning up our powers for some mighty effort has a certain useful vividness, but such usefulness is destroyed if we abuse the word as it is abused above. The flavour of great matters that call for mobilization hangs over proper use of the word 'muster' and it should not be dissipated.

That sort of misfire tends to mar the work of writers who are trying too hard. Here is another specimen:

> The centre of the city comprises cobbled streets, old churches and medieval fortifications, humble reminders of the religious undertones that structure the city.

It makes sense to speak of certain remains as conveying reminders of past attitudes that constitute 'undertones' in a city's atmosphere. 'Undertones' are vaguely detected hints of some theme, giving an additional dimension to the surface implications of whatever is the subject under consideration. But the word 'structure' is essentially concrete in its connotation and collides uncomfortably with that rather nebulous concept. It would be better to end the sentence: 'religious undertones that give character to the city'.

Misfires of this kind can be found in comparatively sophisticated prose. One comes across descriptive efforts, what are called 'purple patches', that do not quite stand up to logical analysis. Here is a journalist's account of the appearance of Lady Archer at her husband's trial:

> What an entrance, what a star. Like Portia all in black. Her glossy hair gleamed with well-cut health, and her voice's timbre, honed on university tutorials, was clearly enunciated, modulated, composed.

The word 'timbre' is used for the distinctive quality distinguishing one vowel sound from another and also for the particular tone colour or quality of musical sounds. It is a fair enough exercise of the imagination to speak of the well-honed quality of a voice's timbre. But a 'timbre' cannot be 'clearly enunciated'. Only vowels and consonants can be 'enunciated', that is to say, clearly pronounced and articulated. The writer should have been content with fewer imaginative leaps. Where 'modulated' might justly be applied to 'timbre', 'enunciated' could apply only to the quality of the articulation and 'composed' seems to belong more to the general bearing of the speaker and the clarity of her speech.

In culmination, let us look at a specimen of near verbal anarchy from an advertisement for the appointment of a Senior Resuscitation Officer to a hospital:

> This is an excellent opportunity to lead this well established Resuscitation Service into the future and to implement an agreed strategic direction that includes additional staff and expanding the service.

To begin with, the words 'expanding the service' do not, in their construction, properly parallel the words 'additional staff'. If 'expanding the service' is kept, then the words 'additional staff' must be replaced by 'adding to the staff'. On the other hand, the sentence might be amended to 'includes an increase in staff and expansion of the service'. But the sentence fails in ways more relevant to our present subject, for a 'direction' cannot be said to 'include' additional staff, nor can one 'implement' a 'direction'. The words 'into the future' are redundant, since all planning and all appointing of staff are done for the future. You could scarcely lead an established service 'into the past'. The word 'strategic' is also redundant. It is one of those words added by administrators and managers in order to ensure that paper will be adequately covered with print and all simplicity and directness avoided. The word 'agreed' invites the same criticism. The reader ought to be able to take for granted that plans for the future have been 'agreed'. I suggest the following simplification: 'Here is an opportunity to lead this established Resuscitation Service and to carry out our plan to increase the staff and expand the service.'

Thoughtless Misconnections

It is impossible neatly to categorize all the various ways in which the wrong word is attached to the wrong word. There are sometimes quite simple slip-ups which the speaker would have avoided had he or she been listening to the words uttered, as in the statement 'The population of London is very dense', which assumes a comic ambiguity because of the various connotations of the word 'dense'. A persistent habit of checking up on every word written or uttered is the only safeguard against this kind of lapse. It is quite likely to occur when the writer or speaker is using a familiar vocabulary, a vocabulary so familiar that it issues from the tongue or the pen in a self-perpetuating flow. Here is a specimen of such carelessness:

> There are, however, a number of avenues for victims of office rage
> to pursue.

We do not 'pursue' avenues. We may seek them out. We may locate them. We may walk on them. But the idea of chasing them is not on. Better write: 'avenues for victims of office rage to follow'.

Handling for argumentative purposes the ready-made vocabulary represented by words like 'avenue' requires a special kind of watchfulness against such illogicalities. A comment on a document released by the Royal Society for the Protection of Birds complains that:

> . . . it was seen by many others as a sad reflection on how aspects
> of this matter had been conducted.

In the expression 'aspects of this matter' we have another instance of 'ready-made vocabulary'. And it is not used logically. You may 'conduct' an orchestra. You may 'conduct' a campaign. You may 'conduct' yourself agreeably. But you cannot conduct 'aspects'. They are quite resistant to efforts of control or organization. The writer is really criticizing how certain matters have been handled. And here is another failure to use a familiar vocabulary accurately. The sentence applauds the achievement of the Weetabix Women's British Open in being granted a major championship by the Ladies Professional Golf Association:

> It is a huge boost for the women's game here and is the culmi-
> nation of a lot of time, effort, enthusiasm and expenditure.

A 'culmination' is the final or highest point reached in some endeavour or activity. The achievement described here could certainly be said to be the culmination of a lot of 'effort', but neither 'time' nor 'expenditure' represents an endeavour or activity which can reach a culmination, and the same must be said of 'enthusiasm'. What is meant is: 'It is a huge boost for the women's game here and is the culmination of long-sustained effort, keen and costly.'

Whatever the vocabulary, ready-made or otherwise, the clear thinker does not use words so as to attribute to anything some function or activity which it could not possibly perform. Even when using what we call 'dead metaphors', that is, words from which the original meaning has been washed away by long forgetfulness of it, care should be taken in this respect. Here, a journalist is introducing a series of articles on health:

> It will place special emphasis on the latest medical developments
> in fields which move at dizzying speeds.

'Fields' is a useful term for areas of study and research, but the good writer will not present the reader with the spectacle of fields which move at dizzying speeds. The collision of concepts is too violent. The sentence might better have read: 'It will place emphasis on fields in which research moves at dizzying speed.' It is true that such misconnections, though they offend against logic, are not of a very damaging kind, being both transparent and obvious too. They do not mislead. Nevertheless they jar when the reader is one who doesn't skip, but actually reads what is written.

We turn from fields which move at dizzying speeds to look at a comparably incongruous misattribution of physical movement:

> The Society's tradition for creating original and distinctive
> designs for its literature really took off in the 1960s.

Any admirer of the Wine Society's tasteful catalogues would appreciate what is meant here, but if one savours the composition of words as faithfully as the Society would wish us to savour their products, the nose must be turned up. 'Traditions' do not 'take off'. To image a 'tradition' as a Boeing 747 leaving the ground or even as a fleet record-breaker jumping to life at the sound of the starting pistol is simply insensitive. The very stability and long-lasting quality associated with the word 'tradition' militates against the notion that a tradition might 'take off'.

An area of discourse in which there is today a good deal to criticize in this respect is one in which writers use periods of time as subjects of sentences.

> Each evening also includes a demonstration of flatwork and
> jumping . . .

> The evening is to consist of reception, drinks, a four-course meal,
> disco and the highlight, a celebrity brainteaser quiz.

We have got accustomed to the conversational idiom in which we say
an evening 'includes' or 'consists of' this or that, when what we are
really talking about is some event or celebration that takes place on
that evening. However the usage is surely best avoided in print. And
the following raises a similar question:

> Her time at Mount Holyoke College in Massachusetts was erratic,
> though she showed a certain gift for creative writing.

One may claim that conversationally to use 'evening' to mean 'event'
or 'celebration' is a laxity now sanctified by habit. Must a similar
degeneration of meaning be allowed to the word 'time'? What does
the sentence mean anyway? Can you attribute to 'time' the defect of
being 'erratic'? The fact is that the writer of the above sentence was
not really meaning to talk about 'time' but about the student and
how she spent time. And if you are not going to talk about time, you
should not open your sentence as this writer did.

We have got accustomed in this respect to a usage which is difficult
to defend logically. Here is a remark about the falling population of
badgers:

> Last year's roadkill study was the first time that fox, badger and
> rabbit numbers had been recorded in this way . . .

Why say the study was a 'time'? Why not say: 'Last year's roadkill
study was the first such recording of fox, badger and rabbit numbers'?
One might ask a similar question about the following:

> President Pervez Musharraf has been cautious; indeed he has
> handled the past 100 days of crisis with great skill.

Is it the '100 days' that he has handled with skill? we ask. What
discourages the writer from saying the obvious, natural thing: 'He has
handled the crisis of the past 100 days with great skill'?

Are temporal matters a logical danger area for the writer? The question arose when I heard a BBC newsreader speak of an 'attempt to end the recent fighting'. I began to wonder. When the newsreader speaks of someone's 'recent' death or even 'recent' illness, I realize that the death or the illness is in the past. That is what the word 'recent' conveys. Now it may be that the fighting which is the subject of the announcement is fighting which has not stopped. In so far as it has not stopped, it is not 'recent' fighting but present fighting. The point I wish to make is that it is now too late to end any 'recent' fighting. For that fighting has now transformed itself into 'present fighting'.

Dangers of Ambiguity

There are times when a word acquires a usage that seems to restrict writers from exploiting it in a seemingly natural way. For instance the word 'winning'. As an adjective it has the established meaning of attractive and engaging. We speak of a charming girl as having a 'winning' way, meaning that she readily wins over into sympathy and admiration the persons she encounters. Yet here we have an obituary on a distinguished barrister:

> His winning reputation brought him a succession of high-profile clients and cases.

In view of the more common use of the word 'winning' it would surely be better here to speak of 'his reputation for winning'. And this is not an isolated example of the unhappy usage. We turn to an article on racing:

> Istabraq's winning reappearance at Leopardstown after Christmas met with a mixed reception from the media.

What appears to be meant here is that Istabraq not only reappeared at Leopardstown, but also won his race. Surely the reappearance is one thing and the horse's victory another thing, and the word 'winning' applies to the latter, not to the former.

There is a not dissimilar switching of a word from its familiar usage in the following piece which discusses the recent tendency for more and more schools to adopt a school uniform for their pupils:

But now more and more schools are rapidly adopting uniform policies as surveys reveal that uniforms have boosted morale, improved discipline, reduced theft of expensive clothing and helped identify intruders.

The expression 'adopting uniform policies' conveys the sense that the policies are one and the same. Here is the only possible context in which the expression ought not to be used. You can speak of a 'uniform' policy about anything else in the world, but not about uniforms.

A more awkward kind of ambiguity is that which lies not just in the meaning of a single word, but also in the ordering of the words around it. Here, someone is making a case for greater Government support of hospices:

He said it was wrong that only 17 per cent of the hospice's £1.2 million annual running costs are met by the State.

This might have meant: 'It was false (wrong) to say that only 17 per cent of the hospice's running costs are met by the State.' Equally it might have meant: 'It was bad (wrong) that only 17 per cent of the hospice's running costs are met by the State.' The context made clear that the second reading was intended.

Allowing Meaning to Shift

There is a subtle kind of failure to keep the connotation of a word from sliding away into some seemingly related but really alien use. A letter-writer to the press commits the error we are concerned with:

The lesson of these events is clear. The European Union has achieved important results which must be preserved, but further progress along the road towards a federal Europe is impossible.

It is certainly quite proper to speak of achieving results, but is it logical to speak in this context of 'preserving' results? One could imagine a situation where a housewife went out to pick blackberries and then came home to 'preserve' the results of the expedition, but the subsequent jam would be blackberry jam not result jam. My point is that one could reasonably speak of 'keeping', even perhaps 'preserving', the rules and regulations which the European Union has produced, but these rules and regulations constitute 'results' only in relation to past negotiations, not in relation to whether they are valued or 'preserved'. You will be asked to obey the regulations, not the 'results'. If you met your friend with his arm in a sling and he said 'I was knocked down by a lorry, and this is the result: I've had it set in plaster', you would not be justified in reporting that your friend had had his result set in plaster. It would have been safer here to avoid the word 'results': 'The European Union has made important advances, which should not be lost.'

There are a number of words that can present similar problems in usage. For instance the word 'choice'. It would be appropriate to say 'I was offered a number of CDs, and my choice was Beethoven's seventh symphony', but it would not be appropriate to take the word 'choice' out of that context and to say: 'My choice was first performed in 1813.' Nevertheless we find that kind if error in a survey of new cars:

> The Fanmaster option was not fitted in the demonstrator model
> but was hardly missed for, being more centrally placed, heater
> output seemed to require little fan assistance.

Purchase of the fitted Fanmaster may be an 'option' for a purchaser but it is the Fanmaster that may or may not be fitted. In no cases is the option fitted. Indeed the Fanmaster ceases to be an option once it is selected. Moreover, it is not correct to describe the 'heater output' (instead of the 'heater') as being 'more centrally placed'.

This is not a defect that is hard to find in print. Here is a sentence from a reference book:

> During the Second World War Burtons supplied a quarter of the
> total requirements of uniforms for the armed forces.

The illogicality here should be brought to light. Burtons supplied uniforms to the armed forces. They did not supply 'requirements'. Indeed the armed forces' 'requirements' were satisfied, abolished you may say, by the uniforms. Once the uniform arrives, the 'requirement' ceases to exist. The preference for the noun 'requirement' instead of the verb 'require' lies behind the faulty usage. The natural English version of the sentence would be: 'During the Second World War Burtons supplied a quarter of the uniforms required for the armed forces.'

There are complex and subtle versions of this kind of error in which the mind allows a word's real connotation to slide out of sight. Here is a sentence heard on the radio:

> Mr Jones denied the charges which were alleged to have taken place.

It is fair enough to say that Mr Jones denied the charges. The 'charges' are verbal assertions which call to be proved or disproved and in this case are indeed what Mr Jones 'denied'. But it was not 'the charges' which were 'alleged', for indeed it was the allegations that actually constituted the charges. And neither charges nor allegations could ever 'take place'. What might or might not have 'taken place' were the events described in the charges, the events which constituted the substance of the allegations, in other words the 'offence' said to have been committed. A charge is one thing and an offence another. What 'took place', according to the prosecution, was that Mr Jones robbed a bank. Indeed the statement would have been better if the twelve word sentence had been reduced to five by omission of the last seven. 'Mr Jones denied the charges' says it all.

In speaking or writing about allegations, charges or rumours, it is easy to slide into this kind of error. 'His stated aim was to help the poor.' If you heard that said, you would recognize that the speaker did not necessarily accept that the 'stated aim' was the real aim. 'The reported theft of her diamond necklace has caused a sensation.' There again that statement does not commit the speaker or writer to acceptance that the necklace really was stolen. Because of these reservations it would surely be wrong to expand the sentences above into 'His stated aim was to help the poor, which was most generous of him' or 'The reported theft of her diamond necklace has caused a sensation and has impoverished her'. The point we are making is that the subject qualified by 'alleged', 'stated' or 'reported' is not the same thing as the subject unqualified by such terms. The point is mentioned here in order to raise a query about a sentence in a leading article:

> The reported death of the Taleban's former intelligence chief will
> not be mourned by many.

A certain unhappiness attends the pedantic reader of this sentence. Would it not be better to write 'The report of the death of the Taleban's former intelligence chief will not cause much sorrow'? A death might 'cause sorrow' and the report of a death might 'cause sorrow' but only a real death can be 'mourned'.

Errors of Duplication

There is a failure in coherence that results from duplicating terms illogically. For instance, it is proper to say 'He ordered us to leave' or 'He gave us the order to leave'. Similarly it is proper to say 'He commanded us to leave' or 'He gave the command for us to leave'. In each of these sentences the notion of order or command is present in one word only, either as verb or noun. It would not be proper for that notion to be present twice, and indeed no one would be likely to make that error ('He ordered us the command to leave'). Yet that error is sometimes made with some verbs. A DHSS document sets out notes in connection with retirement pensions and other such benefits:

> Please make sure you read them. They tell you important infor-
> mation about your benefit.

You can 'inform' someone of a fact or 'tell' them about it. You can give them 'information'. But you cannot duplicate the notion of informing by 'telling' someone 'information'. The sentence should read 'They give you important information about your benefit' or 'They inform you about your benefit'. A graver duplication occurred in a radio announcement about the contents of the Queen's speech at the opening of Parliament:

> The most serious omission is the absence of the Mental Health
> Bill.

To 'omit' the 'absence' of something would logically be to include it. It was the Mental Health Bill that was omitted, not its 'absence'.

Sometimes we find a writer running together two constructions which overlap in function but which result in error if they are combined.

> The main town in the immediate area around here is Chatelleraut
> – like so many French towns a mixture of the very old surrounded
> by the new.

The words 'a mixture of the very old' require to be followed by 'and the new'. The words 'surrounded by' introduce a different construction which cannot be combined with that one. The writer had the choice of 'a mixture of the old and the new' and 'the old surrounded by the new'. It was irrational to try to use both.

Closely related to this kind of excess is another brand of illogicality which is the consequence of having too many words.

> The upshot of the president and the committee ignoring any
> contrary views and blindly having meetings until they get the
> result they want is bringing the club into disrepute.

The 'upshot' is the result, or consequence. And the consequence in this case is that the club is brought into disrepute. That is the 'upshot'. Now, if I suffer from stomachache as a consequence of overeating, the stomachache is the 'upshot'. It would be otiose and illogical to say that the 'upshot gave me stomachache' when the stomachache was itself the 'upshot'. It is likewise otiose and illogical to speak of the upshot 'bringing' the club into disrepute when the disrepute is itself the 'upshot'. The meaning could be better conveyed without the word 'upshot': 'The president and the committee ignored any contrary views and stubbornly held meetings until they got the result they wanted. This has brought the club into disrepute.' (The word 'blindly' was out of place in the original.)

It will be obvious that a curious brand of over-wordiness is behind this kind of error. It is the kind of error as likely to be made by the sophisticated as by the unsophisticated, indeed perhaps more likely, as evidenced by the following sentence from a leading article:

> The future viability of the Tories depends crucially on whether
> or not the traditional left/right divide can be replaced by the
> emergence of a new centre.

The description of replacing one object or idea by another requires the writer to keep parallel objects precisely in mind. 'I have replaced my china teapot by a metal one.' The parallelism between the two kinds of teapot is clear. One ought not to introduce any kind of extra element that breaks in between these two parallels. Thus one cannot logically say 'I have replaced my china teapot by the purchase of a metal one' because the original teapot is not replaced by a 'purchase' but by another teapot. What the writer of the leader really wanted to talk about was whether the left/right divide could be replaced by a 'new centre'. Replacing it by an 'emergence' would be politically and logically indefensible.

The Misconnected Start

Of all the failures in coherence, the most common perhaps are false parallels that result from opening a sentence with a group of words that turn out to be effectively disconnected from what follows them. People are easily lured into the trap we are concerned with here. After all, no device in utterance can be more effective than rhetorical opening words that leave the listener or the reader guessing for a moment before it is clear what they apply to. 'Flat out in the gutter, that's how we found him!' The rhetorical words 'Flat out in the gutter' hold the attention, enriched by a touch of curiosity. What or who was flat out in the gutter? In poetry the device can be deeply moving:

> Cold in the earth – and the deep snow piled above thee,
> Far, far removed, cold in the dreary grave!
> Have I forgot, my only Love, to love thee,
> Sever'd at last by Time's all-severing wave?

So Emily Brontë wrote, making powerful use of the device. The effect is so strong because the mind, stirred to expectancy by the initial phrase, 'cold in the earth', finds satisfaction and understanding when what is buried is revealed.

We hope it is not tasteless to move from this exemplification of a striking beginning that proves so fruitful in what follows to examples of how the device, thoughtlessly adapted, can produce the crudest of verbal illogicalities. Let us turn to the Inland Revenue for a case in point:

> Based on the information available to me I have included any
> pages I think you need at the back of your Tax Return.

It may seem a long way from 'Cold in the earth' to 'Based on the information available to me', but the verbal sequences match, or should match. The trouble is that, though we eventually learned who was 'cold in the earth', we never do learn what was 'based on information available' to someone. For indeed 'Based on the information' is left hanging in the air. There are two possible ways of making the sentence logical. One possibility would be to make later reference to something that is indeed 'based on the information available': 'Based on the information available to me, a selection of appropriate pages has been made.' The sequence there is logical because it is indeed the 'selection' that could be said to be so 'based'. But a more satisfactory correction would probably be to change the opening expression to something that could indeed tie in with what follows: 'Acting on the information available to me, I have included any pages I think you need.' For the IR officer ('I') could not in fact claim to be 'based on information available', but he was indeed 'acting' on the information available.

Errors of this kind can be avoided if, before making an introductory flourish as an opening, the writer faces the question, 'What is the subject of this utterance?' Advertisements give us plenty of evidence of the need for this kind of logical approach.

> Aimed at summer use, the Pakka principle combines windproof
> waterproof and breathable AquaDry with extremely lightweight,
> rip-resistant fabric.

It is not the Pakka 'principle' that is 'aimed at summer use' but the garment. The writer should have distinguished between the principle, which was to manufacture something suitable for summer use, and the garment, which was actually to be used in summer. The sentence would be better without the word 'principle': 'The Pakka garment is designed for summer use and combines windproof waterproof and breathable AquaDry with extremely lightweight, rip-resistant fabric.'

The two sentences we have quoted begin with that part of the verb called a 'participle' ('Based' and 'Aimed'). Grammarians rightly protest about what are called 'hanging participles', that is participles detached from a proper connection, as were the words 'based' and 'aimed' in the examples given. The mistakes of this kind which cause most amusement are misconnections in which references to people get wrongly attached, so that they are said to do or be something absurd or impossible. Here the participle is preceded by the word 'when'. It is an advertisement for a caravan cover that can be put in place with the help of telescopic poles:

> When attached to sewn-in loops, two people can guide the cover
> over the caravan.

The poles, to which the words 'when attached to sewn-in loops' apply, are unfortunately not mentioned in this sentence. The result is that we have the picture of two people attached to sewn-in loops and guiding the cover into place. The sentence should be: 'When the poles are attached to sewn-in loops, two people can guide the cover over the caravan.' This failure of connectedness occurs when no participle is involved. It occurs in this advertisement for woodstain:

> Available in 13 standard and 48 tinted colours, you're bound to
> find a colour you like.

The reader is told that he or she is 'available' in these various colours, for there is nothing else in the sentence to which this multicoloured availability can apply. The writer began the sentence not with mention of the subject really in mind (the woodstain) but with an explanatory phrase ('Available in . . .') anticipatory of what was to follow. Anticipatory accompaniments, small or large, must be clearly followed by the subjects to which they apply.

We often make statements conveying that kind of parallelism. You may say 'As a keen golfer, he is away most weekends' or 'An enthusiast for photography, she goes nowhere without her camera'. Whether the word 'as' is included or not the match between the balancing points made is clear ('a keen golfer' matches 'he' and 'An enthusiast for photography' matches 'she'). And yet one can find sentences like this in print:

> I enjoy cooking, but as a working mother of three, the temptation
> to bung a pizza in the oven is often too hard to resist.

The words 'as a working mother of three' are not paralleled in what follows. Logically interpreted, the writer seems to identify herself as 'the temptation'. The parallelism expected after 'as' must be supplied: 'but as a working mother of three, I often find the temptation to bung a pizza in the oven too hard to resist'.

The Wayward Possessive

We have seen that parallelisms of this kind do not always require to be underlined by the use of the word 'as'. Here we find the same confusion in a review of a book by a football enthusiast:

> Resident in Italy for more than 20 years – and a Hellas supporter
> for almost as long – Parkes's idea was to follow Verona the length
> of the Bel Paese and write a travel book that used the Italians'
> favourite sport as a way of reflecting on national character.

Reading this attentively, we protest at once that it was not 'Parkes's idea' that was 'resident in Italy' and a long-time Hellas supporter, as the reviewer mistakenly tells us. It was Parkes himself. All the writer had to do to correct this would have been to delete 'Parkes's idea was' and substitute 'Parkes decided to'. A small change, but it makes the difference between sense and nonsense.

Let us look at this particular brand of false parallelism in an even starker form:

> Founded by the Romans in AD71, the walls of York contain 18
> medieval churches including the commanding York Minster –
> the largest Gothic church in England.

It was of course the city of York that was founded by the Romans, and not the walls, which date back to the medieval period. There ought to be a special name for this error which defaces current usage on a vast scale. Let us call it the 'wayward possessive', exemplified where a writer begins to talk about the 'walls of York' and then continues as though 'York' were the subject. It occurs in a variety of contexts.

> Originally published in 1814, the book's binding had suffered
> damage from wear and tear.

That is the same error. The 'book's binding', instead of the book, is
said to have been published in 1814. If the words 'originally published'
are kept, then the 'book' not the binding must become the subject of
what follows. Better get rid of the anticipatory opening: 'The book
was originally published in 1814 and its binding had suffered damage
from wear and tear.'

We are dealing here with a slightly skewed habit of thought which
causes an immense amount of irrationality in journalism and advertising. Wherever one turns, specimens of this shift of thought occur,
which allows writers to speak as though they have mentioned a person
or a thing when only something possessed by that person or thing is
under direct discussion. Here is something from the world of angling:

> Originally purchased as the Kercock fishings, the addition of
> Delvine allows unhindered double-bank fishing for 12 rods.

I am totally ignorant of the practice and theory of angling, but I
cannot believe this writer when he tells me that the 'addition' of
Delvine was originally purchased as the Kercock fishing. Nor can I
believe him when he tells me that this 'addition' in itself allows
unhindered double-bank fishing for 12 rods. In short, what he said
was one thing and what he meant was another thing. 'Now that it has
added the Delvine, the stretch originally purchased as the Kercock
fishings allows unhindered double-bank fishing for 12 rods.'

Breakdowns of parallelism of this kind occur not only in journalism
but even in the books of academics. Here is a piece about the poet and
critic Herbert Read:

> A friend of T. S. Eliot, the Sitwells, Henry Moore and Ben Nichol-
> son, Read's particular contribution to the artistic theory of the
> twentieth century was his interest in psycho-analysis and its
> application in art and literature.

One feels that a sentence of this kind ought to be presented for
comment in an examination paper testing general intelligence. The
question asked would be 'Who does the writer tell us was a friend of
T. S. Eliot and the other distinguished writers and artists?' And the

sharp-witted, logically minded candidate would answer: 'The writer tells us clearly that Read's particular contribution to the artistic theory of the twentieth century was the friend of T. S. Eliot and co.' For indeed that is exactly what the writer tells us. The sentence should read: 'A friend of T. S. Eliot, the Sitwells, Henry Moore and Ben Nicholson, Read made a particular contribution to the artistic theory of the twentieth century through his interest in psycho-analysis . . .'

We have seen Parkes's idea treated as though it were Parkes himself, York's walls treated as York itself, a book's binding treated as the book itself, the addition of a stretch of fishing as though it were that stretch itself, and Herbert Read's contribution to artistic theory as though it were the man himself. And there is a further category of this trouble, in which words like 'its', 'their' and 'his' introduce similar false parallels. As before, we find the writer supposedly holding a certain subject in mind, yet failing to ensure that it is correctly referred to in the words used subsequently.

> The new pedestrian bridge will span the two carriageways and be
> of enormous benefit to pedestrians. Generously funded by the
> local authority, only a few months will be required for its com-
> pletion.

Here is a case in point. The writer is talking about a new pedestrian bridge and holding it in mind. Having said 'Generously funded by the local authority', logic requires him to complete his statement by mention of exactly what is so funded. Failure to reckon with this leads him to aver that 'its completion' is so funded. It requires only a slight adjustment to write: 'Generously funded by the local authority, [the building of] the bridge can be completed in a few months.'

The error can be less easy to spot when the sentence containing it is longer and more complex. That is the case in this piece from an account of a children's story:

> Pretty much left to their own devices, their well-meaning but
> slightly off-kilter attempts at spells go sadly awry, until their
> all-powerful mother flies in on her broomstick.

When the writer wrote 'Pretty much left to their own devices' her intention was to say something about the children specifically, but she forgot and launched into a statement about their 'well-meaning but slightly off-kilter attempts'. It is not these 'attempts' which were 'left to their own devices' but the children. Although the sentence could be corrected without altering the opening phrase ('Pretty much left to their own devices, the children find that their slightly off-kilter attempts at spells go sadly awry'), nothing would be lost by simplifying the presentation: 'The children are pretty much left to their own devices, and their well-meaning but slightly off-kilter attempts at spells go sadly awry.'

The errors we are examining, like so many surveyed in this book, all testify to the fact that people are not consciously making up their minds what they are writing about and then firmly keeping it in mind. Instead, they are diverted in the very midst of a rational statement into an illogical one. The error turns up at all levels from that of the cheap magazine to that of supposedly educated coverage of the arts. Here is a review of an artist's paintings at an exhibition:

> Working from memory of emotions that he felt in a particular place, his sensual sceneries have a dreamlike quality to them . . .

The critic who wrote the opening words 'Working from memory' had presumably made up his mind to write about the artist, but within three or four words he had forgotten that. We are told that this artist's 'sceneries' were working from memory. There are two things in the critic's mind, the artist and the artist's work. They are not the same thing. If you write criticism you must make sure which of the two you are talking about and not suddenly switch from the one to the other. The mistake is exactly the same that would be made if one wrote: 'Urinating against every lamp-post he came across in the street, the dog's owner looked bored to death.'

The Commonest Failure of Parallelism

We have come to the commonest form of failure to preserve parallelism. The sentence here follows an account of how a horse fell at an event, snapping one tendon and badly injuring the other:

> Fearing the worst, the horse was bandaged and brought back to
> the vet's box where Icyhoser had been set up.

The writer plainly means that this action was taken because those
responsible for the horse 'feared the worst'. But, as the sentence stands,
it is the horse that is said to be 'fearing the worst'. That is the consequence of saying 'the horse was bandaged' instead of 'they [whoever
it was] bandaged the horse'. The reader or writer who is content with
inexactitude may demur, but in the long run the preservation of
reason in utterance depends on exactitudes of this kind.

This business of attributing to human beings feelings and actions
proper to animals and vice versa is more easily understandable than
transferring human thoughts or feelings to inanimate objects. The
opening of the following presupposes a statement about a person to
follow.

> Nonetheless, recognizing true quality, her bedroom walls are
> covered in a floral fabric on an ecru-toned background by Manuel
> Canovas.

The intelligent reader, taking in the words 'recognizing true quality',
is left agog to hear more about this person of taste and judgement. It
is a shock to be told that it is someone's 'bedroom walls' that recognize
true quality. And the way out of this absurd slip is so simple: 'Nonethe-
less, recognizing true quality, she covered her bedroom walls in a
floral fabric on an ecru-toned background by Manuel Canovas.'

In all these varied cases we are concerned with an illicit slide from
one kind of subject implicit in the opening words of a sentence to a
subject of a different kind whose connotation cannot adequately be
a substitute for the forgotten subject. Grammatical rules may be cited
as rescuing writers from this most common of all errors. Yet the truth
is that the mind of the writer, having seized on a subject and all
agog to make a statement about it, promptly forgets and talks about
something else.

> Looking back to when we first came here, the custom was to visit
> friends, but some of the actual visiting took place on the roads.

'Looking back?' And who, may we ask, is looking back? Why, the custom is 'looking back'. When the writer began the sentence with 'looking back' the intention surely was to proceed to some such subject as 'we'. The intention should not have been forgotten. 'Looking back to when we first came here, we were accustomed to visit friends . . .' There is the same forgetfulness in this advertisement for a car park attendant:

> Working alone, the duties involve collecting and accounting for daily parking charges in accordance with administrative procedures.

And who is 'working alone'? we ask this time. And plainly the answer is the duties are working alone. The writer has made that clear. If a different intention had been there, then the writer might have said: 'Working alone, the attendant will be responsible for collecting and accounting for daily parking charges.'

The confusion caused by this forgetfulness may be even greater than in those two examples.

> Watching Amy Hillman running her manicured nails through her immaculately styled hair, she certainly looks like a girl who's got everything.

The 'she' is the only person mentioned here to fill out the words 'Watching Amy Hillman'. The writer did not intend to tell us that the girl was staring into a mirror. If the opening of the sentence is kept, then 'she' cannot be the subject of what is said afterwards. Why not scrap the word 'watching'? 'When Amy Hillman runs her manicured nails through her immaculately styled hair, she certainly looks like a girl who's got everything.'

Openings such as we have examined, like 'fearing the worst', 'recognizing true quality', 'looking back', 'working alone' and 'watching Amy Hillman' are all anticipatory accompaniments to something that is going to be mentioned. If it isn't mentioned, they testify to an incapacity to think straight. All writers and speakers need to bear this in mind. When they don't, you get the absurdity represented by this observation at the beginning of a *You and Yours* programme on Radio 4:

> Being the New Year, we'll be doing a little looking ahead.

The personal claim of the broadcasting team to 'be' the New Year was not really what was in the speaker's mind.

6

'In a Manner of Speaking'

There are times when we respond to what someone has said by asking 'Do you mean that literally?' We recognize that there is usage that is not literal. In other words, there is usage that bears a touch of the poetic, usage with what we call a 'figurative' element. 'He's walking a tightrope' we say, and perhaps add 'in a manner of speaking', for we are not referring to a circus artist. We are describing someone who is treading a difficult path in some business negotiations or some personal quandary. It should be noticed that in elucidating the metaphor 'walking a tightrope' we tend to fall back on another, but less vivid metaphor, 'treading a path'. After all, there is no 'path' for him to 'tread'. And if we tried to put it more literally still, we should probably speak of 'the course he is following', reducing still further, but not totally eliminating, the metaphorical element. The nature of our language is such that drawing a clear line between the literal and the metaphorical is not always possible. The rules governing rational utterance do not vary as one moves from using words literally to using them figuratively, but the writer must make sure that there is no loss of coherence or consecutiveness consequent on using less literal idioms.

Figures of Speech

We are daily dependent on metaphors in our use of language. They give colour and vitality to what we say. The metaphor may be 'dead', in the sense that the expression is a well-worn one that has lost the vividness of the original concrete parallelism, but certain favourite ones are regularly on our lips. We are as likely to say 'Don't beat about the bush' as to say 'Get to the point'. One may argue that there is no great difference in what is conveyed by those two statements. But some favourite metaphorical expressions are less easily matched by more literal replacements. For instance, it would be difficult quickly to think of an alternative wording of equal forcefulness when we ask 'Did he smell a rat?' The expression is a most useful one, but you use it without any clear sense of the proper literal meaning of the word 'smell' or the word 'rat'. You do not picture a dog with its nose to the ground, sniffing away. Yet in origin someone must have first used the expression with that clear picture in mind. In that way metaphor is crucial in the development of meaning. 'I'm studying our family tree,' a friend tells me. Do I – or does he – picture an enormous oak as he uses the words? No, we probably both picture a diagrammatic representation of the succeeding generations. But how convenient it is for us that some poetically aware individual once put the two words 'family' and 'tree' together in that way, exercising imagination in picturing the family lineage as a growing tree.

We rely on the poetic ingenuity of long-dead individuals for the metaphorical expressions which give vividness to our talk. 'Has the penny dropped?', 'I wish she'd get down to brass tacks!', 'He's only sowing his wild oats', 'I suspect he's a bit of a dark horse'. That's how we talk, without ever picturing coinage or tacks, oats or horses. And it is important to notice that these usages are not just colourful and decorative. They are also sharply and economically meaningful.

Common Metaphorical Expressions

We should take care not to follow a metaphorical expression with something that can be misread in connection with it. That is what happens in the following sentence:

> The book kept me on the edge of my seat with lots of unexpected twists.

The reviewer should not picture herself on the edge of her seat 'with lots of unexpected twists'. The word 'twists', another metaphor, is an aspect of the novel's narrative not of the reviewer's posture: 'Full of unexpected twists, the story kept me on the edge of my seat.'

Some metaphorical expressions achieve great popularity for a time and are done to death. For many decades people in authority would say 'We must explore every avenue'. The 'avenue' was the image for a possible new way forward to achievement. The usage is still with us. I have now heard a party leader quoted on the subject of American threats against Iraq, and arguing that war should be undertaken 'only when all other avenues are exhausted'. In the last chapter we heard talk of 'pursuing' an avenue as though it were something that could be hunted, and now we learn that it can become 'exhausted'. Clearly the metaphorical force of the expression has totally disappeared if an avenue is subject to exhaustion.

For the most part we are now less attached to 'exploring avenues'; we are keen on 'opening windows' instead. In this connection there was an interesting radio account of a speech made by the Queen on an official visit to St Petersburg:

> But now Russia's window on the west was open again, and was being joined by other windows throughout the land.

The image was appropriately used here in the first instance, but to talk of an opening window being 'joined' by others throughout the land kills the effect by overdoing it. Windows don't collaborate like that.

The effect of overuse of such figures of speech is evident in the way that nowadays everybody is talking about 'raising profiles' when they mean that they are trying to increase the importance of certain matters in the public mind. ('We need to raise the profile of TB' I read.) The clear-headed thinker will tend to eschew the expression as overdone. And surely the same now applies to an only slightly less abused expression, 'rearing its ugly head'. This was written by an angler:

> I'm told that the poaching at Randlestown has reared its ugly head once more, with fish being removed illegally by various methods.

I do not know what creature it was, snake or crouching tiger, that first inspired poetic use of its threat but the image created was a powerful one. However, all power is lost when the phrase is used prosaically of any inconvenient issue that arises. An indication of how readily we have recourse to the image is provided by my newspaper. Over its account of some events on the first anniversary of the destruction of the Trade Center in New York, it prints the headline 'Hostility rears its head as nations join global tribute'. So familiar is the expression that the word 'ugly' can be dropped.

Metaphorical expressions have to be appropriate to the context. Here is a description of a new caravan and its equipment:

> Exterior features don't let the side down.

In the right context it can be effective to speak of someone 'letting the side down'. When a person has failed to operate up to his potential, thereby damaging the performance of the body of people he is involved with, the image is exactly the right one. But to use the image, as here, to express approval of the way access to spare wheel, gas locker and water tank is arranged on the outside of a motor caravan is to cheapen language irresponsibly.

Metaphorical expressions of that kind are so frequently used that we need to remind ourselves that they are metaphorical. We don't picture a cricket team on the field when we speak of 'letting the side down'. And when we speak of 'taking steps' to do this or that the image of physically stepping forward or upwards never strikes us. However, if we use such an expression and then follow it by another metaphor which does not fit logically with it, there is a danger that the careful reader will register its inappropriateness. The following statement in a local authority journal provides a case in point:

> It is therefore very encouraging that steps have already been taken, and more are in the pipeline, that will help to breathe new life into the local economy and create new jobs.

The image of taking steps begins to sound odd when further steps are described as being in the pipeline. And the sequence becomes really comic when these steps, issuing from a pipeline, are said to be about to breathe new life into something. The reader seems to be asked to picture a step-ladder or a staircase easing itself forward through a pipeline to tackle a job of mouth-to-mouth resuscitation.

Even the commonest of such metaphorical expressions can be misused. And it is not always just a question of what verbal company they are made to keep. Sometimes the expression does not in itself make sense. We speak of 'bridging the gap' when we are wondering how people holding two opposing views can have their attitudes reconciled, but a journalist uses the metaphor thus:

> At present, it seems almost impossible to bridge the anger of
> India and the resentment of Pakistan.

If you were charged with the task of designing a new road from a city centre to a suburb and there was a railway in between, you would not talk of the problem of 'bridging the city centre and the suburb'. You would talk of 'bridging the railway'. It is what stands between two positions that has to be 'bridged'. Even so we should not talk of 'bridging' the anger of one side and the resentment of the other. The metaphor here is the wrong one. Better write: 'At present it seems almost impossible to reconcile the angry Indians and the resentful Pakistanis.' The same writer dives into a metaphorical whirlpool thus:

> There are no fewer than six tension points in the Islamic world,
> each of which interacts with the others, though none of them
> offers a key to a settlement.

I cannot myself identify exactly what technological situation is imaged by the words 'tension points' and their habit of 'interacting' with each other, but whatever their status, it is surely unwise to expect them to start offering a 'key'.

Single-word Metaphors

We turn from letting sides down, breathing new life, rearing ugly heads and the like to the more common matter of the single-word metaphor. Most errors in using figures of speech occur in less tangled contexts than those we have just been considering. Frequently used single-word metaphors can easily trip up the thoughtless. A Tory journalist was questioned in a broadcast about left–right divisions within the Conservative party. 'People don't think in those pigeon-holes,' he replied.

Pigeon-holes have long represented a useful image for organization that is too rigid and petty. But they are not sites that anyone could 'think' in. St Simeon Stylites meditated on top of a pillar, we are told, but brooding in a pigeon-hole remains an unexplored mode of ascetic self-discipline. Even so, it often happens that a single word, heavy with connotative baggage from its past, is tossed into use with scant recognition of what it really means.

> The Italian-born jockey is also developing a range of ice-creams and mousses, along with sauces, dressings and pastas which will be unveiled throughout the next 18 months in major supermarkets.

The word 'unveiled' carries overtones from dignified ceremonies at which new statues or works of art are disclosed to public view by eminent people or by royalty. The notion of 'unveiling' trays of desserts and delicatessen is quite incongruous. The items will not be 'unveiled'; they will be 'put on sale'. Sensitivity to the figurative basis of a word like 'unveil' is part of the thoughtful writer's equipment. There is a kind of 'wastage' of connotation which the good writer recoils from.

Many instances of ill usage occur simply because a single obvious metaphor is followed by words which cause the reader to question it. That is what happens here:

> There is no doubt that the treatment meted out to the financial services industry in the wake of the personal pensions debacle has left bruises, many of which were justified.

The writer chose a suitable metaphor in describing the losses as 'bruises', but she washed away our sensitivity to the image by then describing many of those 'bruises' as 'justified'. She might better have said 'many of which were deserved'. But that failure to allow an image to do its proper work without being undermined by what follows it is all too common today. Here is something from a leading article reflecting on results in the annual A level examinations. The writer wonders whether new regulations may have allowed students to adopt a 'less demanding route' in their choice of options and thus to defeat the intentions of those who made the changes:

> The iron law of unintended consequences may have struck again.

The image of the 'iron' law is somehow wasted by what follows, for 'laws' do not 'strike'. The word 'strike' belongs to imagery of battle, not of legislation.

We turn to a slightly less obvious failure of sequence:

> I was always pleased to see him. The spark between us was defi-
> nitely growing.

The image of a spark is no doubt appropriate to describe, as here, the beginnings of a love affair. But the primary significance of a spark is that it is the beginning of a fire. The notion of 'growing' seems to belong to a different context from that of ignition. For similar reasons the following passage from an editorial calls for comment:

> Looking specifically at my first editorial, way back then, I see I
> encouraged you all to deluge me with your thoughts, criticisms
> – anything really that might spark off a new tangent for the
> magazine.

We properly use the word 'tangent' now of a new line of development. Even so, it carries about with it the flavour of its origin in the world of geometry. Tangents are not fireworks. The most determined arsonist could not ignite one. The collision of images is insensitive.

Wanting to express how some thought or venture grew and prospered naturally leads us to imagery of setting things in motion or lighting a fire. In this connection the verb to 'fuel' has become popular. 'Her long devotion to the cause of child-welfare had been fuelled by her own experience as an orphan.' The use of the word 'fuelled' is appropriate in that context, but a lax development has occurred in that kind of usage. We find writers abusing the overlap in meaning between the colourful word 'fuelled' and the colourless word 'caused'. If the word 'fuelled' begins to be handled simply as an alternative to 'caused', this kind of usage results:

> Standard Chartered, the emerging markets bank, revealed a 20
> per cent fall in annual pre-tax profits, fuelled largely by a steep
> rise in provisions against bad loans.

To talk of 'fuelling' a 'fall' in profits does not make sense. It is almost as absurd as talking about a failure in a motor race 'fuelled by lack of petrol'. And here is another instance of that kind of incongruity:

> The first single by Will Young, who won the television talent show
> *Pop Idol*, became the fastest-selling debut yesterday.

To dignify the appearance of a first compact disc from a known performer as a 'debut' is fair enough. But the force of the word is totally destroyed by calling it the 'fastest-selling' debut. The word 'debut' still carries colourful associations of dignified first-time appearance in the world of popular entertainment if not any longer of high society. The words 'fastest-selling' destroy any connotative quality the word may carry. You may 'attend' a debut, you may 'make' a debut, but you cannot 'sell' one.

Inexact Metaphors

If you use the word 'debut', you should mean debut. That is the basis of appropriateness in the use of metaphor: clear thinkers mean what they say. The words handled will be allowed to carry their meaning with them. Then sentences like the following will not be uttered:

> The death of President Assam is an enormous milestone in the
> Middle East.

Although milestones have largely disappeared from our roads, they linger in the language of those who keep us informed. The whole point of a milestone depends on its significance in the making of a journey. But no journey is mentioned here. A milestone placed vaguely in the Middle East is a concept of peculiar uselessness. What route does it mark? Who is supposed to be going where? Moreover the significance of a milestone is wholly dependent on the message it conveys. This milestone is said to be 'enormous' as though that added to its significance. Use of the metaphor has simply not been properly thought out. If the writer meant that the death of President Assam was of great moment for the Middle East, that is how it should have been put.

What applies to the use of the word 'milestone' there applies, if to a lesser degree, to the use of the word 'landmark' in the following:

> Toddler Club is free and offers members advice and support on toddler landmarks, such as potty-training, going to first nursery and school, eating and coping with the terrible twos!

A 'landmark' is a fixed point, like a milestone. One might indeed describe the point at which the toddler is potty-trained as a landmark or a milestone. First going to school is happily so described too. But 'landmarks' seem to be forgotten when we come to training the young to eat healthily and 'coping with the terrible twos'. This is one of those contexts where an overworked word such as 'problem' or the colourless word 'matter' might have served the writer better than the 'landmark': 'Toddler Club is free and offers members advice and support on such matters as handling potty-training, eating, introducing children to school, and coping with them at the difficult age of two.'

A degree of consistency is always required in the use of metaphor. What is called a 'mixed metaphor' can easily become ridiculous. This radio commentator is expressing some doubts about the Government's attitude to acceptance of the euro:

> The figleaf of the economic tests is looking ever more hollow.

Now the 'figleaf' metaphor was well chosen to suggest a formula that could conveniently be used to cover whatever policy lay behind it. But the effectiveness of a figleaf in providing cover lies in its opaqueness and its positioning. The proper way to express the reservations here would surely be to convey either that the figleaf is looking ever more transparent or that the figleaf is increasingly in danger of dropping off. The notion of hollowness belongs to a different sphere of phoniness from that represented by the figleaf. We may not be in the habit of concretely picturing our metaphors, but they should lend themselves to proper conceptualization, and hollow figleaves do not. Sometimes such mixing of metaphor is less stark.

> A wave of violence across Israel, the West Bank and Gaza threatened yesterday to derail the prospect of peace talks between the Israeli Prime Minister and the Palestinian leader.

The word 'wave', used of spreading violence, perhaps still brings with it the image of a turbulent ocean, but the metaphor of derailing is now so well established that it can be used without bringing to readers' minds any pictures of trains wrecked on the permanent way. In any case, trains do from time to time get derailed by floods. Liquid imagery, however, has to be handled with forethought. Read what a speaker on Northern Ireland had to say:

> The government has watered down its stance.

As a way of protesting against a softening of policy in relation to terrorist bodies, the image of 'watering down' is not inappropriate. But watering down 'a stance' represents a clumsy venture into the unpicturable, if not perhaps as inappropriate as the following remark about a new model of a car by someone who uses the vehicle for drawing a caravan:

> I blame the engine. Solo, it feels reasonably pokey, but with a caravan in tow, the anticipated 192 lb ft of torque turns out to be a watered-down facsimile in practice.

A watered-down facsimile is even less picturable than a watered-down stance. Neither stances nor facsimiles lend themselves to dilution.

As a last piece of advice in this connection, writers are recommended not to take up a metaphor and then drop it like a hot brick, so that the very point of its use on the page or in the air is lost. For instance the following announcement was broadcast in connection with the Israeli–Palestinian peace process:

> The pathway was not only carefully thought through but by and large agreed stage by stage.

If the image of the pathway is put before the listener or the reader, then what follows must make sense of it. And we do not 'think through' pathways, or even 'agree' them.

Some Caveats

We ought not to leave this section on metaphor without just mentioning one quite rare slip-up that can occur in the use of figurative expressions. It is exemplified in this sentence from a magazine for anglers:

> With cod fisheries in their current dire straits, baby cod need all the help they can get.

We use the expression 'in dire straits' freely to describe a situation of crisis. We use the words unthinkingly, without picturing a narrow sea passageway dangerous to negotiate. In most contexts that thoughtlessness does not matter. But here the writer's mind and the reader's mind are focused on fish in the sea, so that the words 'in dire straits' inevitably call up their literal meaning. The metaphorical expression 'rock-bottom' also comes to mind without bringing pictures along with it, and although it is really a metaphor from mining, one ought to be wary of using it in a nautical context.

> The one-size-fits-all regime run by the European Central Bank does not allow the Germans to try to float their economy out of the doldrums on a sea of money at rock-bottom interest rates.

It is a 'one-size-fits-all regime' that is said to prevent something – i.e., any attempt by the Germans to float their economy on a sea of money out of the doldrums. Having established this image, it was surely a mistake to picture interest rates as 'rock-bottom'.

We take liberties with vocabulary for the best of reasons when a figurative vein is tapped, however lightly. I read these opening words in a piece in praise of a former journalist:

> John Holmes was a phenomenon . . .

That seems to me to be an unexceptional use of a liberty taken with vocabulary, but that is not the end of the sentence.

> John Holmes was a phenomenon, whose work selling advertising space and features for *The Times*, particularly in the Middle East was conducted at the highest level.

This continuation seems to me to spoil an effective opening. If the reader responds sensitively to the word 'phenomenon', with its imaginative suggestion of something rare and *sui generis*, the effect is cancelled out by what follows. A 'phenomenon' does not sell advertising space. The implication that it does is out of place. I am suggesting that if the writer had put a full stop after the word 'phenomenon' and begun a new sentence with the words 'His work', the reader's imagination would have been better satisfied.

The reader may argue that this is too fine a point, but a word like 'phenomenon' deserves respect of its connotative content, as does the personal name 'John Holmes'.

Verbal Transvestism

Our concern here is with a kind of debased metaphor, usage in which verbal practice can verge on the 'metaphorical', but not satisfactorily so. There are words and idioms that belong to the realm of the personal and would be inappropriate if used otherwise. You might say of someone's failure to get a new job 'Oh, he's missed the bus'. But you would not say of a failed scheme 'Oh, it's missed the bus' because people can miss buses but schemes can't. If one visualizes the image of arriving at the bus stop only in time to see the bus departing, then it makes perfect sense, provided that what is left at the bus stop is a person and not a plan. Failure to use the right words and idioms in that way is logically unsatisfactory. Instead of producing a genuine metaphor, the words pass themselves off as fit to do a job they cannot properly do, in a kind of illicit verbal transvestism. For instance, I have just read a piece on the various websites connected with the World Wildlife Fund, which tells me that one of these sites is 'the best of the bunch'. That image is perfectly satisfactory. But then this follows:

> It stands out from the crowd because it allows visitors to go as deep into a subject as they'd like to.

A website may well be the 'best of the bunch', for it makes some sense to compare a website in a group of websites to a banana in a bunch, but the situation of standing out from the crowd is surely a human (or perhaps animal) prerogative to which websites can have no logical claim.

We are not, of course, setting limits to the proper use of metaphor. For in poetry conscious confusion of personal and impersonal idioms can be a powerful device, comic or pathetic. Think how Keats addresses the Grecian Urn at the beginning of his ode. He personalizes the work of art:

> Thou still unravish'd bride of quietness,
> Thou foster-child of silence and slow time,
> Sylvan historian who canst thus express
> A flowery tale more sweetly than our rhyme . . .

The urn is addressed in turn as a bride, a foster-child and a historian. As such, she is congratulated on her narrative ability, surpassing that of the poet. The move into the personal idiom is intentional and sustained, genuinely metaphorical. And what applies to poetry applies too to prose in which such transferences are consciously made as a stylistic device. See how a walker who has risen before daylight awaits the dawn:

> The sky is tiger-striped with orange, but the distant eastern hori-
> zon isn't shaping up precisely as planned . . . Up above me there's
> a patch of blue-black open sky, but it's going to have a job making
> it over to the sun's side in time.

Clearly in 'cold' prose a horizon can't be criticized for failing to 'shape up' properly. But the prose here is not 'cold'. We accept the lively, half-humorous response of the walker for whom the sky assumes a personality as he sees it failing to shape up as he had hoped and seemingly 'going to have a job' getting over to the sun's side in time.

Here, however, we are concerned with careless moves between the personal and the impersonal idiom which derive, not from imaginative vision but from logical laziness and verbal insensitivity. There are many words used of human experience processes which, except in a poetic context, cannot be attributed to inanimate objects. Misuse of the personal idiom may occur at many different levels of propriety, but the sensitive writer who weighs each word will be strict in this respect. The subject is worth pursuing because laxity in this matter invariably produces imprecision. Let us look at some of the personal wording proper to human experience which gets carelessly applied to the inanimate world.

prompting

Here is a broadcast account of a road accident:

> A strong side-wind prompted the vehicle to veer off the carriage-way.

The dictionary defines the verb 'prompt' first as 'to urge (someone to do something)' and all subsequent examples presuppose that it is a human being who can be 'prompted' to do something. The notion of urging, encouraging or reminding conveyed by the word is a matter of influence upon a person. In short, you can 'prompt' your husband to go and pay the Council Tax, but you cannot 'prompt' your vacuum cleaner to proceed under the dining-room table. If the sentence is not amended to 'A strong side-wind forced the vehicle off the carriageway', it should be amended to 'A strong side-wind forced the vehicle to veer off the carriageway'.

experiencing

Another verb primarily applicable to living beings is the verb 'to experience'. It is human beings and animals that 'experience' things, but I read this in an advertisement for a holiday firm:

> Fatima is one of the most recent sites to experience an apparition of the Virgin Mary by three Portuguese children on May 13, 1917.

The children, not the site, had the miraculous experience. And in this sentence there is a further awkwardness in that the word order makes it sound almost as though these three children were in the habit of regularly being granted sight of apparitions. Better: 'It was at Fatima that one of the most recent apparitions of the Virgin Mary was granted to three Portuguese children on May 13, 1917.'

remembering

The following sentence about the poet Alfred Noyes is taken from a reference book:

> He received many honorary degrees and is remembered at Exeter
> College, Oxford, by a window in the hall.

It is customary for a departed husband to be 'remembered' by his
widow, but surely not by a window. Where the widow 'remembers' the
deceased, the window 'commemorates' him. The difference between
remembering and commemorating is the difference between acts
which only living beings can perform and processes which can be
properly attributed to inanimate objects.

showing disregard

> The terror network had shown a complete disregard for human
> life, they killed several thousand people.

Just as winds cannot 'prompt' vehicles to do anything and sites cannot
'experience' miracles, so networks cannot 'show disregard' for human
life. For the clear thinker it was the terrorists, not the network, which
showed that disregard. And having mentioned the 'network', the
exact thinker would not refer back to it as 'they'. There is of course
no need for the word 'network' at all. Better stick to talking about the
terrorists if attitudes and feelings are going to be attributed to them.

learning lessons

A comparable laxity can be found even in a leading article, commenting on the progress of the war against terrorists as action was
taken in Afghanistan against them:

> The long-planned assault has learnt lessons from the mistakes of
> the operation to trap Osama bin Laden and his followers in the
> Tora Bora caves three months ago.

To attribute to an 'assault' the capacity to learn lessons is extremely
lax. Those who planned the assault cannot be equated with their
assault. If a student failed an examination and then, after a time,
resat it and did much better, you would not say 'His well-written
thesis learnt lessons from the mistakes in his first attempt a year ago'.

being incapable

> The system is incapable of managing grand projects, as with the
> Dome or Wembley Stadium.

'Incapable'? My dictionary defines 'capable' wholly in personal terms,
'having ability, competent, having the skill, the temperament, to do
something'. It is the people who operate the system that should be
pronounced 'incapable'. If the word 'system' is kept as subject, then
the word 'incapable' must go: 'The system is inadequate for the
management of grand projects.'

failing to understand

Even more inapt is the following sentence, deriving from the controversy caused by foot-and-mouth disease:

> We must give more help to rural firms as the package so far is
> inadequate and fails to understand the long-term impact of the
> disease.

I do not know whether to accuse a 'package' of a lack of understanding
is more or less insulting than to accuse a 'system' of being incapable.
If the verb 'to understand' is to be kept, then it must be removed from
its connection with the package: 'the package so far is inadequate
and shows that the long-term impact of the disease has not been
understood'. But it would probably be better to change the verb
'understand': 'the package so far is inadequate and fails to cater for
the long-term impact of the disease'.

struggling to cope

We turn to an article in the press on the controversial issue of funding
university students:

> There are examples of superior funding methods elsewhere –
> notably Australia – but these demand a large initial investment
> from taxpayers and would struggle to cope if half of those at
> school were expected to move on to higher education.

Alongside packages that don't properly understand things, funding
methods that 'struggle to cope' seem too to be over-endowed with the

characteristics of the living. Why not: 'but these demand a large investment from taxpayers which might prove insufficient to meet the demand'?

meeting with hospitality

> Our four-week trek to Kanch's south and north base camps met with nothing but smiles and warm hospitality.

What is it that persuades the writer to make the trek rather than the trekkers the recipients of the smiles and the hospitality? Indeed the words 'and warm hospitality' doubly underline the laxity of making the trek the thing that is welcomed rather than the trekkers. Why not say the obvious: 'On our four-week trek to Kanch's south and north base camps we met with nothing but smiles and warm hospitality'?

celebrating

> All of our departures join villagers in celebration of local festivals.

The shorthand employed here is perhaps natural to people who write brochures for holiday firms. The words 'all our departures' have come to mean something like 'all the customers flying in all the time-tabled planes'. This practice ought not to be allowed to extend to accounts of celebrations.

being conscious

Yet the practice seems to be widespread:

> In Kenya the eco-safari has thankfully replaced big game hunting and conservation-conscious tours running from energy-efficient camps are on the increase.

Clearly the tours are incapable of being conscious of anything. The writer should have said: 'and tours for conservation-conscious tourists, running from energy-efficient camps, are on the increase'.

being sensible

Sometimes the personal and impersonal categories get confused in a sentence by misplacement of a single descriptive term. Here is a letter to the press written after the air attacks on New York and Washington:

> Following the horrific events of last Tuesday there will be many
> painful lessons to learn with the wisdom of hindsight. One of
> these must be that people should not be asked to work in build-
> ings that cannot be easily evacuated over a sensible period of time
> in the event of terrorism.

A 'sensible period of time' is not an exact or felicitous expression. People can be sensible and by accepted verbal transference a plan may be sensible or foolish. But a period of time should not be described as 'sensible' when what the writer means is that it should be of sufficient length to allow of escape in an emergency, in other words a period of time such as sensible people would calculate to be appropriate. There is no satisfactory way of avoiding the need to spell this out: 'One of these must be that people should not be asked to work in buildings that cannot be evacuated easily and quickly enough to meet the emergency in the event of terrorism.'

being lenient

We are of course treading here where perhaps only pedants will persist in treading. Nevertheless, infelicities of this kind will not occur in the work of really precise thinkers. When we are informed that in a children's hospital at Christmas time 'the visiting hours are lenient' we recognize that the needed point has been clearly made, but is 'lenient' really the best word? 'Showing or characterized by mercy or tolerance' my dictionary declares of 'lenient'. Why not the currently very popular word 'flexible'?

experiencing trauma

The following is taken from a letter of resignation:

> The railway has been through the most traumatic of times over
> the past seventeen months.

In spite of the popularity of Thomas the Tank Engine and his fellows, it remains foolish in cold prose to attribute the experience of trauma to a railway system. Why not attribute the experience of trauma to the railway employees? It is plain that it would more accurately represent the writer's meaning, for he goes on: 'I have found it increasingly evident that I cannot work alongside my fellow directors.'

being encouraged

In another piece of news from the same industry we read:

> If the Underground is looking for further self-encouragement that it is getting things right, 77% of passengers say they are happy with the quality of information provided at stations.

There is a peculiar usage here. What would be the difference between saying 'Mary is looking for encouragement' and 'Mary is looking for self-encouragement'? Surely the word 'self' is redundant. Even without it, attributing the capacity for human responsiveness to 'the Underground' seems lax at best.

keeping things in mind

Exact thinkers weigh every word used, but there are expressions which spring so easily to our lips that we cease to treat them as proper material for careful examination. Take this use of the expression 'in mind' in the following statement from the Wine Society:

> With the Millennium in mind the Autumn List ran to 156 pages and was the biggest we have ever published.

Clearly the Autumn List cannot be said to have had the Millennium 'in mind'. If the sentence had been rephrased to run 'With the Millennium in mind we increased the Autumn List to 156 pages', all would have been well. As it is, the printed list is endowed with powers of reflection.

being responsive and careful

Two expressions heard on the radio when commentators were speaking of the air attack on New York's skyscrapers are worth recording here. The first is: 'On the Stock Exchange share prices have fallen in response to the crisis.' My question is whether prices act 'in response', which surely suggests a reaction by living beings. 'In response' is not in all circumstances the equivalent of 'as a result of'. The behaviour of the share-dealers might be said to represent a response to the crisis, but not the movements of the shares. The usage stands interestingly alongside that of the commentator who spoke metaphorically of the policy of using the 'big stick' against terrorist organizations, and added the qualification 'The big stick has got to be careful'. The personal expression for being careful springs to mind although no agency has been mentioned that could indeed exercise it. It is lax to say that a stick should exercise care when what you mean is that those who wield the big stick must exercise care.

being self-serving

It is not only in popular journalism and broadcasting that verbal transvestism confuses the personal and impersonal categories. Some who would claim to be 'highbrow' writers seem capable of letting themselves down in this respect. I cite a critic's review of a book by Kenneth Tynan:

> As Tynan said, a good critic 'sees the way but cannot drive the car'. As he also said, a good critic sees what is happening in the theatre; a great thinker sees what is not happening.
>
> Perhaps that's a self-serving dictum, for remarkably little of serious interest was happening in the British theatre when Tynan launched his career in the 1940s and early 1950s.

Now a 'dictum' is a 'formal, authoritative statement' or 'a popular maxim'. How on earth could such a statement be 'self-serving'? Only living beings can be 'self-serving'. The writer chose a clumsily inexact way to imply that Tynan was flattering himself for his understanding of what the contemporary theatre lacked when he began his career.

being cautioned

We may cite a comparable, but far more sophisticated, specimen of confusion between the personal and the impersonal from a work of academic literary criticism:

> Any psychological interpretation of the poem must be cautioned by the recognition that its personal elements are pressed into utterly conventional material that Wordsworth borrowed from other poets.

To 'caution' someone is to warn them in advance of what may be to come. One can 'caution' a person, but one cannot logically caution an 'interpretation', a passage of argumentative prose on a piece of paper. The object of the 'cautioning', the person 'cautioned' cannot be logically bypassed, but must be mentioned: 'Any critic making a psychological interpretation of the poem must be cautioned by the recognition that its personal elements are pressed into utterly conventional material that Wordsworth borrowed from other poets.'

being self-conscious

From the same source we take the following comment on the eighteenth-century poets Beattie and Thomson:

> Like all the writers of Sensibility, they were mild rebels, proffering their works from the margins of contemporary literature as self-consciously minor productions hopeful of acceptance by mainline culture symbolized by the 'Great Cham', Samuel Johnson.

We have heard of tours that are 'conservation-conscious' and of tourist sites that 'experience' apparitions. Here we have works of literature described as 'self-consciously' minor though such products are incapable of consciousness. The critic meant that the writers themselves were self-consciously producing minor works. The expression is right for people, but wrong for artefacts of any kind. One could allow: 'proffering their works from the margins of literature as frankly minor productions', for when a person speaks 'frankly' we properly describe the statement itself as 'frank'. But self-consciousness cannot be transferred from writer to production. We must add that the error here is compounded by the description of the productions as 'hopeful' of acceptance. Poems are as incapable of optimism as of self-consciousness. The whole baggage of misapplied description should be transferred to where it belongs: 'Like all the writers of Sensibility, they were mild rebels, self-consciously proffering their works as minor productions from the margins of contemporary literature, and hopeful of their acceptance by mainline culture symbolized by the "Great Cham", Samuel Johnson.'

the gradual slide
There are occasions when a writer slides gradually from an impersonal
idiom to a quite unsuitable personal one.

> A really strong friendship is both open and flexible. It thrives on
> the differences between you, not just the similarities. It encour-
> ages you to be independent. It values loyalty, but doesn't expect
> exclusivity.

'Friendship' is here clearly characterized as a relationship 'between
you' thriving on differences. The succeeding verbs applied to it,
'thrives', 'encourages', and 'values', gradually assume a more personal
flavour. We are used to speaking of people who thrive and ventures
that thrive, of people who encourage us and developments that
encourage us, so why not speak of a relationship that thrives and
encourages? But when we get to the word 'value' we sense that only
living beings can value things and when, finally, we get to the words
'doesn't expect' we sense the total incongruity in the relationship
between the impersonal subject and the personal verb ('It . . . doesn't
expect').

7

'What are You Talking About?'

This is one of the questions which ought never to be put to you when you have said or written something. Indeed the purpose of this book as a whole is to ensure that readers become immune to such challenges. How often do we feel like putting the question to a writer whose words we have just been reading? Is current usage generally such that the question need rarely arise? To take stock of what gets into print today, with an exact eye to that question, is to discover that the answer is no. To begin with, there is a group of words which have a 'stand-in' function. 'I love it', I say, or 'They're a nuisance'. And it is crucial that whoever I am addressing, on paper or by word of mouth, knows exactly what 'it' or 'they' refers to. We must look at current usage of such words to discover how accurately they are being employed.

Who are *they*?

This is perhaps the most frequently misused of all the words with the stand-in function. Tired of repeating in conversation the words 'the Smiths' or 'our neighbours' we say simply 'they'. Which is fine so long as the people we are talking to know who 'they' are. We take the same liberty on paper. The function of this useful short word 'they' is that it carries a reference outside itself to something that has already been mentioned. The mentioned neighbours become 'they'. So do the mentioned items at the supermarket ('They were more expensive today'). And already we see a source of possible confusion. For if you want to explain to your wife that you met her parents at the supermarket and that the roses you had intended to buy for her were looking rather droopy, it would be as well not to misplace the word 'they' in your account. It has to be said that this is not unnecessary advice to judge from today's press. Nothing is more remarkable than the frequency with which the word 'they' is confusingly misused.

This is not just a matter of grammatical correctness. It is a matter of knowing what you are talking about and making it clear. There must never be any doubt about what the word 'they' refers to. Here is advice to parents about preparing young children for school:

> Make sure school clothes are easy to put on and take off, that they're confident going to the toilet on their own, and that they can recognize their name when printed on a name tag.

The wording conveys that school clothes need to be confident about use of the toilet. The writer had used the word 'child' (not 'children') in the previous sentence, but the word 'they' will not carry the mind so far back anyway. This sentence begins as a statement about 'school clothes' and any following use of 'they' will first direct the reader's mind back to the clothes. The writer's basic mistake at the beginning of this sentence was to make her subject the children's clothes and not the children themselves: 'Make sure the children can put their clothes on and off easily, that they're confident going to the toilet on their own, and that they can recognize their name when printed on a tag.'

In the same journal we find this advice about handling teenagers:

> If you keep lines of communication open, you may decide that some of your 'rules' are negotiable. However, they also need to know your limits.

The only words here to which 'they' could possibly refer back to are 'lines of communication' and 'rules'. Those are the things at issue as the reader comes to the word 'they'. The change of subject must be made clear: 'Your children also need to know your limits.' And comparable treatment needs to be given to this recommendation for an electric toaster:

> Although just a two-slot, they are long enough to toast two slices
> in each.

What is long enough? To speak of a 'two-slot toaster' is to speak about a toaster, not about its components. The truth is that 'they' refers back to a word that isn't there, the word 'slots'. You would not say 'This is a four-star hotel and they were awarded by the AA'. There is no place for 'they' in either sentence. 'This is a four-star hotel, and the stars were awarded by the AA.' 'Although it's just a two-slot toaster, the slots are long enough to toast two slices in each.'

There are certain adjectives which we use in two different ways, either personally or impersonally. For instance we may say 'Are you comfortable in those shoes?' or 'Are those shoes comfortable?' Now clearly, where a word has these two usages it is possible for confusion to arise. If you wanted to abbreviate 'Is that chair comfortable?' to 'Is it comfortable?' no difficulty would arise. The word 'it' can apply only to the chair. But in the question 'Are they comfortable?' someone might be enquiring either about the sitters or the seats. Hence we get sentences such as the following from the world of caravanning:

> Reclining in the double bed is the only comfortable way to watch
> TV as there are only two seats in the dinette which face the telly,
> and after sitting upright for a couple of hours they become
> uncomfortable.

Since we have had no recent reference to the occupants, we naturally read 'they become uncomfortable' as a comment on the seats. There is nothing else for them to refer to. But if the word 'they' does indeed refer to the seats, than we are being told that these seats have been 'sitting upright for a couple of hours'. Unless the construction is changed there is no escape from some such correction as 'after being sat on in an upright position for a couple of hours, they become uncomfortable'. The alternative of course is to write 'after sitting upright for a couple of hours, we found them uncomfortable'.

The Generalized *they*

There is a temptation to reach for the word 'they' and insert it to stand for an unspecified group of people or things so that, instead of saying 'There's a new and better smoke-detector on the market', people will say, without reference to any specific firm, 'They're making a new and better smoke-detector now'. To use this freedom on paper is unwise. The unidentifiable 'they' should we avoided.

> The Compact is a folding aerial, measuring about 6" x 4" x 1" when packed away and can easily be stored in a drawer. They make two different types of aerial . . .

Here is a case in point. There is no need to introduce the unidentifiable 'they'. Replace the words by 'Two different types of aerial are made'.

A slip-up which is not uncommon occurs when there is no proper word for the word 'they' to refer back to because a singular subject has been used, but used in a generalized sense – the usage represented by 'mobile phone' in the sentence 'The mobile phone is a menace'. For instance, here is a passage about dealing with congenital port-wine stains:

> This birthmark remains flat but darkens with age and is twice as common in girls. Over time they may become thicker and have raised bumps.

The writer here did not really intend to tell us that some girls may become thicker over time and develop raised bumps. Yet that is what is said – and it sounds almost like a warning of the coming teenage puppyfat. Having chosen to speak of the 'birthmark' in the singular (but meaning 'birthmarks' in general), the writer forgot the decision so that the pronoun 'they' has nothing to refer back to except the word 'girls'.

The reader may be inclined to think that the points being made here are too obvious, but in fact confusion of this kind between singular and plural is very common when the singular form is used in that universal sense (the words 'this birthmark' for this kind of birthmark, not this individual birthmark). Having the universal usage in mind as covering all instances, the writer then forgets to stick to the singular and lapses into the plural. It happens in the following example:

> Everyone loves a conservatory. Quite simply, they transform your home . . .

Since two sentences are used, this would be best corrected by getting rid of 'they': 'Everyone loves a conservatory. Indeed conservatories transform your home.' In the following that collision between singular and plural occurs within a single sentence:

> People want to aspire to holding a little place by the sea in England, but they are too expensive.

The word 'they' will again have to be sacrificed here and, incidentally, the words 'want to' should also go: 'People aspire to holding a little place by the sea in England, but such homes are too expensive.'

More Complex Misuse of *they*

Let us turn from these fairly elementary specimens of misconnection with the word 'they' to show how the mistake can mar the work of a distinguished journalist writing on grave political matters. The italics are mine:

> The leaks of Downing Street memoranda seem to have dried up for the time being, but no doubt *they* are much less complacent than Downing Street's public response. *They* will certainly be discussing a number of threats to Labour's support at the general election. *They* must be very concerned at the damage done to Tony Blair's image.

There is only one word in this passage that the word 'they' can logically refer back to, and that is the word 'leaks'. First we are told that the leaks are 'much less complacent' than Downing Street's public response, then that the leaks are discussing threats to Labour's support at the general election, and finally that the leaks are concerned about damage done to Blair's image. Since the writer does not make clear who he is talking about as the subject of these various claims, I cannot offer a corrected version of this. It would appear that the first 'they' refers to some such unmentioned persons as are covered by the generalized use of the words 'Downing Street'.

It is clear that in a passage of reasoning a failure of this kind may damage the argument irreparably. Here is an account of a figure-skating final in which a Russian couple were awarded the prize rather than a Canadian, and the journalist clearly thinks an injustice was done to the latter. The italics are mine:

> Elena Berezshnaya and Anton Sikharulidze won gold in the pairs figure skating, the eleventh time in succession that the prize has gone to a couple from Russia or the Soviet Union. But did *they* really skate better than Jamie Sale and David Pelletier, of Canada? On the whole and taking one thing with another, *they* did not. *They* made a couple of errors visible even to me. *They* wuz, I am pretty sure, robbed.

It seems clear that, of the four uses of the word 'they' in that passage, the first three refer to the Russian couple, whose victory the journalist deplores. 'They' didn't skate better than the Canadian couple and 'they' made errors. But the last sentence tells us that 'they' were robbed of something. The error appears to undermine what has been already said.

What is *it*?

There are certain contexts in which we use the word 'it' and no clarification of what 'it' stands for is required. That applies to statements such as 'It is raining' or 'It is summer now'. But in many contexts what applies to 'they' applies to 'it'. What the word refers back to must be clear to the reader so that the use of the word 'it', like the use of the word 'they', requires the utmost watchfulness by the writer. That watchfulness was plainly lacking in the writer of the following:

> Birdwatchers are crucial to scientists trying to understand the complex and sometimes mysterious process of migration – it

might even give us some clues as to whether spring really is occurring earlier.

What does 'it' refer back to? Grammatically speaking, 'it' must be the 'process of migration'. But what the writer appears to mean is that the activities of birdwatchers can shed light on the mysterious process of migration. The subject of the sentence should be changed: 'Bird-watching is crucial to scientists trying to understand the complex and mysterious process of migration – it might even give them some clues as to whether spring really is occurring earlier.' One can readily light upon comparable misuses of the word 'it'.

> The common problem throughout the clubs is how much the clubs pay the players. It is not imposed on them, but in a very free, highly competitive market, people take bigger and bigger risks.

This is not directly from the writer's pen, but from the mouth of someone the writer is quoting. Nevertheless a salient point is being made, a contribution to a continuing controversy, and any contributor to such a debate will be ineffective unless the line taken is clearly expressed, and here neither the listener nor the reader would know what 'it' referred to. Strictly interpreted, 'it' must refer back to 'the common problem' cited above – how much the clubs pay the players. But the speaker does not mean to convey that the 'problem' is not 'imposed', rather, surely, that no policy in relation to the problem is imposed.

What is *this*?

What applies to 'it' applies equally to 'this' and 'that'. Wherever the words are used on their own (as opposed to with other words, 'this house', 'that picture') it must be clear what they refer to and there has to be some precision about this linkage.

> A Swiss doctor who specializes in foot problems realized that feet need to be properly supported and cushioned, yet most of our shoes today do not provide this.

What is 'this'? There is no word to which it can clearly relate back. If the sentence had read 'A Swiss doctor who specializes in foot problems realized that feet need to have proper support and cushioning', then it would have been correct to write 'yet most of our shoes today do not provide this'. The word 'this' there exactly relates back to the words 'support and cushioning'.

The need for a cast-iron point of reference when the word 'this' is used is crucial. Without it logical sequence can be broken, and one can find lapses of that kind in quite sophisticated writing.

> In response to George Dyer, I disagree entirely that proportional representation in the Commons would be a good idea. If this were to happen, the minority extremist parties would hold the balance of power – totally undermining the parties which have the majority of public support.

'If this were to happen' raises the question 'If what were to happen?' No possible 'happening' has been mentioned. What has been said is that proportional representation in the Commons 'would be a good idea'. To make 'If this were to happen' correct, it would have to be preceded by 'I disagree entirely that proportional representation should be introduced into the Commons', then the happening referred to would have been mentioned. The reader should note too that the word 'majority' is not happily used in reference to the word 'support'. There is no gain from not writing 'undermining the parties which have most public support'.

The error we are investigating is far from rare even in generally literate journals. In a recent exchange in the press a parent, who told how her daughter worried about her studies at school, complained that a teacher had written 'Rubbish' against a piece of written work. She was seeking advice from the experts, and one of them replied thus:

> There are times when a caustic remark can serve as a useful corrective to a student who is coasting, but this should be done only when the child is likely to respond positively and there is little likelihood that fragile confidence will be undermined.

The question arises, What is 'this' that should be 'done'? A caustic remark cannot be 'done'. A useful corrective cannot be 'done'. Nothing has been specifically mentioned that could be 'done'. If that expression ('this should be done') is to be kept, then there must be some such opening as 'There are times when a teacher may make a caustic comment as a useful corrective'. After that, 'but this should be done' would make sense.

What is *that*?

We are dealing with a kind of illogicality which can enter into the work of knowledgeable people. Let us examine a piece of news about archaeological discoveries made as a result of excavations on the site of a Roman fort:

> The current debate is concerned with the desire to preserve 'the commanding officer's house', although whether that is the correct interpretation, or whether it was something else is not clear at all.

The use of quotation marks here invites the reader to assume that the writer is not himself committed to what is said inside them. Nevertheless, the word 'that' is thrown into the communication with no sure focus on what it is supposed to relate to. It is like a coat seeking a peg to hang on. It should have been preceded by the peg. 'The current debate is concerned with what has been called "the commanding officer's house", although whether that is the correct description . . .' So far, so good. But what about the word 'it'? We realize that 'it' does not mean 'the interpretation', as it should by its placing, but the 'house'. Therefore the word must be replaced to make sense: 'The current debate is concerned with the desire to preserve what has been called "the commanding officer's house", although whether that is the correct description, or whether the building was something else is not clear at all.'

To turn to an even subtler specimen of this laxity, here is a piece of reasoning in a leading article about the relationships between the economies of the European countries in connection with the development of the single currency:

> For if the assumptions about the compatibility of the 12 founder
> economies are contestable, then that between the British econ-
> omy and euroland is even more so.

The writer seems to have been unable to decide whether he or she
was writing about certain 'assumptions' or about the 'compatibility'
of the various economies. The words 'If the assumptions are contest-
able' are soon followed by 'then that between the British economy
and euroland', which suggests that 'that' is an assumption. But, if it
means that, then we are being told that the assumption is something
that stands 'between the British economy and euroland', which does
not make sense. If, however – as surely must be the case – 'that between
the British economy and euroland' refers to 'the compatibility', then
the sentence should have begun differently. What the writer appears
to have meant is: 'If the compatibility between the economies of the
12 founder countries is a matter of doubt, then that between the
British economy and euroland is even more so.'

Talking About People

We ought not to leave this discussion of the part played in the
connectedness of sentences by words such as 'one', 'they' and 'it'
without touching on a related matter. The equivalent stand-in words
for reference to people ('he' and 'she' and so on), the personal pronouns, are in some cases ill used today on a surprising scale.

she and *her*, *he* and *him*
We generally remember to say 'This is my mother; she lives with me'
and not 'her lives with me'. We equally remember to say 'This is my
mother; I live with her' and not 'I live with she'. Yet we find that
sound practice in this respect is not universally followed. For instance,
I read in a magazine:

> The only person who worries about it is her.

This should be 'she', for it is 'she' who does the worrying. Just as you
would not say 'her worries about it' instead of 'she worries about it',

so you will say 'the only person who worries about it is she'. And the converse error can be found too.

> Moving into the penthouse has made both she and Peter reassess their lifestyle.

This should be: 'Moving into the penthouse has made both her and Peter reassess their lifestyle.' A remarkable thing about errors of this kind is the way they tend to occur when two pronouns are put together. The journalist who wrote the above would probably not have made the same mistake if the reference to 'Peter' had not been included. He would not have written 'Moving into the penthouse made she reassess her lifestyle'.

What applies to 'she' and 'her' as subject and object applies equally to 'he' and 'him'. Yet I read this in a magazine:

> They'd gone from pub to pub, first as part of the gang, then just him and Lisa.

It was not 'him' that went from pub to pub but 'he': 'then just he and Lisa'. The same correction applies to the following:

> Sorry, Pen, we'll stop harassing him. But it's him who keeps calling us.

That should be: 'But it's he who keeps calling us.'

If readers feel offended to be instructed in matters whose complexities they mastered in the junior school, let me explain why I deal with the matter here. Because an account in *The Times* of the Archer trial spoke of the attitude of the judge towards Lady Archer as a witness, saying that he:

> . . . chimed in, rebuking her for failing to answer the question, or for answering on behalf of her husband too ('you are being cross-examined, not him').

Did a high court judge really say this, instead of the correct 'You are being cross-examined, not he'?

I and *me, we* and *us*

It appears to be when we are talking about ourselves that our usage is most likely to go awry in this respect. I find numerous sentences of the following pattern in a magazine story.

> 'Come in love. Me and Paddy will look after you.'

'Me' of course should be 'I'. And one cannot argue that the author is intentionally representing colloquial dialogue with all its faults, because her own voice adopts the same usage as that employed in the dialogue:

> Me, Mary and both our families went to the inquest together.

Again 'me' should be 'I'.

Such misuses of 'me' in place of 'I' may perhaps be comparatively rare. However, if we are to judge from speakers in pulpits, on platforms and on the radio, there is now a widespread general conviction among people who would consider themselves educated, that to say 'you and me' in any context would be wrong. 'That applies to you and I', we hear instead of 'That applies to you and me'. People who would never think of saying 'He gave I a box of chocolates' will nevertheless say 'He gave my wife and I a box of chocolates', which is just as ungrammatical. This is now a literacy scandal on the national scale.

> Mum used to promise my sister and I a tenner for every storyline
> that we came up with . . .

This child's mother is a professional writer. And the following comes from the same magazine:

> When Oliver arrived, it was a fantastic moment for Oliver and I
> to share with her.

In each case the 'I' is misplaced. The first sentence should read 'Mum used to promise my sister and me a tenner' and the second sentence should be 'it was a fantastic moment for Oliver and me to share with her'.

An odd by-product of the current misuse is the discomfort many people now seem to have with the word 'me'. You will hear them falling back inappropriately on 'myself' instead of 'me' in such statements as 'you'll have to talk to John or myself'. However, one of the main reasons for reverting here to this topic, which I have dealt with elsewhere, is that a new strand seems to have appeared in the web of public illiteracy. For the corruption that has affected choice between 'I' and 'me' now seems to be affecting choice between 'we' and 'us'. If readers think I am exaggerating, let them attend to the following sentences taken from recent magazines:

> First-timers load up with potatoes, whereas us seasoned visitors only take a couple.

> While Simon and Terry's chatter is alcoholic, us girls try to identify the weird squawking coming from the grounds of nearby Kiftsgate Court Gardens.

> We were scared that if we reported what Adrian had seen, word would get around that it was us who'd phoned.

> 'Thanks Mum,' said Penelope. 'And since us witches are casting spells, together we may yet save the world.'

In each case the word 'us' should be 'we'. And the last sentence is particularly interesting. The writer had at least the good sense to change tack ('*we* may yet save the world') and not turn one error into two errors by sheer consistency.

The converse error is probably rarer, yet here is a specimen:

> These days, it seems that caravan manufacturers can't do enough to pamper we sybaritic caravanners.

This should be 'can't do enough to pamper us caravanners'.

Pointless Retrospection

If a companion on a walk lays a hand on your shoulder, swings you round and points to the scene behind you, saying 'That's the building I'm talking about', you would expect there to be a building in sight. If there were not, you would begin to question the rationality of your companion. Yet a common failing in logical sequence on paper precisely matches that behaviour. Writers point to something that just isn't there. They refer back to something they think they have already mentioned, when in fact they have not mentioned it at all. Here is a typical specimen of the lapse:

> In his later years Conan Doyle became a convinced spiritualist, and wrote and lectured much on the subject.

What subject? None has been mentioned. The writer, having said that Conan Doyle became a spiritualist has assumed that 'spiritualism' has been mentioned, but it has not. The logical writer could not refer to lecturing 'on the subject' unless the subject had been defined ('In his later years Conan Doyle was a convert to spiritualism, and wrote and lectured much on the subject'). We find the same error committed at a more sophisticated level, more wrapped about with words, in a book of reference:

> The next 20 years, up to the time of his wife's death, were Elgar's most creative period. W. H. Reed, who was leader of the LSO and one of Elgar's closest friends at this time, has spoken of the decisive influence she had on him.

The writer speaks of the influence 'she' had on him, as though he has in fact referred to Elgar's wife. But he has not. He has spoken only of 'his wife's death'. Strict logic requires the use of 'she' only after a clear, unambiguous mention of a person. Here it is only necessary to amend the first few words of the sentence: 'The next twenty years, up to the time his wife died . . .'

This particular illogicality can be found in many different forms, some subtle enough for good writers to overlook them. For just as the use of the word 'wife's' seduces the writer into believing that he has referred to the 'wife' as such, so the use of a word such as 'Irish' may seduce a writer into thinking that he has referred to 'Ireland'. Indeed that is probably the commonest form this particular illogicality takes. Consider this sentence from a leading article:

> Libyan cooperation with the West is likely to remain patchy and sporadic. It is eager to expand trade links with Britain . . . but it is likely to remain at arm's length politically.

'It' here is intended to refer back to the word 'Libya', which has not been used, so that strictly speaking 'it' must mean 'Libyan cooperation'. This error really represents another version of the 'wayward possessive'. One must never make statements like: 'He took a great interest in South African affairs because he was born there.' It would have to be: 'He took a great interest in the affairs of South Africa, because he was born there.' How easily it may seduce even a skilled writer may be seen in an extract from the *Journals* of Anthony Powell. He speaks of recording the visit of a television crew to his home. He describes one of the interviewers as:

> ... quite attractive with that slightly African look, loose limbs, even features regions impose after some years, like Margaret Hayward developing a faintly Indonesian appearance after living there for seven years.

The note is among a series of jottings but it usefully illustrates the illogicality here at issue. One doubts whether Powell would have been so lax in a novel as to speak of Margaret 'living there for seven years' as though he had mentioned 'Indonesia', when in fact he had used only the word 'Indonesian'.

In this matter of retro-reference to something that has not been said, a rather strange new habit of usage has lately become widespread. It is to write as though the basis for some comparison has been laid down when it fact it has not. Here is the first sentence of a leading article:

> The advantage of low expectations is that they are less likely to be dashed.

The logical mind asks 'less likely than what?' Had there been a reference to some issue involving a larger degree of likelihood the sentence would make sense. As it is the reader's common sense has to supply the answer. Clearly the writer means that low expectations are less likely to be dashed than are high expectations. Surely this ought to be said. I cite another leading article:

> It is not necessarily true that the 43rd President of the United States will be a lame duck from the day of his inauguration. The impression left abroad may, though, be more disturbing.

Again the logical mind asks 'more disturbing than what?' Nothing has as yet been said to be disturbing. A view has been conveyed that the new President may not prove to be a lame duck. That is scarcely a 'disturbing' statement. What the writer is trying to say (I'm guessing) is that an 'impression' is being conveyed that might actually be more 'disturbing' than would be the dismissed notion of there being a lame duck President. If this was intended, it should have been said.

Illogical Afterthoughts

A device is sometimes used of making a simple addition to a statement which concentrates the meaning epigrammatically or which acts as a kind of footnote. Whatever the function of the addition, epigrammatic force must not be obtained at the cost of logic. Here is an attempt at the device which fails. It is from an encyclopaedic entry on King Edward VIII:

> The Duke made infrequent visits to England, the Duchess never.

The contrast should be between making 'infrequent' visits and making no visits. Therefore it would be correct to say: 'The Duke made infrequent visits to England, the Duchess none.' If it were desired to keep the word 'never', then the word to contrast with it must precede it: 'The Duke visited England infrequently, the Duchess never.'

In the sentence just quoted the offending last three words are a kind of afterthought, but a very pointed one. In the addition of such postscripts the illogicality we are investigating easily occurs.

> In our health special there are ways to notch up energy and feel fitter than you have in a long while. It's worth trying – I have and it's so easy.

It makes sense to write 'Have you ever tried jogging? I have and it's so easy' because the words 'I have' relate directly back to 'Have you tried jogging' with the comment 'I have' (tried jogging). There is no such combination of words for 'I have' to relate back to in 'It's worth trying', which would have to be followed by 'I've tried it myself'. In the above sentence, however, it is the plural 'ways' that are recommended for trial and, strictly speaking, the reading would have to be: 'They're worth trying: I've tried them myself.'

Retrospective postscripts take many forms. The practice of adding to a statement a kind of terse condition, such as 'if desired' ('A taxi will be provided, if desired') is never very elegant, but its brevity can make it useful. Care must be taken to ensure that its meaning is not ambiguous.

> We will tell you how long it will take to deal with your enquiry
> or claim, if appropriate.

This statement from officialdom leaves a question in the mind. Do the authorities mean that they will let you know how long it will take to deal with your enquiry or claim, if it is 'appropriate' for them to do so? That is what the sentence conveys, and it smacks of condescension ('We shall communicate with you if we think you deserve it'). Or does the conditional 'if appropriate' really refer back to the words 'enquiry' and 'claim'? 'We shall let you know how long it will take to deal with this enquiry or claim if we think it is such that it would be appropriate for us to deal with it.'

Afterthoughts involving *so* and *otherwise*

There are many afterthoughts which take the form of expressing a detached additional comment on something already said. Very often the retrospective comment depends on the word 'so', as in: 'My father left me this enormous house, and frankly I wish it were not so.' The word 'so' clearly refers back to the event regretted. The following sentence from a letter to the press illustrates a faulty use of the same sequence:

> Sir, Why should not 'traditional defence policies' (Sir Patrick
> Duffy's letter, September 21) be subject to strong criticism? Were
> it not so, we should still have Dreadnoughts and a Camel Corps.

The first error here is to use the expression 'Were it not so' after a question. It would make sense to say: 'You must have murdered your wife. Were it not so, she would be here.' But it would not make sense to say: 'Have you murdered your wife? Were it not so, she would be here.' That is because 'so' requires a factual statement to refer back to. The writer of the above asked a question to which the word 'so' could not refer. He should have written: 'Traditional defence policies must be subject to strong criticism.' He could then have used the word 'so' retrospectively. But strict logic would have required a change of tense: 'Had it not been so, we should still have Dreadnoughts and a Camel Corps.' An alternative to that change of tense in the second sentence would be the insertion of the word 'always' in the first sentence: 'Traditional defence policies must always be subject to strong criticism. Were it not so, we should still have Dreadnoughts and a Camel Corps.'

In this matter of the use of 'so' in retro-reference, what applies to a direct question applies also to an indirect question. The Inland Revenue issue this advice:

> Decide if you want me to calculate your tax for you. If so, make sure that your completed Tax Return reaches me by 30 September 2000.

This is not very different from saying: 'Decide whether you want to go. If so I will make proper arrangements.' There is no more finality about 'if you want me to calculate your tax for you' than there is about 'whether you want to go'. Indeed the implicit meaning of the tax inspector's sentence allows clearly of the two alternatives, calculation by the taxpayer or by the inspector. The official instruction should have read: 'Decide whether you want me to calculate your tax for you. If you do, make sure that your completed Tax Return reaches me by 30 September 2000.'

The commonest form of this illogicality occurs in such public pronouncements as the following:

> This ticket permits you to park in accordance with the Regulations and must be displayed inside the windscreen of the vehicle.
> Failure to do so may render you liable to enforcement action.

Here is a very familiar slip. One may write 'You must display this ticket inside the windscreen' and then speak of the 'failure to do so' because 'to do' refers to your duty to place the ticket on the windscreen. However, if there has been no such preliminary verb as 'display' but only the passive verb 'be displayed', it is illogical to refer back to that as 'doing' something. If the last sentence is kept, it must be preceded by 'You must display the ticket inside the windscreen'. That is the only way to make sense of 'failure to do so'.

The frequency with which this error is found in public announcements suggests that the relevant rule needs to be hammered home in a book of this kind. For instance, it is quite correct to say 'He wanted me to sing at the reception and I was happy to do so'. The words 'to do so' reflect back on the words 'to sing' with perfect logic. But it is not correct to say 'Singing was required at the reception, and I was happy to do so' because there is no word for the words 'to do so' to connect with. Even skilled writers sometimes slip up in this respect.

> A myth is nothing if it's not repeated. And the power to do so has
> never been greater.

If the journalist had written 'A myth is nothing until people repeat it. And the power to do so has never been greater', the sentences would have been correct, because 'to do so' would accurately reflect back to the verb 'repeat'. 'To do so' means 'to repeat'. But 'to do so' cannot logically connect back to the words 'it's not repeated'. The writer must keep in mind the exact words used from sentence to sentence.

What applies to the word 'so' applies to the word 'otherwise'. Just as the word 'so' must connect logically and positively with what has previously been stated, so the word 'otherwise', in comparable retro-reference, must connect logically and negatively with what has previously been stated. 'My wife always supports the Tories, but I vote otherwise.' There the word 'otherwise' indicates a contrary attitude. Yet I hear this on the radio in an exchange about crime fiction:

> Most readers want moral endings with good triumphant, but
> crime writers know otherwise.

Logically considered, by thus using the word 'otherwise', the speaker here is telling us that crime writers dispute what 'most readers want'. In fact the word 'otherwise' is totally out of place for any other purpose. What the speaker presumably meant was 'but crime writers know that life is not like that'. To make the second part of the sentence applicable, the word 'want' would have to go, for what readers 'want' cannot be thus disputed.

Other Kinds of Inconsequentiality

A degree of ambiguity can sometimes result from inadequately thought-out references to what has just been said.

> Over the years, I have watched the hounds in full cry from my
> stile vantage point and I believe, very strongly, that no one has
> the right to take away that privilege.

A question is left in the reader's mind. Is the writer anxious to preserve the privilege of being allowed to watch the hounds from her favourite stile? That is what a strict reading of her sentence would suggest. Or is she more basically defending the privilege enjoyed by the hunters? If the latter is intended, then she should have mentioned the hunters for, as the wording stands, if it is not her privilege she is defending, then it must be the privilege enjoyed by the hounds.

Whenever an afterthought takes the form of a contrast with what has just been said, it is crucial that it is firmly tied into the context.

> While the wedding of the year, and surely the decade, was being
> celebrated in one part of town, other Dundee 'citizens' were going
> about their lawful business.

The word 'other' takes the reader's mind back to 'some' or to words with equivalent status. Unless 'some' Dundee citizens have been mentioned, the words 'other Dundee citizens' are misplaced. One might argue too that the element of contrast suggested by the construction (While this was happening, 'other' doings were afoot) rather fails in that the wedding of the year was presumably no less someone's 'lawful business' than the activities of these other citizens. The word 'other' should be replaced, perhaps by 'many', and 'lawful' would be better replaced by 'ordinary'.

A construction which has to be carefully handled if retrospection is to be logical and exact is the use of the words 'former' and 'latter'. The following is from a letter to the press:

> The director of Liberty fails to draw the distinction between users
> and abusers of drugs. As a comparison with alcoholism will verify,
> the former does not necessarily lead to the latter.

As the first sentence stands, 'the former does not lead to the latter' in the succeeding sentence means that users do not lead to abusers. So, if the first sentence is kept, then the second sentence should end: 'the former do not necessarily turn into the latter'. However, the writer probably did not mean that. He no doubt said what he meant in the second sentence, which would be correct as it stands if the first sentence were changed to: 'The director of Liberty fails to draw the distinction between use and abuse of drugs.'

We turn to a last example of the error we are dealing with, again involving two separate sentences:

> This novel, although nominally about disfigurement, shows how
> fundamentalism can destroy society. She reveals a religion that
> is adept at absorbing the most disparate characters, but unable
> to brook dissent.

There are four substantial sentences in this review before the ones quoted. They do not contain the writer's name, but refer several times to the narrator, Natalie Baron. Since Natalie was the subject of the sentence previous to the ones quoted, the reader might assume that 'she' is the subject mentioned above. But plainly the reviewer's 'she', who reveals the religion under fire, must be the novelist. There is a kind of double error in that the first sentence above is about the novel, and 'she' cannot be a novel, and that the previous sentence was about the novel's narrator, and 'she' cannot be that narrator. Clearly the second sentence above must read: 'The novelist reveals a religion that is adept . . .'

Numerical Discrepancies

Sometimes an incorrect retro-reference may be caused by confusion between singular and plural forms. There are two kinds of slip-up in this respect. The first is caused by sheer forgetfulness. A plural subject may be paralleled by a singular one ('Cornish tin mines, one industry crucial to the county') and then the writer continues as though 'one industry' were the subject, and not 'Cornish tin mines'. That is what happens in the following:

> The principal shareholders of the Explorer Group Ltd, a Surrey based investment and property company, has decided to place the Explorer Group up for sale.

As a result of the writer's forgetfulness we find ourselves reading 'The principal shareholders . . . has decided' instead of 'have decided'.

The converse form of the error occurs when a writer moves from a genuine plural to a generalized singular. Here is a sentence about 'weekend gardeners':

> They don't want to become a slave to their garden.

There is no advantage there in not saying 'slaves to their gardens'. And the same applies to the following:

> These attractive and easy-to-grow plants have been a constant companion of mine.

Once more, why not 'have been constant companions of mine'?

There is one complicating matter which ought to be raised in this connection. Sometimes a formally plural subject is really intended as a singular concept. Obviously no one would say *The Three Musketeers* 'are' a novel by Dumas on the grounds that there are 'three' musketeers. There are less obvious instances of that kind of seeming mix between singular and plural.

> Marketing people like organized events. They're easy to use in promotions, and herds of people doing the same thing can look dynamic, exciting and implies a large potential market.

The writer does not mean that herds of people can each and all 'imply' something, but that the event, the spectacle of their doing the same thing 'implies' something, in the singular. The sentence could be much improved. It would have been better to write 'herds of people doing the same thing can look dynamic and exciting, and implies a large potential market', thus usefully separating the final point by the punctuation. But it would have been better still to end: 'and the spectacle implies a large potential market'.

8

Compression and Omission

Many of the faults examined in this book have to do with overwordiness. The good writer values conciseness. However, there are mistaken attempts at economy in the use of words that can produce awkwardness and illogicality. The wrong kind of supposed shortcut can leave the reader guessing. In seeking to save words a writer may leapfrog over a crucial element in the utterance and produce an incomplete sequence. The clear-headed writer will always ensure that there is never any gap in a passage of prose that the reader is left having to fill in mentally in order to make sense of the passage. The writer must not transfer to the reader the task of clarifying what has been said by filling it out or disentangling its drift.

Shortcuts that Misfire

We are concerned here with omissions that reveal basic confusion in the writer's or speaker's thinking, and we look first at specimens of the error in its most transparent form.

> Her name cannot be revealed because of a court order banning
> her identity.

This broadcast statement shows a kind of mental leapfrogging process in action. No court order could ever 'ban' someone's 'identity'. It could never have an effect at all on anyone's identity. What was 'banned' was not the woman's 'identity' but revelation or publication of what the woman's identity was. What it amounts to is that there is no exact account in the original sentence of what happened. Moreover, since the word 'name' is used in the beginning of the sentence, it is unnecessary to introduce the word 'identity' at all. The last three words of the sentence could be omitted. Alternatively, the sentence could read: 'A court order prevents us from publicly naming her.'

At this point the reader will notice that, although we are concerned with a kind of 'compression' which I have called 'mental leapfrogging', the bad usage can sometimes be corrected in such a way that the number of words is thereby reduced, not increased. In short we are sometimes concerned with a bogus kind of 'compression'. Writers *think* they are being economical with words, when in fact that is not always the case. All car drivers are familiar with the recommended shortcuts that sometimes prove costly in time and leave one mentally at a loss. We are at times concerned here with their verbal equivalents.

Here is a stark instance, provided by a piece of printed information conveyed to members of the audience at a concert:

> Orders for interval drinks will be taken and served in the Secondary Hall.

This specimen illustrates how dangerous a thoughtless use of 'and' can be in linking two processes, the taking of orders with the serving of drinks. In effect the orders for drinks are said to be taken and served in the same place. Certainly the orders are 'taken', but it is not the 'orders' that are served, it is the drinks. A more natural word-order would have obviated this problem: 'Interval drinks will be ordered and served in the Secondary Hall.' Taking a seemingly shortcut in linking together two or more concepts in that way (the ordering and the serving) can easily lead to confusion. Whenever concepts are tied together by the word 'and' the writer has to make sure that the partnership is logical. At its crudest, failure to make a proper linkage results in announcements such as this, heard on the radio:

> My impression is that this case doesn't add or detract anything to the euthanasia debate.

Since common usage requires us to speak of adding one thing 'to' another, and common usage of 'detract' requires us to follow it by 'from', there is no logical escape from using both constructions fully ('add to' and 'detract from'). The reader should note that, if we try to correct this sentence in that way ('doesn't add to or detract from the euthanasia debate'), we reveal that the speaker used the wrong word ('debate'). What was meant, presumably, was that the case in question 'doesn't add to or detract from the case for euthanasia'.

We turn to a more complex example of this error:

> The Eighties were an age of ambition – fostered by the boom, the change of pace in the workplace brought about by technology and promotion coming faster and younger.

It is justifiable to speak conversationally of promotion coming faster, but it cannot be said to come 'younger'. Promotion does not arrive one year in a wheel-chair and the next year in a track-suit. The word 'and' is required here to link two concepts that cannot be thus partnered, because one ('faster') applies to the word 'promotion' and the other ('younger') to the unmentioned candidates for promotion. To keep the existing pattern of the sentence, one would have to write something like 'fostered by the boom, by the change of pace in the workplace and by the fact that promotion came more quickly and to younger people'. However, that is awkward and, in any case, to say that promotion now comes more quickly to growing human beings automatically implies that the human beings it reaches will be younger than once was the case. In short, the words 'and younger' could just be omitted from the original sentence without any loss.

Where false linkages of that kind occur ('faster' and 'younger') the argument that the listener or reader 'will know what is meant' is not enough to excuse the sloppy thinking. One should not seek to save breath or ink at the expense of logic. Here is another such lapse:

> Some time ago I bought a multi-band TV from a dealer for £358.00. The first repair took nearly four weeks – awaiting a part from Switzerland. The warranty was extended only through total embarrassment and pressure.

In this case the embarrassment was presumably felt by the dealer, but the pressure was applied by the customer. To couple the two without differentiation represents another lax use of 'and'. If the warranty was extended 'because I exercised pressure on the dealer to the extent of embarrassing him', that should be made clear. A different kind of

failure to keep a logical grip on the wording appears in this sentence
from a magazine article tracing the career of the actor John Cleese:

> Television fame came first as a member of the team alongside
> David Frost in the satirical 1960s programme *The Frost Report*.

We seem to be being told that television fame was a member of an
acting team. Not many words have been omitted, but they are crucial.
'Television fame came to him first as a member of the team alongside
David Frost.'

More Subtle Failures

The effect of mental leapfrogging is not always so directly evident as
in that instance. Here we have an account of the discovery of the body
of a male, seemingly murdered, and the journalist wants to tell us
that the victim may have been older than was originally thought:

> Although he may still be as young as 14, detectives say it is possible
> that the unidentified victim, whose naked body was discovered
> last week, was an adult aged in his mid 20s.

What we must object to is the wording, 'Although he may still be as
young as 14', which is an inapt thing to say of a dead person. What is
really meant is 'Although the detectives believe he may have been as
young as 14'. It is the omission of 'the detectives believe', or some
such similar wording, that causes the trouble.

That kind of shortcut, employed at a more sophisticated level of
reasoning, occurs in this quotation from an article on the subject of
the Greenwich Dome:

> There was another project to provide a new Underground link
> between East London and Westminster. Somehow that project
> became entangled with the Greenwich site, without the pollution
> problem being solved. On top of that came the National Lottery,
> with its vast sums outside Treasury control.

The distinguished writer quoted here scarcely does justice to his topic.
You can 'entangle' one project with another perhaps, but you cannot

entangle a project with a 'site'. Moreover the reader may well query what 'that' refers to in the words 'on top of that'. For a moment the reader may even wonder whether there was a plan to build something called the 'National Lottery' on top of the Greenwich site. For just as the writer forgot that you cannot 'entangle' a project with a site, so he then forgot that the National Lottery is one thing and controversy about the National Lottery a different thing. He needed to fill out his text in this respect: 'Somehow that project became entangled with questions about the Greenwich site . . . Added to that came the controversy about the National Lottery.'

What happens in a passage such as that in the way of sliding over crucial steps in the fabric of the logic may perhaps be acceptable in conversation, but not in print, however conversational the style. Here is a tribute to a much-liked journalist:

> He was a truly beloved figure and an admired one too. I've never
> known more women say that John Morgan was their best friend.

What the writer is speaking about here is a certain *situation*, in which women in considerable numbers have spoken about the deceased. That is what the writer has not previously come across, but he makes it sound as though he has been taking regular soundings among women about their view of the deceased. The choice of words brings the pollster to mind. Indeed the sentence would be logical and appropriate were it the case that he had been regularly taking surveys amongst women on their attitude to John Morgan, and that the polling graph indicated that the number of those approving of the 'He was my best friend' option had now reached a historical peak. But what the writer really meant to convey was something like: 'I have never known of a case where so many women spoke of the deceased as their best friend.'

Shortcuts with the Verb 'to be'

There is a kind of economical verbal leap which we readily adopt in conversation when using the verb 'to be'. We use the device partly so that we shall not sound too formal and partly out of sheer laziness. It is not the kind of economy which we ought to import into the English we write. That is especially the case when the practice offends gravely against logic. Here is a piece from a light-hearted leading article on the subject of the UK fashion industry and how profitable it is:

> The fashion industry quotes around £700 million. The relatively low figure is not for lack of talent.

Would a contemporary English examiner these days let that second sentence go? What is meant, of course, is: 'It is not lack of talent that makes the figure low.' That would do. The abuse of the verb 'to be' in the original is insensitive. Elementary grammar requires the verb 'to be' to be followed by something to match the subject. The words 'not for lack of talent' could properly be used after an appropriate verb ('He lost the match, though it was not for lack of talent') but it would be wrong to write: 'His loss of the match was not for lack of talent.' The words 'is for', used together, have their own colloquial connotation ('She is for Bridge; I am for tennis').

We find a comparable misuse of the verb 'to be' in the following:

> The last evening on the trek was a good reason for a celebration and an opportunity to thank our companions for their support.

It was the 'fact' that it was the last evening on the trek that 'provided' the good reason. One must not be over-pedantic about this habit of verbal economy. We say 'The short evenings made after-dinner croquet impossible' when what we mean, strictly speaking, is 'The shortness of the evenings made after-dinner croquet impossible'. Such colloquial usages do not cause raised eyebrows. It is our preference for the verb 'to be' and for the word 'reason' that causes the trouble. The logical pedant might say that the actual meaning here is 'The "lastness" of the evening provided a good reason for a celebration', but that is hardly decent usage. If we were in the habit of expressing our meaning directly and saying 'Because the evenings were short, after-dinner croquet was impossible' and 'Because it was the last evening, we decided to have a celebration', then the laxities in question would not appear.

We can find even laxer uses of the word 'reason'.

> Overbecks, our main reason for visiting Salcombe, is an elegant
> Edwardian house at Sharpitor.

Although the writer does not directly say 'Overbecks is/was our main
reason for visiting Salcombe', the appositional construction amounts
to the same thing. Directly or indirectly to define the house as 'our
main reason' may not leave any uncertainty about what is meant, but
it is a sad liberty to take with the word 'reason'. To say Overbecks
'provided' the main reason for visiting Salcombe would be better, but
probably the best thing of all would be to get rid of the word 'reason':
'Overbecks, which was what chiefly drew us to Salcombe, is an elegant
Edwardian house at Sharpitor.' Again, as so often, replacing a noun
by a verb ('reason for' by 'drew') constitutes an improvement.

There are omissions which come naturally to us in conversation
but which look bare and even confusing on paper. Here is a letter
dealing with a suggestion that tax relief should be granted to community amateur sports clubs:

> Would such groups, especially those operating in deprived areas,
> derive significant benefit from this? I suspect that their resources
> and budgets are too small and too informal to make any great
> difference.

A vital stage in the reasoning has been lost here. The argument is not
about what 'difference' the 'resources and budgets' can make, but
about what difference the granting of tax relief would make. 'I suspect
that their resources and budgets are too small and too informal for a
tax relief provision to make any great difference to them [to have any
effect].'

Recording Changes and Improvements

A very common version of the 'errors by shortcut' which we are
exemplifying is that involved in the use of words such as 'change' and
'improvement'. In conversation we perhaps tend to say 'The greatest
change was the pedestrianized city centre' when what we really mean
is 'the pedestrianization' of the city centre. The careless usage is not

really excusable in print or in formal speaking. The clear-minded speaker or writer will not refer to the result of a change as itself a change, although the practice seems to be irresistible by some of our contemporaries.

> She has seen a lot of changes over the years, and many for the better when it comes to a jockey's life – rider safety and the Jockey of the Year Awards are to name just two.

The writer is supposed to be listing some specimen 'changes'. But neither 'rider safety' nor the 'Jockey of the Year Awards' are 'changes'. They are, presumably, both the result of changes. The sentence must be rewritten. 'She has seen a lot of changes over the years, and many for the better when it comes to a jockey's life – changes which have improved rider safety and given us Jockey of the Year Awards.'

What applies to the word 'change' applies to the word 'improvement'. You will hear people say 'The great improvement we made this year was the new bathroom' when they mean that the 'making' of the new bathroom was the great 'improvement'. On paper we need to beware of this colloquialism.

> Minor improvements at the West Anglia Great Northern station include a new waiting room and extended WH Smith shopping area.

The 'improvement' was the construction or provision of these new facilities: 'Minor improvements include the provision of a new waiting room and extended WHSmith shopping area.'

Statement and Fact

A curious but now most common kind of verbal shortcut is that which confuses statement with fact, report with event, plan with action. Official announcements all too often offend in this way. We find the error in the reporting of government decisions and business meetings.

> British industry will today call on the Chancellor to appoint a 'tax tsar' in his Pre-Budget Report (PBR) next week . . .

Here is a plain case in point. It is not an appointment that will be made on this occasion. No Chancellor could 'appoint' someone to public service in a statement such as the Pre-Budget Report. All the Chancellor could do would be to 'announce' such an appointment. What is meant is: 'British industry will today call upon the Chancellor to announce the appointment of a "tax tsar" . . .'

There seems to be a settled habit in recording such matters of allowing the mind to slide indiscriminately between handling statement and deed or between handling plan and action.

> Petrol vouchers and mobility allowances are being studied by ministers to help to alleviate transport difficulties for the poorest people in rural areas.

Now clearly we are not meant to take it that ministers are sitting with petrol vouchers in their hands and really 'studying' them. What they are 'studying' is a plan for possible action. That should be said: 'Ministers are considering the introduction of petrol vouchers and mobility allowances to alleviate transport difficulties for people in rural areas.' It is surprising how easy it is to find specimens of this kind of verbal shortcut in political arguments about policy. Here is a letter to the press looking back to the failure of sanctions at the time of the crisis in Rhodesia before the establishment of Zimbabwe:

> The reason they failed then was the sanctions were incomplete, particularly in the supply of oil. Blockade by sea, covering the port of Beira, and the use of force were passed by the United Nations Security Council. And indeed enforced.

To say that 'blockade by sea . . . and the use of force were passed' represents exactly the kind of shortcut we are investigating. It was not 'blockade' that was 'passed' by the Security Council, but a resolution ordering a blockade. What was 'passed' was a resolution. This does not mean that the only way to correct the sentence would be to write: 'Resolutions authorizing blockade by sea, covering the port of Beira, and the use of force were passed . . .' The verb 'passed' could be changed and the original wording otherwise kept: 'Blockade by sea, covering the port of Beira, and the use of force were authorized by the United Nations Security Council.'

And here is a comparable specimen of cutting corners in a news item about the royal family:

> The Earl of Wessex's fight to stay in his 57-room Berkshire mansion, in the face of opposition from other senior Royal Family members, will be raised with the Queen next month.

The prospect of a 'fight' being 'raised with the Queen', whatever the topic, sounds treacherous. What will be raised with the Queen is, of course, not the fight but the subject of the fight. The writer should have said so. One must not allow the state of mind to develop to which issues and the reporting of issues are one and the same thing.

What applies to the political and social field applies also to the business field.

> Profit warnings issued by UK companies have risen for the first time in two years, with the ambitious sales targets set by fledgeling IT companies partly to blame.

Business, like any other department of life, has its right to its own idioms and indeed its own brands of shorthand, but it is an area where precision ought to be valued. 'Warnings' are not the kind of things that 'rise' or 'fall'. What has 'risen', presumably, is the 'number' of profit warnings.

The confusion between statement and fact occurs in discussing literature. It might be helpful here to illustrate this error at its crudest and then at its most sophisticated. For the crude instance we turn to an article on new books from a magazine. The article comments on a publisher's recent output of titles 'covering natural history, gardening, travel and place, health and leisure'. It then adds:

> The countryside and crafts have just been announced by the family-run company which works on a no-membership, no-obligation system . . .

It is not, of course, 'The countryside and crafts' that have just been announced but 'the publication of books on the countryside and crafts' that has just been announced. The omission of the word 'books' does not in this context confuse the reader, but it is plainly an abuse of language to leave the reader mentally to fill in the gap.

For a somewhat more subtle version of this laxity, here is a sentence from a review of a new work of fiction:

> Most of the stories take place in provincial German cities.

The 'stories' do not 'take place' in German cities. The 'stories' are printed in a book and that's where they stay located. It is the events recorded in the stories that take place in German cities. You would not say of Shakespeare's *Hamlet* 'The play takes place in Denmark' when you meant 'The action of the play is set in Denmark'. You would not even say 'Hamlet kills Claudius in Denmark' though you might say 'Hamlet kills Claudius in Act V'.

'Read My Thoughts'

The professional writer may sometimes slip into the error of making an unjustified shortcut through trying to give a light touch to a stage in a piece of reasoning. Here is an article on the subject of proposals by the Mayor of London to institute a system of charging motor vehicles for driving in London. The writer lists the objections to the new plan, and comes to the subject of the technical machinery involved in identifying motorists:

> The prepayment options will cause confusion, the identification
> of violators from car number-plates may be unreliable and the
> accumulation of fines promises to make the enforcement of park-
> ing tickets simple.

To begin with, the writer presumably does not mean us to understand that the new system is going to make the enforcement of parking tickets simple, but that is exactly what he says. He means, we must assume, that the difficulties involved as the number of uncollected fines accumulates is going to make the present difficulties over enforcing the use of parking tickets look 'simple' by comparison. He ought to have said so. The expression 'the accumulation of fines' is infelicitous shorthand and so is 'the enforcement of parking tickets', and the implied parallelism between the two constructions is illogical. Enforcing the payment of parking fines may look simple compared to something in the new system, but what is that 'something'? It cannot be the 'accumulation' of fines, as is said here, but it might be the 'problems' caused by that accumulation. Our point is that there is here a whole-sale exploitation of shortcuts which fail of their object, in that the meaning is obscured by them. If only journalists would use verbs more frequently: 'As unpaid fines accumulate, the practical difficulties will make the enforcement of parking ticket regulations look simple by comparison.'

We are here concerned with the habit of leaving the reader to fill out the meaning when the writer has made a leap in utterance that defies logic by omitting crucial steps in the articulation of the argument. As a striking example of this habit I cite an article on the political situation, which takes an overview of the Blair Government's performance. It measures Mr Blair's achievements in the educational field and ends thus:

> But tricky problems remain, for example, over student finance
> and higher education, and transport is as far from improvement
> as ever. Most voters would be much less charitable.

'Much less charitable' than who? The reader can work out what the writer means, but the writer has not said it. Presumably he wants the reader to pick up the unspoken comment 'That's what I say about it' or 'That's one way of putting it', inserted after 'as far from improve-ment as ever'. To some such understood observation the writer adds the final comment that most voters would judge the Government's performance more harshly. Without some such insertion the conclud-ing sentence does not make sense.

That is an interesting and, unfortunately, not all that rare version of the 'illogicality by omission' mistake. Here is another example:

> But before I get a sackload of mail from campervanners and
> other oppressed minority leisure groups, I have travelled in the
> campervan and, yes, we will carry a feature on the trip to Belgium
> early next year.

If one were to take this at its face value, the writer is saying 'Before I get a sackload of mail I have travelled in the campervan' which makes nonsense. There is clearly something not said which the writer meant to be understood. He meant: 'Before I get a sackload of mail from campervanners and other oppressed minority leisure groups, let me say yes, I have travelled in the campervan.' The words 'let me say', or some equivalent, are crucial if the statement is to make sense on paper. In conversation intonation and gesture might enable the speaker to take shortcuts of this kind which cannot be risked in print.

And here, a sports writer is warning us about the immensity of the task facing the English cricket team in a forthcoming series of matches against Sri Lanka:

> To underline the enormity of the task, Australia lost a three-match
> series in Sri Lanka last year.

It is simply not true that Australia lost the series in order to underline the immensity of the task now faced by the English cricketers. No team would go about losing matches in order to make such a point. Yet that is what happened according to the writer. The truth is that the words 'to underline the task' do not attach properly to anything said in the sentence. They attach to something that is not said, for there is a crucial point that the writer has left out. What he really means is: 'To underline the enormity of the task, let me tell you that Australia lost a three-match series in Sri Lanka last year.' Those words ('let me tell you') or their equivalent are essential if the statement is to make sense. It is not satisfactory on paper to leave that omitted point to be just understood.

Other Gaps Left by Writers

We keep having to repeat that writers ought not to leave work for the reader to do that they should have done themselves. Yet one can find gaps left for the reader to fill not only in the daily press but in books by academic writers with high literary qualifications. I cite a specimen from a book on Wordsworth:

> Yet Carter and Barbauld were typical of Wordsworth's earliest
> influences in another way: they were women . . .

The words 'Wordsworth's influences' would generally mean just what they say, the influences exercised by Wordsworth. The untutored may be forgiven for thus using the word 'influences' as the equivalent of 'people who exercised influence upon' and it is acceptable to say loosely in the lecture room 'Barbauld was another influence'. But to put on paper a reference to 'Wordsworth's earliest influences' when one really means 'the writers who influenced Wordsworth in his early days' does not mark the writer as a person of literary sensitivity.

It is very often the case that the errors of omission we are dealing with in this section are so readily corrected by the mind of the reader that it may seem over-pedantic to point them out, but this is a book about clear thinking, and the clear thinker leaves nothing to chance.

> I knew where I'd be heading. To the home of Cheddar, the most famous cheese in the world. Cheddar Gorge is the biggest in Britain and renowned for being an area of natural beauty . . .

We cannot fail to take in the point that Cheddar Gorge is the biggest 'gorge' in Britain, but the writer doesn't say that. The point is made clear only by what follows, namely that the place is 'renowned for being an area of natural beauty'. The subject of cheese is at issue in the previous sentence, and a reader unacquainted with the world of cheese may wonder for a brief moment whether there is a cheese called 'Cheddar Gorge'. If there is, we seem to be learning that it's the biggest cheese in Britain.

Comparably easy for the reader to fill in is the omission from the following:

> Last September we asked you whether you had ever been the victim of the following seven sex crimes: attempted rape, rape, child abuse, stalking . . .

The first quick reading of the opening here suggests that victims of horrendous multiple assaults are being asked to come forward. But from what follows in the article it is clear that victims of all seven crimes are not being sought for. Why should it be left to the reader to examine the context as a whole and then to insert the words 'any of' before the words 'the following seven sex crimes'? That is the writer's job.

Gaps left by writers are not always so easily filled in by the reader as that.

> A friend has just come back from rafting in Ecuador, while family conversation at Christmas included an acquaintance who frequently travels in Nepal for trekking. Neither are explorers but common or garden people . . .

Surely a sentence beginning 'Conversation included' might be expected to continue along such lines as 'discussion of the future of the House of Lords'. And indeed it is only when we get to the sentence 'Neither are explorers' that we fully realize that the 'acquaintance' took part in the conversation and was not the subject of it. The word 'included' should go: 'A friend has just come back from rafting in Ecuador and at Christmas an acquaintance who frequently travels in Nepal for trekking took part in family conversation.'

It is perhaps worth adding at this point that of all omissions made in the interests of economy, the omissions of the short words which good English so much depends on is to be regretted. The freedoms taken in conversation in this respect should not be taken on paper. And anyway some of the freedoms taken in conversation are offensive to the logical mind. Take the following:

> When the couple moved into the Gosforth house, 'it was in a complete state of disrepair', recalls Carolyn, 'livable but grim.'

No house can be said to be 'livable'. We do not 'live' houses; we live 'in' them. Yet the habit of taking such illogical liberties seems to be spreading.

> The issue of accommodation is worth giving careful thought.

As the sentence stands, omitting the final word 'to' ('worth giving careful thought to') is to reduce sense to nonsense. Ironically enough, if the word 'giving' had been omitted, all would have been well: 'The issue of accommodation is worth careful thought.' The habit of making that kind of economy in utterance seems to be spreading. A radio commentator complains that a football match took place on 'a pitch verging on the unplayable'. No one attends a match in order to play a pitch. Logic requires a pitch to be 'playable on' or perhaps 'unplayable on'.

Jamming Words Together

A slightly different brand of uncomfortable compression is the rather crude new habit of jamming nouns together in a kind of verbal hotchpotch.

> However, any proposal to put the fiercely competing Mail and Express titles under common ownership would lead to immediate competition concerns.

We know that a 'concern' may be 'grave' or 'trivial', but what kind of concern is a 'competition concern'? It is not more logical to turn a 'concern over competition' (or possible lack of it) into a 'competition concern' than to turn 'concern over grandfather' into a 'grandfather concern'. And it is not more logical to turn 'immediate concern over competition' into 'immediate competition concern' than it would be to turn 'concern for a dying grandfather' into 'dying grandfather concern'. Yet the saving in words by the elaborate evasion of simplicity is minimal. The words 'would lead to immediate competition concerns' can become 'would lead at once to concerns over competition'.

A more serious question of meaning seems to lie behind this announcement on the radio:

> Lawyers acting for General Pinochet appealed against an order for his house arrest.

We are here looking at a coupling which popular usage is rendering seemingly respectable, yet the word 'house' is jammed against the word 'arrest' with surely less rational justification than there was for jamming the word 'competition' against the word 'concerns'. What was ordered in this case was not an arrest at all, but a confinement. Nobody was being 'arrested'. Somebody was being 'confined' and it was not a house but a human being. 'An order confining the General to his home' is what is at issue and there is no reason for not putting it like that.

Yet increasingly we come across attempts at this brand of compression which defeat their own objective by sacrificing clarity.

> The modern forestry, saw-milling and wood-processing industry
> has a good story to tell. It makes an important contribution to
> the economy by providing rural employment and contributes to
> the balance of payments by import substitution.

By no degree of elasticity in the logic of utterance can 'import substitution' be treated as a satisfactory combination of terms. What the writer means, presumably, is that the products of the home forestry industry reduce the need for the import of wood from abroad. That point should be made directly. The roundabout notion that the home products are 'substituted' for might-have-been imports is really rather a cumbersome superfluity than a clarification of what happens.

Yet the lure of supposed compression leads to such awkwardnesses. The following is taken from an article on the NHS, recommending the so-called American 'magnet' hospitals as a new model for the UK:

> But they also achieve better patient outcomes by giving nurses
> the lead.

It is a pity that the medical profession has allowed the development of this kind of usage in which the word 'patient' is taken into new compounds, since the word has its own meaning as an adjective. Talk of achieving better patient outcomes as a way of saying that patients will be better treated introduces a mindset that the world of healing would be better without.

We may cite an even more tangled attempt at this technique of jamming nouns indigestibly together in a comment on developments in nursing:

> This provides an indication of some of the trends in nursing
> innovation and changes that have been taking place, for example
> skill mix changes and staff development, and identifies gaps in
> developments.

If individual nurses are being encouraged to turn their hands to a variety of different medical activities, well and good, but there is surely no such logical entity as a 'skill mix change'.

There is a further kind of uncomfortable verbal combination that leaves readers scratching their heads about what is actually meant. I quote a letter to the press on the subject of the increasing traffic congestion on our roads. Action is needed, the writer insists, and then adds:

> Punitive penalties will only exacerbate the problem and do not tackle key issues. The reality is that our population habits are changing.

The last sentence has that kind of vagueness in its meaning which is always to be avoided in controversy. 'Our population habits are changing.' What does that mean? The word 'habits' generally refers to the conduct of living beings. But our method of populating the planet remains essentially what it always was. There can be no 'change' in that. If I were to ask one of my friends what his 'population habits' are, what topic would he take up? I do not even know what my own 'population habits' are, let alone to what extent they are or may be 'changing'.

Questionable Couplings

We have broached the subject of verbal couplings. The fashion for such partnerships extends far beyond the practice we have just looked at, of jamming two nouns together. Wherever we turn in the world of publicity we find words run together in couples with sometimes little regard to the total effect the combinations are making. There is an epidemic of verbal promiscuity that challenges traditional constraints on the marrying of terms. And the promiscuity does not end with couplings. There are multiple linkages in orgies of verbal congress.

One must not be too pedantic about this. There are unorthodox couplings with a light-hearted flavour, like the compound 'mountain consumers', used of enthusiastic climbers. Such innovations, thrown off to lighten the tone of a passage, are acceptable enough. The English language has always allowed for imaginative couplings of that kind. A new venture in catering specifically for women in the business world is described as 'an eye-opener, a paradigm shifter'. One cannot praise the elegance of the phrasing but the two compounds blend the long-established with the comparatively recent in the manufacture of compounds. Yet sometimes novel couplings seem merely to reveal misdirected ingenuity. When 'multi-tasking flexibility' is recommended to a certain profession, do the words mean more than the word 'versatility'?

Redundant Couplings

There is a category of couplings that seems to serve little purpose in that what they convey is, or ought to be, self-evident. Consider the following sentence about a railway:

> First Great Western's HST fleet is now benefiting from a purpose-built train wash at St Philip's Marsh depot in Bristol.

We must now expect combinations such as 'train wash'. Since the word 'laundry' is so firmly associated with the washing of clothes that the words 'train laundry' would seem comically wrong, the use of 'wash' as a noun, more or less meaning 'laundry', has to be accepted. But surely it ought almost always to be unnecessary to describe something as 'purpose-built'. If a thing is not so built, not built to serve the purpose in building it, what is the point of the exercise? Yet I find this advertisement in a magazine for walkers and climbers:

> Eagle axe with Spring leash sets a new benchmark in mountain axe technology. It is the ultimate purpose-designed axe combination for the dedicated winter walker and incorporates several unique innovations.

Again the words 'purpose-designed' are used as though it were not every day that you could lay your hands on a product that was designed to serve the purpose it was intended for. We have elsewhere criticized the appearance of the word 'functional' when used as though serving its function were a noteworthy aspect of a product. And we seem to be in the same world of designer redundancies in the following sentence:

Even traditional goal-orientated workshops which train executives of both sexes are beginning to include such components as yoga and 'soul training'.

Surely the compound 'goal-orientated' belongs to the same category of otiose expressions. A goal is, *ipso verbo*, something to be aimed at. Therefore 'goal-orientated' means 'aimed at what has to be aimed at'. And no workshop would be of any use if its activities were not aimed at what has to be aimed at.

While we are concerned with redundancy, the following piece is worth attention:

> The sale is part of a strategy to shift the operational emphasis of the group, which is controlled by the Weston family, towards cash-generative business with sustainable growth potential.

The outsider's view of the commercial world could scarcely entertain the notion of a business that was not 'cash-generative'. Since the aim of business is to make money, all businesses that are not failing will be 'cash-generative'. Talk of shifting the operational emphasis of a group towards cash-generative business is surely just a roundabout (and rather unbusinesslike) way of saying that the move is towards making the business profitable. In short, what the sentences means is 'The sale is part of a move to make the business profitable'. Whether the words 'with sustainable growth potential' add much to the meaning is doubtful. A profitable business will presumably have that potentiality. Incidentally, the words 'sustainable' and 'potential', like the words 'strategy' and 'operational', derive from the all-purpose Thesaurus of Current Verbiage.

Other Awkward Couplings

One comes across verbal couplings that raise questions of meaning rather than of possible redundancy. The literalist might regard the following as dangerously close to the ambiguous:

> He replaces June Crown, the public health doctor who has been a
> staunch advocate for nurse-prescribing in reports on the issue
> commissioned by the government.

'Nurse-prescribing' is an unhappy verbal compound. Well established
compounds of that kind have a common pattern. 'Name-calling' is
the calling of names. 'Sock-darning' is the darning of socks. 'Wood-
chopping' is the chopping of wood. On that basis 'nurse-prescribing'
would be the process of prescribing a nurse for a patient. It may well
be that there are patients who would be only too happy to have a
nurse prescribed for them instead of another dose of antibiotics, but
the usage is not verbally defensible.

The fashionable use of the word 'self' in new couplings seems
sometimes to outreach the scope of logic. We have long had compounds such as 'self-service', 'self-examination', 'self-assessment', 'self-
consciousness' and so on. But here is a comment on do-it-yourself
house-building which surely breaks new ground:

> With the drama of self-building, it is easy to overlook the cost of
> furnishing . . .

Couplings like 'self-development' refer to the development of the self.
On that basis 'self-building' ought to mean something similar, that
is, building the self. Designing and building your own house belongs
to a different category of activity. However, there are now further
developments in verbal couplings involving the word 'self', as is
illustrated in the following sentence:

> A while ago, a friend of mine self-medicated by taking a combi-
> nation of St John's Wort, zinc and echinacea – on top of her usual
> liquid iron supplement.

It is the compound verb 'self-medicated' that raises questions. We have
not tried to turn compounds such as 'self-service' and 'self-expression'
into verbs. You do not say 'I self-served at the motorway service station'
or 'She self-expressed in a new outfit'. There is no gain at all in saying
someone 'self-medicated' instead of 'treated herself' or 'prescribed
for herself'.

It is clear that the fashion for inventing new couplings is now flourishing, and it can produce very uncomfortable combinations.

> From puppyhood we teach the dogs to make assumptions and how to generalize because dogs are context-specific and get confused when they have to do the same thing in a different place.

Although it is clear what the writer is getting at, the compound 'context-specific' is neither elegant nor precise. Used of dogs, it would seem to suggest that there are limitations on where they can exist. Wherever compounds of this kind are made, the adjectival element (in this case 'specific') should be strictly applicable to the subject it applies to. The popular compound 'customer-friendly' describes something which is 'friendly' to the customer. But dogs are not specific to any particular context. They can exist happily in the home and happily on a country walk. It would have been better to say that the 'responses' or 'reactions' of dogs are 'context-specific', but better still to drop the word 'specific' and say that dogs are 'context-sensitive'. The use of the words 'same thing' is also imprecise. The writer means that dogs get confused 'when they are required to repeat a familiar routine in an unfamiliar situation'.

It is obvious that in some contexts new couplings can be economical, but sometimes the very reverse is the case, and what is said gains nothing from experiments in coupling.

> Systems authorities have been established to look at issues such as the wheel-rail interface where it is vital the train operators and the infrastructure owner work together.

The word 'interface' is now a popular toy in the hands of word-spinners, but the above sentence seems to wrap up a very simple and obvious matter in inflated vocabulary. That the wheels of trains must run smoothly on the railway lines is surely a fact that must have been established long ago. The layman is apt to suspect that there might not be an awful lot that is new to be said on the topic. But to define this crucial mechanical locus where the wheel meets the track as a spot where train operators and the infrastructure owners must work together sounds like a comically ironic way of proposing to get rid of them all. There is always a danger that novelty in the manufacture of verbal compounds will seem comic. Innovation surely goes too far in the following sentence from the racing world:

> A very smart two-year-old bred by Robert Sangster (Swettenham Stud) and trained by Peter Chapple-Hyam at Manton, Woodborough won the Anglesey Stakes and was group-one-placed three times, including runner-up in the Middle Park Stakes . . .

Here we see a well-established threefold compound ('two-year-old') and an experiment with a new one ('group-one-placed'). One may argue that the relationship between 'group one' and 'placed' ('placed in group one') is no different from the relationship between 'thunder' and 'struck' in 'thunderstruck' ('struck by thunder'), but there is no gain in economy and a great loss in smoothness from not writing 'placed in group one'.

Telescoped Expressions

Another brand of illogicality produced by thoughtless compression is represented by this broadcast statement made at the time of the 2001 outbreak of foot-and-mouth disease. It brings to light a truly regrettable verbal habit.

> Many restricted areas are still in place.

Just as, in sentences quoted right at the beginning of this chapter, it was not really a woman's identity that was banned and not really television fame that appeared on *The Frost Report*, so in this case it was not areas, whether restricted or not, that could be appropriately described as 'still in place'. The local stability of the areas was not brought into question by the outbreaks. The only things that could appropriately be said to be in place were the 'restrictions', and unfortunately these are not mentioned. This is a curious brand of illogicality, by which the mind assumes that because the descriptive word 'restricted' has been used, therefore one can proceed as though the word 'restriction' has been used. The sentence should read: 'In many areas restrictions are still in place.'

Talk of 'restricted areas' seems to lead writers astray. Liberties are taken with the reader's understanding on a startling scale. Here is a comparably unsatisfactory usage from a Himalayan source:

> Trekkers and climbers should feel perfectly safe in the region next year, as long as they are far away from the Seachan Glacier, and other obviously restricted areas such as those in force in parts of the Nanda Devi area.

Here the reader is required to do the work the writer ought to have done, to work out the real, intended meaning from a seeming confusion. 'Areas' whether restricted or not, cannot be said to be 'in force'. It is restrictions that are in force, not 'areas'. If the words 'such as those in force' are kept, then the word 'restrictions' must somewhere precede them to make sense of them. In fact the words are not needed if the words 'in force' are omitted: 'and other obviously restricted areas such as those in parts of the Nanda Devi area'.

This practice of leaving the reader to do the work is evident on a similar scale in the now increasingly common practice of making such statements as the following:

> Police were alerted to the missing climbers when a member of the public reported an abandoned car in Glen Doll car park on Sunday night.

What police were really 'alerted to' was the fact that the climbers were missing. And 'the fact that the climbers were missing' is not an equivalent of 'the missing climbers'. We can see the difference clearly between 'The police discovered the missing climbers' and 'The police discovered that the climbers were missing'. What is interesting here is that the error is repeated in a milder form later in the sentence. What the member of the public really reported was the fact that a car had been abandoned in Glen Doll car park. And 'the fact that a car was abandoned' is not an equivalent of 'an abandoned car'. The sentence should read: 'Police learned that the climbers were missing when a member of the public reported that a car had been abandoned in Glen Doll car park.'

Advertisers are frequent offenders in a similar kind of laxity.

> The pre-publication sale price is £15 . . . After publication the price
> will rise to £18, so your early order is encouraged.

The writer wants to encourage people to order early, and really the
uttering of such a suggestion ought not to strain the mind's capacity
for preserving logical sequence. It is 'earliness' that is at issue and is
primarily being encouraged. In itself the act of ordering is encouraged
under that priority. Nothing at all is gained, but a good deal of
common sense is sacrificed by not writing quite simply 'so you are
encouraged to order early'.

9

Sense and Nonsense

In general this book can be said to be concerned throughout with the difference between sense and nonsense. However, it is only notable degrees of failure to be logical and coherent that usually bring the word 'nonsense' into play. How easy is it to deviate into such writing? What are the practices which can trip us up in this respect? After all, some of the most glaring lapses are revealed when a seemingly rational statement will not stand up to exact probing of its literal meaning. It is worthwhile to look at certain areas of usage and habits of usage which are likely to undermine our best intentions to avoid making statements of that kind.

Negatives

One danger area is that of expressing negatives. Use of the word 'all' can easily lead to trouble in this respect. Here is a public notice dating from the early days of the foot-and-mouth epidemic in Cumbria:

> It is currently an offence to use all footpaths and bridleways across farmlands, including the fells, in Cumbria.

The logical mind wants to accept that a ban on using 'all' footpaths means what it says. That is, you must not go about using 'all' the footpaths. Indeed an offender found on one of the footpaths might logically protest, 'But I haven't used *all* the footpaths and bridleways in Cumbria. I've only used this one.' Obviously what was really intended by the notice was a ban on using 'any' of the footpaths. That should have been made clear: 'It is currently an offence to use any of the footpaths and bridleways across farmlands, including the fells, in Cumbria.' The pedant may wish to add that, strictly speaking, farmlands do not 'include' all the fells. Since the writer of the notice wanted to make clear that the areas to which the ban applied 'included' the fells, the notice should have ended 'across farmlands. This applies to the fells too'.

One should mention in parenthesis here that the word 'all' may be subject to the same mistreatment in a positive as in a negative statement.

> Linoleum is a sheet product made from all natural ingredients.

Plainly this will not do, for not all natural ingredients are present in linoleum. The word 'all' should be replaced by the word 'only'.

There are negations of other kinds than those using the word 'all', which can be thoughtlessly thrown out at the beginning of an argument only to be nullified by what follows. Here is a letter to the press:

> I disagree with the assertions of Ms McCormack that respect should be shown to those who earn it. Every human being, irrespective of behaviour or social class, deserves respect merely by dint of their intrinsic human dignity.

There is a total breakdown of logic here. If the writer believes that every human being deserves respect, then he cannot disagree with the correspondent who said that respect should be shown to those who earn it, because they too are human beings. The way to rescue the sequence from illogicality is to insert the word 'only' in the first sentence: 'I disagree with the assertions of Ms McCormack that respect should be shown only to those who earn it.' Without that word the statement is indeed nonsensical.

Where a point is made using the words 'neither . . . nor' it is tempting sometimes to combine two notions in an illogical relationship.

> For all the talk about valuing staff, and the money and investment in management courses to get senior managers to see the importance of the contribution of the individual in the organization, it would seem much of this has been neither heard nor heeded.

We are concerned here only with the end of the statement. The piece is concerned to reflect rationally on developments in the business world. It regrets the seemingly slight pay-off from all the talk about administrative attitudes. All that is fine. But then we are told that the good advice has been 'neither heard nor heeded'. If a message has not been 'heard', it cannot possibly be 'heeded'. You cannot take any notice at all of a message which has not been communicated to you. Ironically enough, reversing the order in the last clause might rescue it: 'it would seem much of this has been neither heeded nor even heard'.

Especial care must be taken when linking a negative point to a positive point using the word 'and'.

> Greek media reports have suggested that the trial of the 17th November group would not start until spring 2004 and last many weeks, as mountains of evidence and testimony were sifted through.

If you say 'I shall not come next week and sing at your concert', the word 'not' applies equally to the words 'come' and 'sing'. You could not possibly mean that you will not 'come' to the concert but will readily 'sing' at it. Yet the sentence above makes that kind of assertion. The 'trial would not start ... and last many weeks' should become 'the trial would not start until spring 2004 and would last many weeks'. Thus the negative 'would not start' is cancelled out in the positive 'and would last'.

This kind of illogical follow-up after a straightforward negative can sometimes assume a complex character. Here we turn to a grave leading article printed at the time when people were questioning how far Tony Blair would commit himself in support of President Bush's campaign against Iraq. The article was urging the Prime Minister to be fully supportive:

> He [Tony Blair] has not shirked in the past from confronting awkward international situations, not least in Kosovo three years ago when at times he appeared to be dragging along a reluctant Bill Clinton.

In the first place, although the verb to 'shirk' can be used intransitively

('He is shirking'), its regular transitive form would work here ('... he has not shirked confronting awkward situations'). More immediately relevant at this point, however, is the extraordinary double negative. You would not say 'She has not neglected her shopping, not least in Marks and Spencers', though you might say 'especially in Marks and Spencers'. The logic requires positive specification of what he or she did not shirk or neglect. 'He has not in the past shirked confronting awkward international situations, as was evident in Kosovo three years ago ...'

Another leading article made a comparison between a Nuclear Disarmament demo during the 1980s and the Countryside Alliance march in 2002, pointing out that as Mrs Thatcher ignored the first, perhaps Mr Blair could afford to ignore the second. And the leader went on:

> This is a superficially appealing argument but the comparison is not exact for both practical and political reasons.

We do not use the construction 'both ... and' thus after a negative. Very often the construction 'either ... or' can replace it, but here it would have been better to get rid of the negative: 'the comparison is inexact for both practical and political reasons'.

Familiar Expressions Misused

A lapse into nonsense can occur because one of those familiar phrases that come all too readily to mind is carelessly used where it is totally inappropriate. Sometimes a familiar expression that we tend to fall back upon is inserted into the text in such a way that it subverts the intended meaning, even by contradiction. Here a journalist is dealing with the plight of American-Somalis who emigrated to the US with their families as babies or young teenagers and have been forcibly sent back to Somalia. Some of them are trying to make their way back to the USA.

> But even if they survive the journey, they have no money nor papers to prove their existence.

'To prove their existence' is a phrase that comes readily to mind. But of course no official is going to require these asylum-seekers to 'prove their existence'. The immigration officials are only too fully aware of 'their existence'. It is ironic that what is wanted here is a word overused in contexts where it is really inappropriate: 'they have no money nor papers to prove their identity'.

Care is needed in handling such expressions as 'at the least' and 'at the most', 'at the best' and 'at the worst'. It is not all that unusual to find phrases of that pattern used in a way opposite to what is intended. I quote a reissue of a press article dating from 1930 when Lord Beaverbrook was trying to lure Conservative Members of Parliament to join his new Empire Party:

> But that the Conservative Party should be seriously weakened by desertions is considered in the highest degree unlikely. It is not a party which splits easily at the best of times.

Surely 'at the best of times' really means 'at the worst of times'. At the 'best' of times for the party it would not split at all. It could conceivably split only at a bad time for the party. The case must be that it would not split 'easily' even with things at their worst.

Expressions like 'at the best of times' flow through our minds so smoothly that the brain falls half asleep, but such familiar phrases have to be dead right in their context. Here is the beginning of a letter to the press in a controversy about tennis and the way it is supported in the UK:

> Tennis authorities should stand up and be counted for much of the criticism they receive.

The expression to 'stand up and be counted' is generally used in a context where some issue is at stake and those who have a strong view on the one side or the other are not making themselves heard, so that their case is likely to go by default. The words are a call to people who have a strong view to make themselves known. But in the sentence above the expression is not a call to worthy people to be bold about their beliefs, but a call to people under judgement to acknowledge their failings.

And here we have a travel writer taking us to some of the delights of Vienna:

> Spanning the river is Henri IV Bridge which, with its nine arches
> and a length of 144m gives you some idea of its size.

The useful expression 'gives you some idea of' enables us to impress someone with the dimensions or beauty of what we are recommending. But the writer here has used the construction in a topsy-turvy manner. To begin with, the dimensions presented give an exact account (not 'some idea') of the size of the bridge. And it is these dimensions, not the 'Henri IV Bridge', that convey the idea of its size. You would not say, 'My brother John, with his size eleven boots, gives you some idea of his size'. We cannot allow the notion to survive that idioms such as 'gives you some idea of' have a kind of independent existence as verbal counters that can be brought into use whenever one wants to impress a reader with some description.

Sometimes a common expression is misused simply because it is misunderstood. When Ken Livingstone announced plans to charge motorists for entry into central London, a voice on the air said:

> Mr Livingstone's proposal is falling foul of criticism from
> motorists.

To 'fall foul of' is to quarrel with someone. The expression is derived from the entangling ('fouling') of their respective ropes which occurs when two ships get too close together. Mr Livingstone's proposal no doubt 'fell foul' of various motoring lobbies, but the word 'criticism' does not make sense here.

As a last example of a familiar expression misused we take the following comment about developments in the food retail business:

> Distribution systems have become more centralized, with food
> travelling even further in pursuit of efficiency.

Huntsmen chase across the countryside in pursuit of a fox and a man may work himself to the bone in pursuit of promotion, but food cannot pursue efficiency, however far it travels. To make sense of the familiar expression the writer must place the motive of pursuit elsewhere: 'food being transported even further in pursuit of efficiency'.

Misplaced Phrases

If we clearly sort out our intentions before we begin to speak or to write, we shall not get our words or phrases into such a tangle that our meaning is not obvious. Yet the misplacing of a phrase is one of the commonest ways of introducing a nonsensical element into a text. At its worst, ill-placing of a word or a phrase can cause ambiguity and indeed unintended humour. Consider the following in the obituary notice of a much-mourned husband:

> Died peacefully on 17th September in the home where he was born with his wife by his side.

The sentence makes it sound as though the deceased had been born in the presence of his wife. Had a comma been placed after the word 'born' all ambiguity would have gone, but it would be better to reposition the words 'with his wife at his side': 'Died peacefully on 17th September, with his wife at his side and in the house where he was born.'

There are times when one lights upon a sentence which contains no structural error of that kind but which presents its material in such a way that the reader becomes aware of a great incongruity. The following is from an entry in a reference book:

> On 9 December 1980 John Lennon was shot dead outside his New York apartment leaving an enormous fortune.

There is something bathetic about this sequence. Is it just that the reader does not want his mind moved so brusquely from the tragic fact of the corpse on the pavement to the matter of financial abundance? It seems to me that an appropriate change in tone would be effected by ending the sentence after the word 'apartment', and adding 'He left an enormous fortune'.

There is of course no problem of actual meaning there, but the same kind of phrase, tacking an additional item of information on to the main statement, can mislead if ill-positioned. Here is a sentence about diminutive crocodilian animals:

> They burrow in territory adjacent to agricultural land and take
> small livestock, such as ducks, making them unpopular with
> farmers.

Here the word 'making' introduces just such a postscript, but unfortunately it is so placed that the sentence reads as though the creatures make ducks unpopular with farmers. The simplest way of improving the sentence would be to change 'them' to 'themselves'.

From that we turn to another sentence from the farming world, in a letter critical of the EU's Common Agricultural Policy:

> But with the UK now in the EU, Britain's £5bn CAP contribution
> still has to be paid. The government can allow cheap food imports
> in, but that would lead to UK farmers being paid not to produce
> food in the form of set-aside payments instead of area payments
> for what they did produce.

This reads as though farmers are being discouraged from producing food in the form of set-aside payments. It is the words 'in the form of' that do the damage. Change to: '. . . that would lead to UK farmers being given set-aside payments for not producing food instead of area payments for what they did produce'.

A leading article gives us another such misplacement:

> The Home Secretary concentrated not on punishment but on
> pre-emptive action to prevent young people getting caught on
> what he has called 'the conveyor belt of crime' and rehabilitation
> for those who have slipped through the net in order to reduce
> reoffending.

The misplacement of the last five words suggests that young people have 'slipped through the net in order to reduce reoffending'. (A comma after 'net' would have left less room for misreading.) Another leading article, however, gives us a more taxingly questionable misplacement:

> In a new publication from the Centre for Policy Studies, Robert
> Darwell, former adviser to Norman Lamont, argues that the Conservative Party has suffered from its failure to have a proper
> intellectual debate about the causes of its two recent election

defeats. He is quite right, something that the law of averages suggests had to happen at some point in his otherwise pointless pamphlet.

It is the second sentence that bemuses the reader. Superficial reading suggests that something suggested by the law of averages had to happen somewhere in this man's otherwise pointless pamphlet. One must assume that the words 'in his otherwise pointless pamphlet' do not stand where they should.

It is sad to see that carelessness over word order invading literature put out by an Oxford college, but here is part of an appeal circulated by one:

> Christ Church is, of course, a registered charity and it may there-
> fore be helpful to inform Old Members about some of the new
> opportunities for UK taxpayers wanting to give to the House
> brought about by these changes.

Again, after reflection, there is no confusion in the meaning here, but the gap is awkward between the word 'opportunities' and the descriptive qualification 'brought about by these changes'. This is one of those cases where the reader, instead of instantly registering what has been said, has to go behind the text for a moment and sort out what the writer was conveying. There would have been no cause for such reflection had the piece read: 'and it may be helpful for Old Members who want to donate money to the House to be informed of some of the new opportunities for UK taxpayers brought about by these changes'.

Finally, let us examine a statement unlikely to confuse readers, yet both awkward and gravely at fault through misplacement of a phrase:

> My husband, Frederick Moore, RAF, was one of the 1650 British
> POWs slaughtered by their Japanese captors between January and
> August 1945. This atrocity has never been recognized, as in Borneo
> no prisoner survived on the direct order of the Emperor.

In saying 'This atrocity has never been recognized' the writer really means 'This slaughter has never been officially recognized as an atrocity'. The rest of the sentence raises a relevant point of word order.

There is a great difference in meaning between 'Nothing was done to appease the tyrant' and 'To appease the tyrant, nothing was done'. The meaning of the one statement is totally irreconcilable with the meaning of the other. The problem here is that to say 'No prisoner survived on the direct order of the Emperor' might mean that there was no prisoner who survived as a result of a request from the Emperor, which would yet allow for the fact that many prisoners survived without any such request being made. A simple change in word order would get rid of this ambiguity: 'as on the direct order of the Emperor no prisoner survived in Borneo'.

Misplaced Clauses

It is misplaced explanatory clauses, those beginning with 'who' or 'which', that are most likely to produce confusion. They can make the meaning of sentences difficult to unravel. The thoughtful writer will not put the reader into the position of coming across the word 'who' and not knowing what person it refers to, or coming across the word 'which' and not knowing what it refers to. This applies even when a moment's backward research in the passage read makes the matter clear.

> The wealthy widow of an American financier who moved to England last month has married a drug-using sadistic, womanizing alcoholic according to psychiatric reports presented to a court at which he was appearing.

The reader first receives the words 'an American financier who moved to England last month' and then recalls that the financier's wife was a widow, and that it must have been she who crossed the Atlantic. A couple of commas, placed before and after 'who moved to England last month' would have helped a bit, in that the word 'who' would not then so closely follow the word 'financier'. In fact, however, the sentence is a characteristic specimen of the fatal penchant for not telling a story in the simplest possible way, that is, by recounting events in chronological order without recourse to any relative clause. Take out 'who' and insert 'and': 'The wealthy widow of an American financier moved to England last month and has married a drug-using sadistic, womanizing alcoholic . . .'

Readers ought never to have to rack their brains when they come across the word 'who' or the word 'which'. Yet it is not unusual to find specimens of such problematical cases where an uncomfortably placed relative clause mars the flow, and where it would be better to get rid of the construction involving 'which' or 'who'.

> She also treasures two 19th-century Meissen kittens in a basket
> of posies that she spotted in a Brussels antique shop 10 years ago
> which is now worth around £300.

Although no one is likely to make the mistake of thinking that the Brussels antique shop is now worth £300, the sentence ends awkwardly. That is because the writer was not content with one relative clause ('that she spotted in a Brussels antique shop 10 years ago') but added a second ('which is now worth around £300'), and placed it so that at first sight it seems to hang on the word 'shop'. The word 'which' should be taken out and the last point made in a separate sentence: 'It is now worth around £300.'

Even when there is no serious risk of confusion, an ill-placed clause beginning with 'which' or 'who' can be drawn into an improper, even comic, connection with the wrong word.

> Many of the paintings in the house were bought by Laura's mother,
> one of which hangs above the fireplace in the dining room.

Here the clause beginning with 'one of which' requires to be closely attached to the word to which it applies, in this case the word 'paintings'. Instead of which, it is confusingly cheek by jowl with the words 'Laura's mother'. Although the context prevents any misunderstanding, the reader is jolted by the misplacement into having to think twice about what is being said. This is one more of those carelessnesses which compel the reader to do work that the writer should have done. In this case the use of 'which' was unnecessary: 'Many of the paintings in the house were bought by Laura's mother, and one of them hangs above the fireplace in the dining room.'

The writer should avoid 'theoretical' ambiguities of this kind, that is, ambiguities which cannot seriously confuse the reader because common sense guides to the right interpretation, but which it would be easy to make fun of by pressing a seemingly equally valid interpretation. Some instructions from the DHSS can be used to illustrate the point:

> Your money will be paid into the account you told us about on the last working day in each week, 4-weekly period or 13-weekly period.

The words 'you told us about' are unhappily followed by 'on the last working day in each week' as though that were the occasion on which the information were conveyed. Why not 'Your money will be paid into your chosen account on the last working day in each week'?

Direct Breakdowns in Sequence

We are here largely concerned with an error that is called a 'non sequitur', that is, a failure in logical sequence. Throughout this book a persistent theme has been that writers must know exactly what they are talking about in a given sentence and must not shift their ground to talk about something else. Let us look at a specimen of the error in its most transparent form:

> The discovery of a skeleton at Stonehenge dates from AD 650.

This announcement in the newspaper is a case in point. We are told that the 'discovery' dates from AD 650; but it is the skeleton that dates from AD 650, certainly not the discovery. The sentence should read: 'The skeleton discovered at Stonehenge dates from AD 650.' The writer began to talk about a 'discovery' and forgot the fact a few words later. It is surprising how quickly this forgetfulness can operate. We find this in a recommendation for the Tefal Easy Store steamer:

> It starts steaming in just fifteen seconds, can cook a complete meal in one, and with an automatic timer, you just set it to go and it turns itself off when finished.

We have to reread this in order to clear our minds of the obvious first impression that the steamer can cook a complete meal in one second. After all, that is what is clearly stated. The words 'in one', presumably meaning 'all at once', are written in forgetfulness of the preceding mention of 'seconds'.

At their crudest, such failures in connectedness are not difficult to spot.

> Continued scratching, if left untreated, can cause bacterial infection, so it is important that this condition is treated effectively.

This sentence follows after the writer has brought up the subject of itchy rashes. The statement, however, ought to make sense on its own. As it stands we are told what damage continued scratching may do if it is 'left untreated'. No other reading is possible. The writer should have borne in mind exactly what she was talking about, that is to say, the condition of having an itchy rash. Scratching is not something that should be 'treated'; it should be terminated. 'Bacterial infection can be caused by continued scratching, so it is important to treat the condition effectively.'

The pursuit of simplicity and directness is of course the main safeguard against such lapses. But professional writer are not content to produce only simple sequences. The very topics they are treating may forestall such simplicity. Here is a review of a film called *The Lady and the Duke*:

> The skill and beauty of Rohmer's tale about a Scottish gentlewoman stranded in Paris during the Revolution is a sensuous joy and one of the most artful and intelligent films about self-interest that I have seen.

This writer decided seemingly to talk to us about 'the skill and beauty' of a certain tale but within less than a score of words he had forgotten that. 'The skill and beauty . . . is a sensuous joy and one of the most artful films . . .' That is the line his statement takes. But the skill and beauty 'is' neither a joy nor a film. The mistake was that the writer did not begin with what his real subject was, the film. 'This film, based on Rohmer's skilful and beautiful tale about a Scottish gentlewoman stranded in Paris during the Revolution, is a sensuous joy and makes one of the most artful and intelligent films about self-interest that I have ever seen.' That would not be the only possible correction, but it sorts out the meaning obscured in the original.

Reviewing seems to be dangerous terrain in respect of the kind of error we are here investigating. We turn now to the review of a novel, called *Homage*:

> This book is named after a ranch in California, but it might also stand for Rathbone's own homage to Hollywood, and particularly film noir, to evoke atmosphere and mood.

The reviewer starts with a statement about the book. It is named after a ranch in California. But no sooner are the words uttered than the writer forgets what is his subject – the book. For the words 'it might also stand for Rathbone's own homage to Hollywood' seem to be meant to refer to the title of the book and, the character of the English language being what it is, they can't. A further problem arises with the words 'to evoke atmosphere and mood'. To what do they refer? What is it that is designed to evoke atmosphere and mood? Any correction would best take the name of the book, and not the book itself, as the subject. 'The title of this book is the name of a ranch in California, but it might also stand for Rathbone's own homage to Hollywood, and particularly to film noir . . .'

We turn to a slightly more complex change of course, again in the review of a novel:

> In telling the story of Leto, the mother of Artemis and Apollo, and her long journey through the ages, alongside an account of how a mummy displayed in the British Museum becomes the focus for a public seemingly desperate to find a new national symbol, Warner's knowing attempt to raise issues of native identity founders on its own erudition.

Whether the novel does indeed founder on its own erudition I do not know. But this review founders on its own illogicality. A statement about this novel which begins with the words 'In telling the story of Leto' can be followed by only one subject, the name of the writer (or perhaps the title of the book). It was the writer who told the story. But the reviewer thinks that it was her 'knowing attempt to raise issues of native identity' which miraculously told the story. That is what he says, plainly enough. We overlook the seemingly careless sequence 'In telling the story . . . alongside an account', but in English we do not usually 'tell accounts', we 'give' them. Although the sentence could be corrected in its present structure, it would be better to get rid of the opening construction ('In telling'), which causes all the trouble: 'Marina Warner tells the story of Leto, the mother of Artemis and Apollo, and her long journey through the ages, and runs alongside it an account of how a mummy displayed in the British Museum becomes the focus for a public seemingly desperate to find a new national symbol; but her/the author's knowing attempt to raise issues of native identity founders on its own erudition.'

Finally, let us look at what can sometimes happen when the poetic impulse takes over the pen of the journalist. For my example I go to the broadsheet press and to a Christmas piece imbued with the spirit of the season. The writer speaks rapturously of 'the old words and melodies of carols' and how they 'cover the unchanging nature of rebirth and life on Earth'.

> So, in tune with the season of carols, for the next week we shall
> be following some of the dear old traditional songs to see whither
> they lead us into the new century.

It is a pity that the piece should end thus, but the poetic spirit bloweth where it listeth. To begin with, it is not clear how we are to read the word 'follow'. We speak of 'following' a hymn when we hold the book in front of our eyes, but the writer can scarcely intend us to take his words like that, especially since these carols are going to 'lead' us somewhere. And it is because of the route mentioned that I have chosen to follow this piece closely. We are supposed to follow the carols to see 'whither they lead us'. But we apparently know whither they will lead us. Namely 'into the next century'. Not even in poetry can one get away with that kind of sequence: 'I want to know whither this road leads to London.'

More Complex Breakdowns in Sequence

We have found serious breakdowns in logic in reviews of films and novels. We turn now to a piece of artistic criticism:

> Forty years of experience and obsessively hard work have elevated
> Rego's accomplishments from her own modest assessment of
> 'terrible, over the top, *faux naif* things' to paintings described
> today by John Eric-Drax, Director of Marlborough Fine Art, as
> 'absolutely original ... hugely powerful. Her work carries enor-
> mous influence.'

This is like saying 'Forty years of experience have improved John's
driving from his own assessment of "far too fast and furious" to
journeys described today by his mother as "absolutely safe"'. There
is no proper balance between what follows 'from' and what follows
'to'. An 'assessment' of driving capacity does not turn, as time passes,
into actual 'journeys'. Similarly, in the sentence above, the accomplishments must not be described as developing from an 'assessment'
in the early days to 'paintings' later on. The decision should have been
made either to write about the change from one assessment to another
or about the change from one quality of work to another. As it is, the
two are illogically mixed up. Let us attempt to create a proper balance
in the original sentence: 'Forty years of experience and obsessively
hard work have elevated Rego's accomplishments from the "terrible,
over the top, *faux naif* things" she herself modestly judged them to
be, to paintings described today by John Eric-Drax, the Director of
Marlborough Fine Art, as "absolutely original".'

Surveying the lives and achievements of artists seems to lure
writers into that kind of illogicality.

> The exhibition is accompanied by a 58-page publication featuring
> an introduction by Melvyn Bragg, an essay tracing Cooper's devel-
> opment from art school at Goldsmiths in the 1960s to the present
> body of work ...

Cooper did not really 'develop' from an art school to a body of work.
He developed from being a student at Goldsmiths to being an artist
with a substantial body of work to display.

And here is another review from the art world:

> Intriguingly, his mellow landscapes are always framed by thick
> bands of white colour, thus removing the scenes one more notch
> away from reality.

The question arises: Who or what is 'thus removing' the scenes? The sentence proclaims the 'mellow landscapes' as the subject, but these landscapes are surely themselves 'the scenes' painted. So, logically considered, they are removing themselves one more notch away from reality. Now it might well be argued that in fact that is exactly what the writer wanted to say. But what about the word 'thus'? It links back to the verb 'framed', and clearly the writer had in mind that by framing the landscapes as he did, the artist removed them one more notch away from reality. We have one more instance of failure by the writer to decide whether he was going to talk about the artist and what he did or about his pictures. All that was needed to make the sentence logical was to make the artist the subject, and to stick to that. 'Intriguingly he always framed his mellow landscapes by thick bands of white colour, thus removing the scenes one more notch away from reality.'

A review of a film provides another and curious kind of non sequitur:

> Piers Adams is a successful night club owner. He is full of manic energy, common sense and fun – an unusual combination, particularly when you see some of the other characters that inhabit the club scene.

To begin with, there is a straightforward error in the use of the word 'when'. No proper connection is established between the statement that the hero's characteristics represent an 'unusual combination' and what follows. The combination of characteristics cannot be said to become any more or less unusual 'when you see some of the other characters'. It is like saying 'Roast lamb and mint sauce make a fine combination, particularly when you look at the dessert menu'. The fineness of the combination exists irrespectively of your attention to the choice of desserts. Even so, the unusual nature of the hero's blend of characteristics cannot be affected one way or another by the sight of the 'other characters'. What the writer actually meant, presumably, was that the hero's quirky blend of characteristics shows up more notably against the more predictable characters of the other figures.

Switching Constructions

Much of our attention in this section, and indeed in this book as a whole, has had to be given to one of the basic illogicalities in expressing oneself, which consists in switching horses in mid-stream, starting one statement and then finishing another one. If ever the subject of a sentence is not followed up properly by words that relate logically to it, then there is an instance of beginning with one statement and then switching to another one. Here we are going to examine this switching habit. First, let us take a fairly uncomplicated switch. A correspondent is protesting against the unwanted intrusion of a camcorder user into the home.

> It was at the very least misguided and at most extremely impolite
> in not discussing it with the writer beforehand as well as a
> possible breach of home security.

The move from the words 'It was misguided' to the words 'in not discussing' illustrates a straightforward switch in construction. Clearly the insertion of the word 'in' leads the writer astray. You would not say 'It was ungrateful in not saying thank you' but 'It was ungrateful not to say thank you'. So the sentence above should read: 'extremely impolite not to discuss it with the writer beforehand'. But the use of the words 'at the least' and 'at most' raises questions too. The distinction between degrees of error or offensiveness is surely primarily a qualitative one. After all, the most natural use of the 'at the least' and 'at the most' construction is in such usages as 'I should say there were at least five hundred people there, at most seven hundred'. Indeed one feels that the writer really meant 'It was at best misguided and at the worst extremely impolite'.

We turn to a piece from an article in appreciation of an actress who revealed her versatility in performing at the Chichester Festival:

> Few actresses could switch so convincingly between spending
> some nights playing Masha, the repressed lovelorn sister in
> Chekhov's *Three Sisters*, while on others executing a rip-roaring
> turn as Edythe Herbert, the cross-Channel swimming heroine of

Peter Stone and Timothy S. Mayer's zappy musical, *My One and Only*.

There is an English construction basically represented by statements such as 'You must choose between going to the cinema and staying at home'. That is cited as an example to show the parallelism that follows the construction 'between this and that'. In the same way 'between spending some nights playing Masha' needs to be balanced by 'and spending others playing Edythe Herbert' or words to similar effect. But in the sentence above the basic construction is 'You must choose between going to the cinema while staying at home'. For 'between spending some nights' is followed by 'while executing a rip-roaring turn'. In any case, it was a false sequence to move from 'between spending some nights' in a particular way to 'on others executing' this or that. If the originally chosen pattern of the sentence is to be preserved, it must go something like this: 'Few actresses could switch so convincingly from night to night between playing Masha, the lovelorn sister in Chekhov's *Three Sisters* and executing a rip-roaring turn as Edythe Herbert . . .'

Enthusiasm for a cause tempts writers to excess. When the cause is one that touches what is regarded as a way of life, bringing cherished traditions under threat, passion has to be restrained when the pen or the keyboard is seized. Here, a writer protests against a suggestion that the Government may be planning to hold local referendums on the future of fox-hunting:

> Far from letting the Government off the hook or finally resolving the matter, enormous problems for the Government would follow the first sign that a Government bill would be permitted to be used as a vehicle for such a move and anything which did reach the statute book as a result would be largely ineffective and a recipe for a 'running sore' with no final resolution.

When the advertiser who is moved with the desire to fill up space on paper loses control we can all relish it. But one cannot take pleasure in seeing any writer who is moved with emotion for a cause losing control like this. The vagueness of the threat of 'enormous problems' is matched by the vagueness of the concept of trouble arising because of a 'sign' that a Government bill might be used for a certain purpose. There can be no stirrings of the emotions consequent on threats so tenuously phrased. In any case, verbosities such as 'that a Government bill would be permitted to be used as a vehicle for such a move' instead of 'that the Government might legislate' cannot express the kind of passion that seems to flow behind the words. The culminating image of the 'running sore' is ill used, in that running sores are not manufactured according to 'a recipe', and anyway they are not things to be 'resolved' but to be healed. Rewrite thus: 'Far from letting the Government off the hook or finally resolving the controversy, preparing a bill for such referendums would cause great problems and any subsequent legislation would prove both ineffective and a recipe for continuing controversy.'

A Current Bad Practice

A recent development in popular usage has produced a practice which can be said to offend common sense. One of the useful liberties of English usage is the number of verbs which have a kind of dual function. The verb 'to allot' is a case in point. 'The largest portion of the estate was allotted to the eldest son' may be re-phrased as 'The eldest son was allotted the largest portion of the estate'. We perhaps sense a touch of greater idiomatic freedom in the second sentence than in the first. After all, we know that the estate was the thing that was handed over. In the active voice, of course, we can choose to say either 'The trustees allotted the largest portion of the estate to the eldest son' or, more conversationally perhaps, 'The trustees allotted the eldest son the largest portion of the estate'.

There are plenty of verbs which allow of this useful double function. The verbs 'to assign', 'to grant', and of course 'to give' work like 'to allot'. Similarly we 'forgive' or 'pardon' someone his offences, and we say either 'He was forgiven/pardoned' or 'His offences were forgiven/pardoned'.

This freedom has supplied us with some very vivid conversational usages. Someone tells me a long and dubious story and I say 'I was told a tall story', though, strictly speaking, it was the story that 'was told' to me. Someone gets the better of me in selling me something which proves to be unsatisfactory and I say 'I was sold a pup'. The story was 'told' and the item was 'sold' but we choose another way of putting it. The range of usage over which this freedom of choice is exercised seems to be extending, perhaps unwarrantably.

A verb which has already been subject to this development is the verb 'to issue':

> A 35-year-old mother who attacked her nephew when she dis-
> covered he had given her 12-year-old son cannabis has been issued
> with a police warning.

Strictly speaking, of course, it was the police warning that was 'issued', not the mother. A telltale evidence of verbal laxity there is perhaps the use of the word 'with' ('has been issued *with* a police warning'). A decree might be issued 'with a flourish of trumpets'. Indeed a new drug might be 'issued with a health warning', but a woman is surely not likely to be 'issued with a police warning'. Yet this usage is now thoroughly established. In a letter about an experiment to prevent bullying in schools a correspondent writes:

> The children were each issued with a blank piece of paper and
> asked to write down the name of three bullies, underlining the
> worst.

What happened in the school is that blank pieces of paper were issued to the children. It is no doubt too late to resist this usage. We read that members of a society have been 'issued with' new membership cards and firemen have been 'issued with' new uniforms. It is difficult to understand what it is that discourages us from writing 'New membership cards have been issued to members' or 'New uniforms have been issued to firemen'.

In the case of certain verbs this usage is now so widespread that the claim for its acceptability on those grounds can scarcely be questioned. We have long had to regret the now widespread misuse of the verb to 'diagnose' in 'She was diagnosed with shingles' instead of 'Shingles was diagnosed'. In a recent magazine I read:

> I went back to the consultant at the hospital and he diagnosed
> me with Chronic Fatigue Syndrome.

The best way to improve this is simply to omit the two words 'me with'. Here is the place to draw attention to some more novel and, one hopes, more exceptional laxities of this kind. For instance, in an extension of the misuse of 'diagnose', we have already heard the verb 'prescribe' used in such statements as 'She was prescribed a new drug' instead of 'A new drug was prescribed for her' and, on the radio, we have been warned against certain problems that might ensue 'unless you're administered with antibiotics'. Note again the telltale 'with', the word in our language that probably causes more bad writing through its misuse than any other single word. Just as it is the disease that is 'diagnosed' and not the patient, so it is the antibiotics that are 'administered' and not the patient.

It is clear that this questionable construction is being used for more and more verbs. Someone made this announcement about a cancer victim on Radio 4:

> The child will die unless he is donated bone marrow.

It is true that we allow this freedom to the verb 'give' so that 'unless he is given bone marrow' would not offend. Yet it seems perverse to want to speak of the child having to be donated something when what is meant is that something has to be donated to the child. We have not yet, I think, heard 'The church has been donated five thousand pounds for its repair fund'. A recent addition to this kind of misuse involves the verb 'to implant'.

> Two women have had to undergo emergency operations after
> they were implanted with the wrong embryos.

BBC news writers need to be told that it is the embryos that 'were implanted', not the women.

Ever more verbs are being thus misused. My daily paper records that the Royal Society of Chemistry has bestowed the Extraordinary Honorary Fellowship on the statue of Sherlock Holmes. A photograph of the ceremony is captioned 'Holmes and Watson in Baker Street yesterday, where the great detective's statue was bestowed with a medal'. It was, of course, the medal that was 'bestowed' on the statue.

One wonders how long it will be before someone writes 'I have long been delivered with two pints of milk each morning'. After all, we can already find even more horrific instances of the misusage. In the days leading up to the trial of Jeffrey Archer the BBC announcer described how Archer had been taken to a police station, and added:

> He was read five separate charges.

All one can say in reply to this is that it was the charges that were read, not the prisoner. As a specimen of laxity, this is surely on a par with the comment of a person informing the press on the antics of Colombian kidnappers, who demand money in exchange for release of the victim:

> If someone doesn't pay, they get sent the body.

The reader will observe that we have now entered an area of error in this respect in which the offensive word 'with' is jettisoned. It is also an area of error in which seemingly great ingenuity is exercised to make the maximum effect. Could you think of a way of adding the word 'deduct' to the number of verbs misused in this way? There are those working for the BBC who can. This came from a cricket commentator:

> Yorkshire have been deducted 4 points for preparing a poor pitch.

Surely it was the points that were deducted and not the team. If you bought a dress for a bargain price at a sale, you would not say 'I have been deducted ten pounds from the original cost'.

Even so linguistically careful a journal as the *Spectator* managed to disgrace itself on the blurb for *The Spectator Cartoon Book 1999*. It told how the selection of cartoons for the journal had to be winnowed down:

> Every year Michael Heath, the cartoon editor, is submitted over 25,000.

It is surely inexcusable to speak of someone being 'submitted' when one means that items were submitted to him. This seems to have been recognized. The penny must have dropped. The mistake was corrected in the next year's equivalent publication.

10

Reasoning and Explaining

In much of what we say or write we are either arguing a case or explaining a position. That is true not only when we are engaged in business but even in the daily domestic chatter. 'I think we've just got to replace that car, for it's costing a fortune in minor repairs' you say, or 'The more I try to teach him good manners, the ruder he seems to get'. The distinction between the two processes, arguing and explaining, is an artificial one, for we are often involved in both at the same time. Nevertheless, the distinction is worth attending to for theoretical purposes, because whereas arguing a case puts the maximum demand on our powers of logical reasoning, explaining a position puts the maximum demand on our powers of clarification. The enemy of sound reasoning is false logic; the main enemy of clarity in utterance is turgidity. We turn first to look at some of the contexts in which, to judge from current practice, our powers of logical reasoning are tested.

Conceding and Affirming

We often have cause to say things like 'Although I don't like some of his ideas, I shall vote for him'. We concede a dislike for some of his ideas but then affirm something which seems to contrast with that dislike, namely that we shall vote for him. On a more personal level, we perhaps have cause to say of someone 'Although she is a pain in the neck, I realize that at heart she means well'. Again we concede certain objections to a person, but then affirm something very positive about them. That element of contrast is present in all logical uses of this construction. The rule applies to all reasoning which follows the words 'although', 'despite' and 'in spite of'. It also applies to certain statements beginning with 'granted that' and even to some statements beginning with 'if'.

although

Never forget that the proper use of 'although' is to introduce a contrast. 'Although he has broken his leg, he has promised to be there.' The man will be there in spite of the fact that he has broken his leg. Yet we find someone writing to *Gardeners' World* a letter beginning like this:

> Although I am a newcomer to your magazine, my wife and I enjoyed the recycled and creative ideas you featured.

Is there any proper contrast between being a new reader and enjoying a magazine? Surely not. Had the correspondent begun differently – 'Although I hate gardening, I enjoyed your magazine' – the statement would have made good sense. As it is the word 'although' was ill chosen. What the writer should have said was: 'Speaking as newcomers to your magazine, my wife and I enjoyed the recycled and creative ideas you featured.' A similar kind of misuse occurs in the following:

> The park is beautifully laid out, with superb lawns and flower-beds, although the immediate attraction is the unusual, futuristic buildings.

Again there is no contrast between stating that the park is beautiful, with superb lawns and flowerbeds, and pressing the immediate attractiveness of the futuristic buildings. In short, 'although' is once more the wrong word. It should be replaced by 'but', for the sentence 'This is beautiful but that is the immediate attraction' exemplifies a logical relationship between two balancing statements.

The failure to achieve a proper logical relationship between what is conceded by the word 'although' and what is nevertheless affirmed can be found at all levels from the crude to the sophisticated. Here it is found in an obituary notice:

> Although I got to know him well only towards the end of his long
> life, he really was a person of extraordinary charm.

There is no contrast between conceding that you got to know someone
only late in his life and claiming that he was a person of great charm.
Even the word 'but' would be out of place in separating 'I got to know
him well only towards the end of his long life' and 'he was a person
of extraordinary charm'. What is in the writer's mind is the implicit
contrast between the brief span in which he knew the deceased and
the confidence with which he can speak warmly of his personality.
That needs to be said: 'Although I got to know him well only towards
the end of his long life, I can testify that he really was a person of
extraordinary charm.' The reader will recognize that we have here
another instance of the kind of omission dealt with under 'Read My
Thoughts' in Chapter 8.

At a more complex level the mistake can be less obvious and yet
more misleading. Here is a comment about a Government proposal
to draw retired teachers back into the classroom:

> Professor Alan Smithers . . . said that, although schools appreci-
> ated the experience and knowledge of older teachers, they were
> often left with little choice because the pool of willing, available
> teachers under 65 was so small.

If someone said to you 'Although I enjoy muesli for breakfast, I am
often left with little choice because there is nothing else on the table',
you would recognize a misuse of the word 'although', for there is no
element of contrast between enjoying muesli and often finding it on
the table. Similarly there is no proper contrast between appreciating
older teachers and having to appoint them. The determination of the
speaker to be tactful is satisfied at the expense of logic.

despite

It might be argued that the word 'despite' suggests a coming contrast
even more forcibly than the word 'although'. In usages such as 'Despite
his wife's opposition, he insisted on taking the new post' the element
of contrast is plain. One must not embark on statements beginning
with 'despite' unless there is that direct contrast to be enunciated.

One might question, for instance, the validity of using the word 'despite' in this excerpt from an obituary:

> He was enormously successful in the Middle East, and despite his
> RAF career during the war he chose to shun administrative duties,
> preferring the life of a travelling salesman.

The sphere in which this former airman was 'enormously successful' was that of advertising. That he should become a travelling salesman thereafter does not seem incongruous. But the implication, introduced by the word 'despite', that someone who had a career in the RAF during the war would be expected to have a special taste for administrative work is odd.

The use of the word 'despite' comes under question even more strikingly in the following. It is a letter to the press about the need for reform in the police forces.

> Despite massaged crime figures, which suggest that certain
> crimes are falling, there is a danger that rank-and-file police
> officers are becoming badly demoralized.

The contrast implicitly anticipated in 'Despite massaged crime figures, which suggest that certain crimes are falling' is something like 'we know that crime is generally on the increase'. (And, incidentally, the words 'are falling' are ill applied to 'crimes'. The sentence should read 'suggest that the figures for certain crimes are falling'.) The claim that police officers are becoming demoralized does not have the direct contrast with the falling or rising crime figures required by the word 'despite', or indeed with the claim that they are 'massaged'. It would be more logical to drop the use of 'despite'. 'Massaged crime figures suggest that certain crimes are falling, but . . .' And here one must question the words 'there is a danger that rank-and-file policemen are becoming demoralized'. Why 'are'? The danger is surely that something *may* happen. The writer must not seek to combine the argumentative advantages of saying in seemingly measured terms that a certain development is threatened and at the same time implicitly claiming that it has become a reality.

An equally improper misuse occurs in the following:

> At one of the kennels, a small Scotch terrier had to be put down
> after developing stomach cancer. Despite biting two of the kennel
> staff, only one went for a rabies jab, since MAF regulations do
> not make it compulsory.

The logical thinker does not fling about phrases like 'Despite biting two of the kennel staff' without immediately identifying the biter and its subsequent fate. The words 'despite biting' require to be followed by some relevant contrasting statement ('Despite biting two of the kennel staff, the dog was given its dinner'). Obviously the words 'despite biting' are out of place here. What the writer means is that, despite both being bitten, only one of the kennel staff went for a rabies jab. Perhaps 'despite' is a dangerous word to use in argument. Here are the words of some satisfied tourists about their arrival at a camp site:

> We were pleased to note that, despite being the low season, all
> the facilities were open.

Had the sentence read 'We were pleased to note that, despite our being newcomers, we were warmly welcomed' no rules would have been broken. And that is because we are told there to whom the word 'being' applies. The difficulty in the sentence above is that, in spite of what is said, the facilities were not 'being the low season'. So the word 'being' is left high and dry. There was probably no escape from confusion except by getting rid of the word 'despite': 'We were pleased to note that, although it was the low season, all the facilities were open.'

Some Other Usages

Another way of making a concession followed by an affirmation is to use the word 'if'. This is not the most common use of the word, but it serves us well when we want to go halfway in conceding a point before saying something that seems to negate it. 'If she showed great generosity to you, she certainly didn't show it to anyone else I know.' Coloured with the flavour of irony, that statement assumes a powerful thrust. But the power of it depends on the sheer force of the contrast between 'she showed great generosity to you' and 'she didn't show it to anyone else'. If this contradictory element is missing, the construction misfires. And it does so in this press comment on the death of Mary Whitehouse:

> If the liberal Left viewed her as a prude, even those sympathetic
> to her views were sometimes alienated by her sanctimoniousness.

The word 'if' is totally out of place, because there is no element of contradiction or even contrast between the claim that the Left viewed her as a prude and the claim that those sympathetic to her were alienated by her sanctimoniousness. The word 'if' might better have been replaced by 'while', which would not promise the element of contrast. But best of all get rid of such decorations to the direct statement: 'The liberal Left viewed her as a prude and even those sympathetic to her views were sometimes alienated by her sanctimoniousness.'

There is a concessionary element in sentences beginning with 'granted that'.

> Granted that he did his best, the performance was still not good
> enough.

It is noticeable that the element of contrast remains between the fact that he did his best and the fact that the performance was not good enough. The sentence is really just another way of saying 'Although I allow that he did his best, the performance was still not good enough'.

Conditions

The commonest way of introducing a condition is to use the word 'if' ('I shall stay in if it rains'), but there are some other expressions which perform a similar function. Consider the sentence: 'Assuming that I am fully recovered, I shall be happy to attend.' That usage has a clear conditional element. If we were to change the wording, we should fall back on the word 'if': 'If I am fully recovered, I shall be happy to attend.' Nevertheless, it is clear that the usage beginning with 'assuming' is slightly different in meaning from the usage beginning with 'if'. Using the 'assuming' version I imply that I shall probably be recovered and am therefore likely to attend. Using the 'if' version I may leave room for unqualified doubt.

One sometimes find the word 'if' abused for unsuccessful attempts at forcefulness. Here is a passage from an article on Edward Bernays, the nephew of Sigmund Freud, who became an expert on the psychological aspect of marketing:

> Edward Bernays is virtually unknown today. If the name fails to
> ring a bell, he is likely to be the most important person of the
> 20th century that you have ever heard of.

And if not? If the name of Edward Bernays does not fail to ring a bell, then does he lose all hope of ever becoming the most important person we have ever heard of? The suggestion that someone can gain fame only if his name fails to ring a bell is actually what this statement conveys. The use of the word 'if' is here totally improper. What the writer meant to say, presumably, was 'Although Edward Bernays is virtually unknown today, he is likely to be regarded as one of the most important men of his age'. There was no cause for the rather showy venture into campanology.

It is appropriate here to make another point about the use of the word 'if', for logical argument so often relies on it. I quote a press comment at the time leading up to the Danish referendum about adopting the euro:

> In the final fortnight the 'yes' camp hit back by warning of the
> potentially dire economic cost if Danes rejected the euro.

In almost all questions of usage the rules of grammar and the hunches of common sense go hand in hand, but over the question of this construction perhaps they do not. However, it is the business of the writer on usage to side with the pedants. The correct grammatical use of 'if' requires it to connect with a verb, which it would if we amended the sentence: 'In the final fortnight the "yes" camp hit back. They warned that the Danes might pay a potentially dire economic price if they rejected the euro.' The same grammatical correctness could of course be achieved by amending the wording thus: 'hit back by saying what the dire economic cost might be if the Danes rejected the euro'.

That usage, which grammarians must label 'incorrect', is now fairly well established.

> To underline the potential benefits for the people of Yugoslavia if Mr Milosevic were forced to step down, the European Union again pledged to change its policy towards the country if his regime were replaced by a democratic leader.

The sentence is quoted in full because the word 'if' is twice used, once incorrectly in grammatical terms and once correctly. The second use is the correct one. The pledge is to 'change' policy 'if' something happens. The first usage is incorrect because the concept 'benefits if Mr Milosevic were forced to step down' is grammatically unacceptable. One should not hang an 'if' clause of that kind on a noun, 'benefits'. The sentence would be correct if it ran: 'To underline the potential benefits that would accrue for the people of Yugoslavia if Mr Milosevic were forced to step down . . .'

Causes and Consequences

Much of the reasoning we do from day to day involves dealing with causes and effects, intentions and results. These are areas of utterance where strict accuracy in the choice and placing of words always pays off. Yet some of the words we fall back on are quite inadequate to the demands of tight reasoning. Here is a piece about motor caravans.

> Immediately behind the driver is the wardrobe; not a big ward-robe, but a proper wardrobe, which didn't involve climbing over or moving furniture in order to use it.

This lax use of the word 'involve' is all too common today. It is a pity to use it as though it meant 'cause' or 'require' when these other verbs exist. What the writer means is that the shape and positioning of the wardrobe were such that one was not required to climb over furniture or to move furniture in order to get access to it. The word 'involved' has become an all-purpose verb covering all kinds of causal connections. In this respect it is abused as the verb 'to mean' is abused.

> Just because your company has an on-line presence doesn't mean
> you're making an on-line profit.

We have referred earlier to the inexact use of the word 'mean', but there is an illogicality here of another kind. The word 'because' is incorrectly used. We should never make statements such as 'Just because she is beautiful doesn't mean that she attracts me' when strictly what we mean is 'The fact that she is beautiful doesn't mean that she attracts me' or 'The fact that she is beautiful doesn't make her attractive to me'. Similarly here the sentence above should read: 'The fact that your company has an on-line presence doesn't necessarily mean that you're making an on-line profit.' Indeed it would make perfectly acceptable English to cut out the opening words 'The fact' and use a neglected construction: 'That your company has an on-line presence doesn't necessarily mean that you're making an on-line profit.'

Most of us do not run into difficulties when we make statements such as: 'She worked so hard that she made herself ill.' Yet evidence suggests that, except in the barest statements about consequences that follow certain actions or conditions, writers can easily be led astray in handling that construction. Here is a statement about the damage done by smoking tobacco:

> The really frightening thing is, there was enough of an effect
> from my smoking that it caused permanent damage.

We must criticize the sequence 'there was enough of an effect that it caused', which is a clumsily roundabout way of saying simply 'it caused'. If smoking causes damage, then damage is the 'effect' of smoking. That follows. One does not need to use both the word 'cause' and the word 'effect' to make the point. As for the word 'enough', it would seem again to go without saying that if the smoking 'caused' damage then there must have been enough smoking to do the trick. Nothing has been gained by not writing: 'The really frightening thing is that my smoking caused permanent damage.'

It looks as though excessive emphasis on adequacy ('enough of an effect') too easily intrudes into statements about consequences. Here is a statement about a pilot scheme proposed for rail freight:

> It says SWT would make a good pilot because it has a number of
> good secondary operators and busy railfreight around South-
> ampton and is 'sufficiently difficult so as to test the complexities
> of the intended organisational train' according to Stagecoach's
> paper.

Here we must point out that the words 'sufficiently difficult so as to
test' say no more than would be conveyed by 'difficult enough to test'.
The question arises too of what it is that is 'sufficiently difficult'. As
it stands, the sentence tells us that SWT is 'sufficiently difficult', but
surely that is not meant. We must suppose that what is meant is that
SWT controls an operational system complex enough to test the pilot
scheme.

The watchfulness needed in making that kind of case can be well
illustrated by looking carefully at the following about the Lawn Tennis
Association.

> It has long been fashionable to criticise the LTA but it seems to
> me that the LTA has followed David Lloyd's trailblazing example
> and provided an infrastructure that has resulted in a huge expan-
> sion of participants, especially youngsters.

Our complaint here may seem to be a subtle one, but failings in strict
logic often do require subtle analysis. The question is whether an
'infrastructure' can 'result' in anything. Providing an infrastructure
can have results – consequences from that provision having been
made. It is true that in loose conversational use we may say 'That
enormous breakfast resulted in stomachache', when what we really
mean is that 'Consuming that enormous breakfast resulted in
stomachache'. But in print, especially when a line of reasoning is
being followed, that will not do. Although the best correction would
be to remove the word 'infrastructure', it could be preserved if the
verb 'resulted' were changed: 'provided an infrastructure that has
allowed for a huge expansion of participants'. However, that cannot
be allowed to stand because it is not the participants who 'expand'
but their numbers that 'increase': 'provided an infrastructure that
allowed for a huge increase in participants'.

This first sentence in a leading article on the subject of the single

European currency provides a somewhat taxing specimen of reasoning for the reader to interpret:

> The danger of any currency conversion is not only confusion but cheating.

The article goes on to explain how in different countries the change to the euro has produced unjustified profiteering. Our first complaint is that the third word 'of' is out of place. It would be better to speak of the danger 'in' currency conversion. Our second complaint is that the 'danger' must not be identified as 'confusion' ('The danger . . . is not only confusion') when what is meant is that the currency conversion may perhaps 'produce' confusion. The same applies to the word 'cheating'. In short the sentence should read: 'The danger is that currency conversion may produce not only confusion but cheating.'

Wherever a case is being made of a controversial kind it is crucial to move step by step in such a way that opponents of the view cannot ridicule the sequence. I take as an example of carelessness in this respect a passage from an article expressing some doubts about the effectiveness in all respects of the policy of screening women to detect breast cancer. The writer notes how attractive is 'the idea of diagnosing cancer before it has produced symptoms and started to spread' and goes on:

> Finding and removing a small lump on mammography has led to breast-screening programmes in many countries with resultant surgery followed by radiotherapy and chemotherapy. 'Many lives have been saved' is the cry. But have they?

Especially when challenging orthodox thinking, one must use reasoning that is watertight, and here there is a bad start. 'Finding and removing a small lump on mammography' is a faulty sequence of words. A lump may be detected in a mammogram, but it cannot be 'removed' except by a subsequent operation. In any case, the whole sequence, including the point that 'finding and removing' a lump 'has led to breast-screening programmes in many countries', is surely a curious way of saying 'Because small lumps have been detected by mammography and then removed, many countries have adopted breast-screening programmes'.

Preserving Clarity

So far in this chapter we have been concerned for the most part with the kind of defects in the logic of utterance which interfere with sound reasoning. We turn now to look at how the slackness in the choice of words interferes with the clear presentation of a case. The brand of 'slackness' currently doing most damage to English usage is the cultivation of a turgid prolixity that is the enemy of economy and lucidity. The English language is rich in its vocabulary and English usage versatile in its provisions. It frequently happens that we have the choice between two alternative ways of saying more or less the same thing. We may say 'They welcomed us very warmly' or 'They gave us a very warm welcome'. In that case the choice is between the word 'welcome' used as a verb and the same word used as a noun. It is a fact of life that we tend to use the noun rather than the verb when we are being formal and the verb rather than the noun when we are being informal and personal. Very often the habit of preferring the nouns grows with us especially in our public or business affairs. This is one of the reasons why modern utterance tends to have an awkwardness or turgidity that could easily be avoided. I cite here a quotation from a book on Winston Churchill. The writer is dealing with the response to his appointment as Prime Minister in 1940, and insists that Churchill was not the choice of the Whitehall Establishment, of the King or of most of the Tory MPs. He then adds:

> In an inchoate way, however, he was, or quickly became, the champion of the nation in the eyes of both public and press. And those who had initially been reluctant and suspicious quickly came round to his indispensability.

It is reasonable to speak of 'coming round' to this or that realization. But 'came round to his indispensability' is a stilted way of saying 'came to see that he was indispensable'. The point to be stressed here is that, when those important people discussed this matter between themselves, they must have told each other that Churchill 'was indispensable'. But when the thing is put down later in black and white it seems more dignified to talk of his 'indispensability', and of course that is a pity. Yet the taste in words which it represents has established itself in many departments of activity today.

Let us take an extreme example from the medical world:

> The aim of the audit was to determine the adequacy of diagnosis for patients with a continence problem and the provision and appropriateness of treatment, and to assess the knowledge of healthcare staff with regard to incontinence. There should be an emphasis on the promotion of continence rather than the containment of incontinence.

Of the 53 words there, thirteen are nouns which could well be removed and replaced. They are 'aim', 'adequacy', 'diagnosis', 'continence', 'problem', 'provision', 'appropriateness', 'treatment', 'knowledge', 'regard', 'emphasis', 'promotion' and 'containment'. The sentence could then run thus: 'The audit aimed to determine how adequately incontinent patients are diagnosed and how satisfactorily and appropriately they are treated, and to assess how knowledgeable healthcare staff are about incontinence. Promoting continence should be emphasized rather than containing incontinence.' We claim a gain in clarity, simplicity and vividness. But what is more remarkable perhaps is the gain in brevity. For in rewriting the passage thus, the original total of 53 words has been reduced to 38. So the original has been reduced by fifteen words, over a quarter of the original number.

The continuation of this passage shows an appetite for jargon and wordiness that the good writer will avoid.

> A wider, patient-specific approach should be taken to continence, addressing all the individual factors that might contribute to incontinence in each patient's case.

There is little temptation to try to correct this, because the question arises whether it says anything at all worth saying. To speak of a 'patient-specific' approach to medical problems raises the question whether any disease or ailment can be treated without such an approach. What would the 'non-patient-specific' approach amount to in the study of incontinence? Perhaps a study of the plumbing requirements needed to deal with it? As for 'addressing all the individual factors' in a patient's case, is this not what the nursing and medical staff must do whether the problem is a broken leg, a tumour on the brain or bowel disease? Whenever people talk about 'the individual factors that might contribute' to something they are likely to be producers of hot air.

The Spread of Turgidity

Publications in the medical world merely reflect what is happening in the media, in business, in politics and indeed in the literature of good causes, as this extract from a wildlife journal illustrates. The piece discusses a document on planning policy in relation to conservation.

> This states that nature conservation can be a significant issue when determining a planning application but adds that, where possible, local authorities should consider what mitigation measures can be undertaken to minimize the impact on wildlife.

To begin with, to state that something 'is a significant issue' is merely to say that it matters, or that it is important. We could do without the word 'issue'. But more alarming is the latter part of the sentence. To 'consider what mitigation measures can be undertaken to minimize the impact on wildlife' is merely to 'decide how the effect on wildlife can be minimized'. The mind that reaches for expressions such as 'mitigation measures' has little care for clarity and simplicity.

The daily press shares the passion for abstract nouns. I read a leader that says:

> The Tory assault on Mr Brown over taxation is not without legitimacy.

Would there be any loss in exchanging 'is not without legitimacy' for 'is legitimate'? When we say that a situation is 'not without hope', we imply that there are degrees of hope in human experience. One may have a lot of it or a little of it. But it seems doubtful whether one could sustain the claim that there are varying degrees of 'legitimacy' so that an act might be said to have a lot of it or a bit of it. And the leader goes on later:

> There are very real doubts as to whether the Treasury can continue
> to extract taxation at the sort of level which was once considered
> easily achieved.

We shall not make a fuss over the words 'as to' but they would be
better omitted. What is more relevant is the use of the words 'to
extract taxation' instead of 'to tax'. One might reword the sentence
thus: 'It is very doubtful whether the Treasury can continue to tax as
highly as was once considered practicable.' A sentence of 26 words
has been reduced to a sentence of 18 words. But the more important
point to make here is that the nouns 'doubts', 'taxation' and 'level'
have given way respectively to the adjective 'doubtful', the verb 'tax'
and the adverb 'highly'.

We turn to a specimen of comparable excess from the transport
industry. The article is critical of the diversity of operators in the
current system.

> The railway's long-term survival demands more effective and
> co-ordinated management.

It may take a few more words to write 'If the railway is to survive for
long, it will have to be managed more effectively and systematically'
than to write 'The railway's long-term survival demands more effective and coordinated management', but the loss of the nouns 'survival'
and 'management' is surely a gain.

For another specimen of this overuse of nouns I take an obituary
notice on Lady Plowden that looked back to the Plowden Report,
recalling its recommendations:

> The report called for a large expansion of part-time nursery edu-
> cation, the abolition of corporal punishment, more dialogue, and
> greater involvement for parents, the introduction of two school
> starting dates each year, and up to two terms part-time attend-
> ance before full-time entry, to benefit children born in the sum-
> mer months, the recruitment of ancillary help for teachers and
> an inquiry into religious education for young children.

We are not suggesting that this is gravely bad English; we are pointing
out that it is noun-ridden English, and consequently stiff and heavy

in its impact. The nouns that could well be changed into verbs are 'expansion', 'abolition', 'involvement', 'introduction', 'attendance', 'entry', 'recruitment' and 'inquiry'. The new reading would be: 'The report recommended that part-time nursery education should be greatly expanded, corporal punishment abolished, dialogue increased and parents more fully involved. It suggested that there should be two school starting dates each year and that pupils should attend part-time for up to two terms before entering, to benefit children born in the summer months, that ancillary help for teachers should be recruited and religious education for children inquired into.' Again we are not suggesting that the revised version is in all respects superior to the original one. But the prose flows more flexibly. And the gain in fluency is due largely to the reduction in nouns and the increase in verbs.

It may be helpful to point to the kind of construction that leads writers to use nouns where other parts of speech would be better. Consider this sentence from a piece by an economist:

> Even if cheap money was applied to the German economy, however, there is no more certainty of it working than in Japan.

The grammarian would rightly point out here that the sequence 'certainty of it working' should be 'certainty of its working'. But, correctly or incorrectly used, the construction is not nearly so clear and neat as it would be to say 'there is no more certainty that it will work' (replacing 'working' by 'that it will work') or, even better, 'it is no more certain to work' (replacing 'there is no more certainty' by 'it is no more certain' and 'working' by 'to work'). What leads writers to sentences such as the one we have criticized is partly the habit of using nouns like 'certainty' instead of talking about 'being certain' and then the preference for 'of it working' rather than 'that it will work'.

It will be clear that excessive use of nouns is not always wasteful of words: it can be economical; but it is almost always clumsier, or at least less fluent, than the converse reliance on verbs. Here is a statement from the business world provoked by controversy about the euro:

> In such circumstances, there could be an increase in financial
> market volatility at an area-wide level as well as in the frequency
> of occurrences of financial distress at the company level.

If this is rewritten, expunging many of the nouns, it becomes 'The
financial markets could become more volatile over whole areas and
more companies could suffer financial distress.' Getting rid of the
nouns 'increase', 'volatility', 'frequency' and 'occurrences' is stylisti-
cally a gain. As for such usages as 'at an area-wide level' and 'at the
company level', this passion for 'levels' is a recipe for stiltedness.

The business world too often produces statements from writers
who seem determined to litter their pages with easily avoidable
abstract nouns.

> Questions about the sustainability of the Reckitt Benckiser suc-
> cess story emerge every time it posts results.

'Sustainability' ought to be on the list of terms proscribed because
they are as unnecessary as they are unnatural. What the writer means
is: 'Doubt whether the success of Reckitt Benckiser can be sustained
emerges every time it posts results.' There seems to be a reluctance
by writers to put into print the constructions they would (we hope)
use in speech. What is technically called an 'indirect question'
('whether the success can be sustained') is a lively feature of English
usage, yet it is now repeatedly sacrificed in favour of polysyllabic
nouns. Another specimen of this preference for nouns follows in the
same piece:

> Reckitt's strategy is simple. It aims to sell more products at higher
> levels of profitability.

Do we need the nouns 'level' and 'profitability' when we want to say:
'It aims to sell more products more profitably'?

Wherever one looks in business publications evidence of the passion for polysyllabic nouns emerges.

> Every business needs to drive strategic growth, improve processes,
> reduce operating complexity and increase corporate flexibility.

Businesses, it appears, no longer need 'to grow', but to 'drive' growth and, of course, make it 'strategic'. The speakers for this world never talk about making anything more or less complex or more or less flexible. Instead they talk about increasing or reducing complexity or flexibility.

Mumbo-Jumbo

There is a category of turgidity that out-bombasts all others. The business world has perfected its own brand of word-spinning, a category of the phoney, which consists in saying little or nothing as noisily as possible. It has given us the brand of usage known as management-speak, which has spread into many departments of life where meetings have to be held and business has to be done. But the purest form of the dialect is still to be found on the home ground of management. Here is a small specimen recommendation from railway management:

> Finally, it could promote packages of major service upgrades, by
> promoting the implementation of new services by operators.

The verb 'to promote', here twice used, is one of management-speak's favourites, but so of course are the words 'packages', 'upgrades' and 'implementation'. And the juggling with these terms represents an attempt to convey in impressive terminology that services would be improved and new ones added.

That represents but the threshold of the palace of verbiage constructed by management. This is how it recommends a coming 'workshop':

> As an output from the workshop will be identification and priori-
> tization of the major issues, and these will be followed up with
> recommendations as to how these issues can be addressed.

It is difficult to conceive of a business meeting of any kind to which this generalized agenda would be inappropriate. What it all amounts to seems to be that the meeting is going to deal with matters that need to be dealt with. And the communication goes on to promise an introduction to:

> a methodology that can be employed to tackle these issues, and
> focusing on making a significant impact to the bottom line.

The inflated abstract nouns, 'identification' and 'prioritization', the dead-as-doornails terms like 'issues', 'recommendations' and 'significant impact', and the hollow all-purpose verbs like 'addressed' and 'focusing' represent a selection from the set of examples supplied in the businessman's primer *How to Say Nothing and Sound Impressive*.

To plunge deeper into the sea of words is to encounter as a summing-up an insistence that real progress:

> will require a partnership between a logical, integrated and comprehensive methodology that focuses on creating a well-grounded plan for action, and a business mind-set that appreciates both the issues and opportunities inherent in the current situation.

If only, if only one could introduce into the management world a mind-set that appreciates directness, conciseness, clarity and simplicity. What is wanted is a mental world where it is accepted that if a plan is good it is axiomatically 'logical, integrated and comprehensive' and one doesn't need to waste words in saying so, a world where it is assumed that if a plan of action is sound it will be axiomatically 'well-grounded', and where it is recognized that any sensible human being will appreciate the issues and opportunities inherent in the current situation, whatever that situation may be.

But the author of this document pursues his assault on the English language with the persistence of a dog and the subtlety of an elephant. In providing a 'flavour of some of the areas that will be explored' in the workshop, a series of questions is formulated, including the following:

> Who is or will be part of the cross-functional interactive multi-media marketing communications team and how will they operate?

The layman might be tempted to reply 'Search me!' But a cross-dimensional inter-communicative multi-functional proactively responsive and integrated operations team might well agree that the issue should be addressed, a focused approach implemented and an outcome optimization strategy leveraged.

One trouble with business-speak of this kind is that parody is nigh impossible. The real thing out-parodies parody. *Private Eye*, which so assiduously garners specimens of gobbledegook at its worst, quoted a letter to a conference speaker who was due to address a conference and required advice about a suitable topic.

> I would suggest something along the lines of 'Balancing Functionalist and Interpretative Paradigms in Understanding Entrepreneurship'.

There is no one to tell us whether this expert recommendation was followed or whether the occasion turned out to be as productive of gas as the recommendation promised, but as long as there is a 'Pseuds' section in *Private Eye*, the guardians of sane English utterance will not feel totally pessimistic. Indeed, to read the specimens it garners is to realize that the examples we have so far cited of excess in the use of abstract nouns scarcely match up to the most outrageous contemporary extravagance in polysyllabic utterance. Here is something from a European Union source:

> Key Action 3 aims to improve the functionality, usability and acceptability of future information products and services, to enable linguistic and cultural diversity and contribute to the valorization and exploitation of Europe's cultural patrimony, to stimulate creativity, and to enhance education and training systems for lifelong learning.

Mocking rapid wordiness of this kind has long provided humour in our literature. In real life too there have been memorably entertaining instances when wit has cut a pretentious verbalist down to size. After a speech made by Ramsay MacDonald in the House of Commons in 1933, Winston Churchill provided a chilling tribute: 'He has, more than any other man, the gift of compressing the largest amount of words into the smallest amount of thought.'

Index

Words and phrases discussed in the text are indexed in *italics*.

about, 61–3
active/passive function of verbs,
    218–21
adjectives, personal/impersonal use,
    153
affirming, conceding and, 222–9
afterthoughts, illogical, 166–7
against, 61–3
akin to, 72–3
all, in expressing negatives/positives,
    199–200
all-time, 51
also, 87–8
alternation in separation,
    95–8
although, 223–4
ambiguity, dangers of, 113–14
and, as linking device, 78–80
answer, 17
apart from, 101–2
apostrophe, misuse, 76–7
    possessive, 73–6
    to indicate omission, 76–7
approval, expressing, 50–55
as, 68–9
aspect, 17–18
as regards, 69
assembling, 78–102
as well as, 84–5, 88–9

background, 18
balance
    in contrasting, 98–9
    in grouping, 85, 87, 88, 89–90, 93
to be, shortcuts with, 178–80
because, 230
being
    careful, 147–8
    cautioned, 148–9
    conscious, 145
    encouraged, 147
    incapable, 144
    lenient, 146
    responsive, 147–8
    self-conscious, 149
    self-serving, 148
    sensible, 145–6
besides, 88–9, 101–2
both . . . and, following negatives, 202
business language, 239–41
by, 61–3

careful, being, 147–8
causes and consequences, 229–32
cautioned, being, 148–9
celebrating, 145
changes, recording, 180–81
clarity, preserving, 233–5
clauses, misplaced, 208–10

cleverness, inappropriate, 107–8
climate, 18–19
compared to, 72–3
comparisons of magnitude and
    quantity, 45–6
composition, 6–7
compression, 189–91
    failures of, 184–8
    telescoped expressions, 196–8
conceding and affirming, 222–9
concept, 13
conditions, 227–9
condone, 26
connotations, shifting, 55–6
conscious, being, 145
consequences
    adequacy, excessive emphasis on,
        230–32
    causes and, 229–32
constructions, switching, 216–18
contrasts, 98–101
    parallelism in, 98–9
convenience, 19
cope, struggling to, 144–5
coupling, verbal, 189–92
    ambiguous, 193–6
    multiple, 191–2
    questionable, 191–2
    redundant, 192–3
cross-section, 37
cure, 26–7
currently, 51–2
curtail, 27
cutting-edge, 52

deliver, 20–21
deprive, 27–8
despite, 224–6
disapproval, expressing, 50–55
dismantle, 28
disregard, showing, 143
double negatives, 201–2
duplication, errors of, 117–19

element, 37–8
encouraged, being, 147
evaluations, 50–55
exaggeration, 10–12, 14–15
exceptions, making, 101–2
experiencing, 142
    trauma, 146–7
extent, comparisons of, 45–6

fact, statement confused with, 181–4
failing to understand, 144
familiar phrases, misuse, 202–4
figures of speech: *see* metaphors
finite, exaggerative use, 15
fob off, 28–9
focused, 21
followed by, 70–71
for, 58–9
from, 60–61
from . . . to, 93–4
functional, 21

granted that, concessionary element,
    227
grouping
    balance in, 85, 87, 88, 89–90, 93
    devices for, 78, 84–90
    successiveness in, 78–84

happen, 29–30
he/him, 160–61
her/she, 160–61
hinges, verbal, 65–73
hospitality, meeting with, 145

identify, 22
if
    concession followed by
        affirmation, 226–7
    introducing a condition, 227–8
I/me, 162–3
implement, 22
improvements, recording, 180–81

in addition to, 88–9
incapable, being, 144
include/including, 90–93
inclusiveness, 90–94
incredible, 10
in excess of, 38
infinite, exaggerative use, 14–15
in spite of: see despite
install, 30
intensifiers, misuse, 10–12
in terms of, 71
involve, 229
it, identifying, 156–7

keeping things in mind, 147
keeping to the point, 103–7
key, 52–3

learning lessons, 143
legendary, 16
lenient, being, 146
less, 38–9
lessons, learning, 143
like, 72–3
linkages 57–65

magnitude, comparisons of, 45–6
major, 53
majority, 39
management-speak, 239–41
matters of opinion, 46–50
to mean, 46–8, 229–30
meaning
    draining words of, 12–16
    metaphor in development of, 130
    shift in, 114–17
meeting with hospitality, 145
me/I, 162–3
metaphor
    common expressions, 130–33
    context, 139–40
    in development of meaning, 130
    inexact, 136–8

personal/impersonal terms used,
    140–50
reliance on, 129–30
single-word, 133–6
mind, keeping things in, 147
misconnected start, 119–22
misconnections, thoughtless, 109–13
misplaced clauses, 208–10
misplaced phrases, 205–8
myth, 15–16

need, 48–50
negatives
    both . . . and, following, 202
    double, 201–2
    expressing, 199–202
    linking to positives using 'and',
        201
neither . . . nor, illogical relationship,
    200–201
niche, 53–4
non sequiturs, 210–15
nouns
    coupling, 189–91
    excessive use, 234, 237–8
numerical discrepancies, 172–3

oblivious, 30
obscene, 16
obtain, 31
of, 59–60
omission, 184–8
one-off, 54
on the one hand . . . on the other hand,
    89–90
opinion, matters of, 46–50
or, 95–6
otherwise, 167–70
overstep, 31

parallelism
    commonest failure, 125–8
    false, 119, 121–2

parallelism – *cont.*
    in contrasting, 98–9
    in grouping, 84, 86, 89, 90, 93
    in separation, 95–9
part, 39–41
passive/active function of verbs,
    218–21
percentage, 42–3
phrases, misplaced, 205–8
point, keeping to, 103–7
positives, linking to negatives using
    'and', 201
possessives, 73–6
    wayward, 122–5
postcripts, retrospective, 166–7
prompting, 142
proportions, ready-made vocabulary,
    36–45

quantities
    comparisons of, 45–6
    ready-made vocabulary, 36–45
question, 23

raise, 31
reasoning, implied, 184–8
referring back, 163–6, 170–71
    numerical discrepancies, 172–3
relinquish, 31–2
remembering, 142–3
responsive, being, 147–8
retrospection
    numerical discrepancies, 172–3
    pointless, 163–6, 170–71

section, 43
sector, 43–4
self, used in coupling, 194
self-conscious, being, 149
self-serving, being, 148
sensible, being, 145–6
separating, 78–102
    alternation in, 95–8

sequence
    breakdowns in, 210–15
    items listed in, 78–84
she/her, 160–61
shortcuts
    changes/improvements, recording,
        180–81
    failures of, 175–8, 184–8
    implied reasoning, 184–8
    statement confused with fact,
        181–4
    verb *to be*, 178–80
showing disregard, 143
side, 32
size, comparisons of, 45–6
so, 167–70
solution, 23–4
some, 44–5
sound thinking, need for, 3–5
speculate, 32–3
statement, confused with fact, 181–4
struggling to cope, 144–5
subdivisions, ready-made
        vocabulary, 36–45
subsidize, 33
substitute, 33–4
successiveness, failures in, 78–84

telescoped expressions, 196–8
terrific, 10
that, identifying, 159–60
theme, 13–14
they
    generalized, 154–5
    identifying, 151–4
    misuse, 155–6
this, identifying, 157–9
through, 61–3
time, problems of, 112–3
to, 61–3
together with, 86–7
towards, 61–3
trauma, experiencing, 146–7

true, 54
truth, 54–5
turgidity, spread of, 235–41

understand, failing to, 144
undo, 34
unique, 15
us/we, 162–3

verbs, passive/active function,
    218–21
vocabulary: *see* words
voluminous, 34–5
vulnerable, 24

way, 25
we/us, 162–3
when, 65–7

where, 67–8
whether . . . or, 96–8
who, 68
with, 63–5
words
    appropriate relationships
        between, 103–7
    as hinges, 65–73
    coupling, 189–92
    drained of meaning, 12–16
    economy with, 174, 175
    linking, 57–65
    misuse, 9–12
    over-use, 16–25
    ready-made, 36
    redundant couplings, 192–3
    shifting connotations, 55–6
    similar in sound, 25–6